53-6496

Eng. Lit.
2.50

DATE DUE

Literary Masterpieces

of the

Western World

Literary Masterpieces

of the

Western World

Edited by

FRANCIS H. HORN

1953

The Johns Hopkins Press : Baltimore

Foreword

THE ESSAYS in this volume grew out of an experiment in adult education at The Johns Hopkins University. Hopkins has a long tradition of courses for adults at late afternoon and evening hours offered for college credit; from its establishment in 1876 it has also provided occasional public lectures by members of the faculty or visiting scholars. Several years ago when the University reorganized its evening division and appointed the editor of this book dean of the new unit, McCoy College, it was decided to experiment with a program of lecture courses for adults without college credit. The first of these was entitled " Literary Master-pieces of the Western World." The lectures in the course consti-tute the basis. for this volume. They were so well received that similar courses now form the heart of the University's extensive noncredit educational program for adults.

That the new program should have been inaugurated by a series of lectures on " great books " was not accidental. The University has unusually rich scholarly resources in the field of literature. Professor Boas in his introduction notes how these essays testify to " the complexity of Johns Hopkins scholarship." Each essay has been written by a well known authority; each demonstrates the competence of its author. Hopkins is fortunate also in that its outstanding scholars, especially those in the humanities, are also excellent teachers and lecturers. The essays which follow were originally prepared as lectures for a heterogene-ous adult audience. Their uniformly high level is evidence that they were written by professors not disdainful of putting their scholarship to work in the service of the continuing education of adults. The volume indicates that at Johns Hopkins scholars have descended from their ivory tower to the market place, or have, if one prefers, been willing to take the average adult citizen from the busy market place to the scholar's high tower, there to help him probe the meaning and mystery of life as set forth in our great literary classics.

Yet it is a mistaken notion to identify the study of our literary masterpieces with the ivory tower. Though seldom so recognized, the study of great literature is an intensely " practical " subject. Ours, to be sure, is a scientific and technological civilization; no one will gainsay the great material advantages we thereby enjoy. But we shall seek in vain for the ultimate meaning of life in the study of science and technology. It is as true today as in Pope's time that " The proper study of mankind is man." The social sciences, which examine man primarily in his group relations, have much to teach us about the meaning of life and man's place in it. But it is to the humanities—literature, philosophy, religion, history, and the fine arts—that we must turn for answers to the most searching questions regarding man and his destiny. Especially in our great literary achievements do we find the embodiment of human experience that helps each of us to live his life more effectively, more richly, and to greater purpose. In these critical times, it is more important than ever that we turn to great literature, not only for the enjoyment it gives us, but also for the insight and inspiration it provides. This profound need of our time is the primary reason why the new adult education program at Hopkins began with a series of lectures on masterpieces in our literary heritage.

Because this series of lectures was received so enthusiastically, because the lectures themselves seemed to embody so successfully sound critical scholarship within a framework of popular presentation, it was considered advisable to make them more widely available. The professors who had participated in the course agreed to revise the lectures for publication. The result is the baker's dozen of stimulating essays included in this volume, to which Dr. Boas has written a provocative introduction.

These essays will help provide an understanding of Western literature and its great contribution to our cultural life, an understanding sorely needed in the complex and turbulent world in which we live. The essays will be of interest to the specialized scholar and to the college student of literature, but they are intended primarily for the general reader, for the person who wishes sympathetic and scholarly assistance in his reading and understanding of our literary classics. He will find rich rewards in the essays in this book. He will discover even greater treasure if they send him, as they are intended to do, to the masterpieces themselves.

FRANCIS H. HORN

Executive Secretary
Association for Higher Education

Washington, D.C.
April 7, 1953

Contents

* By permission of the Editor of *English Studies.*

Introduction

AN HISTORIAN of philosophy, invited to write an introduction to
a series of essays on literary masterpieces, will be expected to
elaborate some general conclusions about the works as a whole.
It is not his purpose, I assume, either to add or subtract from
the greatness of the works and authors discussed, for he would be
incapable of doing either in a convincing manner. It is not his
purpose to prove that the masterpieces in question really are
masterpieces, for that is granted by all. He might well be asked to
point out what they all have in common which makes them great,
but surely the reader can do that for himself, if he is interested.
It is perhaps more fitting—and certainly more fitting to the capa-
bilities of the present writer—to look at them all and indicate
certain features which might escape the notice of the casual
reader.

To begin with, it is obvious that we have here a series of literary
works which run from the earliest moments of recorded history
to the nineteenth century. It thus represents a longitudinal cross-
section of Occidental literature, with many gaps to be sure, but
on the whole a fair sample. It represents poetry and prose, sacred
and profane literature, drama and novel. But curiously enough
it is not a hodgepodge of books selected simply because a group
of nine professors happened to like them. Each of these books
may be thought of as changing the minds of men, of reorienting
our thoughts. They are corners, so to speak, which Western civilization turned at certain moments in its history. This is obvious
as far as the first of them, the Bible, is concerned, and no doubt
equally obvious as far as the *Divine Comedy* and Goethe's *Faust*
are concerned. But in what sense of the word can Rabelais or
Shakespeare be said to have changed men's minds?

Each of these authors, oddly enough, both recapitulates the culture of an age and gives it new color. One cannot think of Rabelais, or for that matter of Vergil, or even Fielding, without also thinking of dozens of other men whose ideas flowed into him and were welded together into a new amalgam. Rabelais has become a symbol of the Humanism of France in the sixteenth century, of its consuming interest in human beings, of its sense of the ridiculous, of its hatred of bigotry and sham, of its love of classical learning, of its exuberance and tremendous fertility in ideas and words. He is the incarnation of a whole set of thoughts, feelings, and aspirations, which we today think of as the spirit of the time. We overlook, unfortunately, the hard fact that there was no spirit of the time before there was Rabelais. He helped to make his time. But no one more than he rolls all its complexities together and presents them to us in a single bundle.

When we think of the Augustan Age in Rome, we do not think of Ovid, or Horace; we think of Vergil. For the genius of Horace and Ovid was confined to themes smaller in scope than the range of Vergil and because the very compendiousness of Vergil's *Aeneid*, the national epic, gave it a majesty and required a massiveness of detail for its execution. The Augustan Age in literature became the Age of Vergil as the Elizabethan Age in literature became the Age of Shakespeare. There are incorporated in the *Aeneid* a thousand legends drawn from folklore, a score of echoes of Homer, the experiments of earlier poets who wrote in Latin hexameters, a profound devotion and unquestioning belief in the greatness of his national culture, simple popular philosophy expressed in noble lines which soon became proverbial, and that almost naive faith in certain religious beliefs without which no poet ever speaks for anyone other than himself. I am not speaking now of the exquisite finish of much of Vergil—the qualification is needed since the *Aeneid* is still unfinished—but simply of the substance of the poem, that to which the finish is given.

Even Fielding has this scope, this panoramic quality. *Tom Jones*, like many of the novels of Balzac or the plays of Molière, and unlike the *Scarlet Letter* or *The Portrait of a Lady*, is a *summa.* It is true that Fielding's novel is almost an allegory; the very names, given to the main characters, as Mr. Malone points out, are names of moral virtues or vices or types of behaviour. And yet Fielding's genius got the better of him and he could not, except in the case of his heroine, overlook reality. Reality, to be sure, in literature must be reality as seen by a writer and it is quite possible that Sophia is what Fielding actually thought a young lady of her station to be like. Dickens and Thackeray when they came to portray good women did no better, though they too got down to earth in portraying wickedness. The fact of the matter probably is that Anglo-Saxon men did not intimately know good women for the simple reason that they were good. It was not the custom of the Tribe until recent times for good women to leave their homes. They were seen, if not through a glass, at least through a haze.

In any event such women seem to have been acceptable to English and American readers. But no one today would read *Tom Jones* in order to concentrate his attention on the character of Sophia Western, unless he wished to discover what the eighteenth century thought of as the ideal of womanhood. The book is read for its broadly and vividly sketched picture of English life. For Fielding is to Richardson what Hogarth is to Reynolds. This is a society seen through the eyes of a powerful imagination, a world—as the French use that term—with its own geography.

To see more clearly what I am trying to express, one has but to compare such an American novelist as Cooper with Henry James. The former has immersed himself in the very scenery of his country, its mountains, rivers, plains. Most of his characters seem contrived, cut out of pasteboard, purely fictitious. But they did not seem so to Cooper's contemporaries nor to thousands of readers both here and in Europe for several generations after their author's death. Some of the scenes in Cooper, if lifted out of their context, seem downright absurd today. But they were part of the literary convention in their day and we are never aware of conventions when we accept them. I have heard a Belgian look up the Susquehanna at Conowingo, surely one of the most grandiose

views in America, and exclaim, " *C'est très Fenimore Cooper.*"
Cooper had become, like Vergil or Homer or Shakespeare, a
symbol of a society, an historical epoch, of a landscape.

Now no one looking at a river, a mountain, or even an open
field, would ever say, " *C'est très Henry James.*" For the society
of Henry James, so largely uprooted and afloat, is typical of
nothing but the novels of Henry James. He has created his own
world peopled by beings who are so telepathic that they need
scarcely ever speak to one another. A lifted eyebrow, a tone of
voice in a broken sentence, the carriage of a head, inform them
of much more than words could convey. Their landscape is the
drawing-room or the Italian *palazzo*. That there was such a
world, inhabited by somewhat anaemic anthropoids, may very
well be true. But it was a world which it has become difficult to
accept as real or as typical of anything other than itself, whereas
the equally conventional world of Balzac or of Proust, of Homer
and Vergil is accepted without question. Cooper may not have
been the spokesman for a society, but he was at least the spokesman for a tradition, for an historical epoch. James was the
spokesman, exquisitely adequate too, for a group of individuals
of his own creation.

But there is another peculiarity of this cross-section of cultural
history, and that is its fertility in arousing questions of interpretation. There is scarcely a chapter in this volume which does not
point out how various critics and readers have seen in the books
which they have studied a variety of " meanings." We can omit
as a special case the Bible. But Homer himself, surely an apparently straightforward writer, unmysterious, presenting no enigmas
as far as the simple-minded reader can see, becomes to the scholar
a puzzle. Was there one Homer or a group of rhapsodes who have
the collective name of Homer? Are the *Iliad* and the *Odyssey*
single epics or collections of ballads? Vergil is a notoriously mul-
tivalent writer. Was he a spokesman for imperial Rome, a propagandist, servile to the Emperor, an inspired prophet, a magician,
a ridiculous lover? All of these things and more have been said
about him by men of different periods. Is *Beowulf* dominated by

Christian or heathen motivations? Is the *Divine Comedy* the culmination of the medieval world-view, or the initiation of the Renaissance? So it goes. There is scarcely an author or a book in our list which has not presented its puzzle to the historian and critic. One would imagine that a masterpiece would be clear and unequivocal in its meaning, that there could be no doubt about what it "had to say." But men are still quarreling about the meaning of *Hamlet* and it sometimes appears that the life of a masterpiece is prolonged not merely by all people's being agreed in their admiration for it but in all people's disagreeing about what it says.

This is worth at least a moment's reflection. For it will be noticed that when a problem is solved, it becomes obsolete. No one is going to worry over the proof that the sum of the angles of a triangle is equal to 180 degrees or that the earth is an oblate sphere, though young people can be trained in such proofs for the sake of the exercise supposed to be involved in them. The human mind feeds on problems, not on answers, and the great minds are those which perceive new problems, not those which repeat old ones. It may very well be that the reason why these masterpieces continue to interest us is that we do not understand them, that they continue to present problems of interpretation to us. If what I say is true, then a work of art dies when one thoroughly understands what he has studied, but if he is a mature scholar, he is usually willing to admit that his interpretation will be dated.

So long then as a poem or a drama contains an element which is not clear, men will attempt to clarify it. But sometimes the problem arises because a generation has acquired new knowledge about the period in which a book was written, about the language in which it was written, about the psychology of authorship, and this and similar information are projected upon the work of art under examination to give us new information about it. Ironically enough, the new information arouses new problems too and thus the work of art gains a new lease on life. For instance, Fielding wanted *Tom Jones* to show that virtue triumphs over vice, but few would read it with that in mind nowadays. The reason is that we do not believe in the efficacy of virtue unaided by a certain strength of will and sometimes we believe that on this earthly plane vice usually triumphs over virtue, especially if the wicked are clever enough to conceal their wickedness. But we who are remote from eighteenth century England may be simply interested in the vivid evocation of life during that period and, switching our attention from the target of our ancestors, who lived at that time and hence did not have to read books about it, we find a new center of interest and thus keep the book alive.

Why some books feed the imagination in this way and others do not has no certain answer. But one possible answer may be worth noting. It must first be couched in philosophical language and then illuminated by concrete examples. Philosophically the answer may be that the passage from essence to existence is always absurd, non-logical. One can argue that if certain things are so, then certain consequences will follow. We can argue that if all men were good, they would be happy, but we cannot prove that all men are good, though we may discover it, which is quite a different matter. Or again, we can say that if on top of a building eighty feet high there is a brick weighing half a pound, if it is dropped it will hit the earth with a calculable force. But by argument alone we cannot prove that the stone is on top of the building or that it actually will be dropped, or that if it is dropped it will not be caught before it hits the ground. These things also are discovered, observed, not deduced. If now one makes a sharp distinction between what one might call history as distinguished from science, one can say that historical events are observed, not deduced. And since they are always individual and unique events, never completely describable in general and abstract terms, they are more fittingly described in art than in science.

But that there should be any exemplifications of general terms continues to be a problem and the human mind is caught between the illogicality, the absurdity of the individual, and the necessity of giving it a name. We can call Abraham Lincoln a man, but he was more than a man; he was also a president, a statesman, a great writer of prose, a humorous man, a somewhat uncouth individual, and so on almost *ad infinitum*. By heaping up the adjectives, by increasing the classifications, we can always approximate a complete description but we never reach it for there is always the stumbling block of existence before us. But if Abraham Lincoln were only a man, the simple representation or exemplification of *Mankind*, any biologist could give us a complete account of one of the most complex characters in history. Since, however, he was complex, as we all are to some extent, an individual, born at a certain date and murdered on another, there will be as many interpretations of Lincoln as there are biographers, and historians will never tire of writing his life. The individual is the greatest problem of all. He tantalizes us by his very individuality. We are inquiring curious animals; we want answers to our problems even when we know that none are available. Hence the work of art which is farthest removed from science will be the work of art which will demand most reinterpretation and which will probably have the longest life. This is merely a guess on my part, but it is a guess which is not entirely without foundation.

Finally it will be observed as one goes through these essays that each writer has his own approach. How many possible approaches there are to literature is beyond counting, but in general it may be said that there are at least the following. One may treat a book as a document illustrative of its times, as a kind of historical evidence of what the people of that time felt and thought. One may treat it as the concrete embodiment of a philosophy. One may treat it as a symbol, conscious or unconscious, of a set of religious beliefs. One may treat it as evidence of the author's state of mind, of his aspirations, his repressions, his desires, his ambitions. One may treat it as essentially a moral treatise, since it is bound to show human beings in interrelations. It may thus be said to be inevitably a moral judgment on the human race. Or one may treat it simply as a formal arrangement of ideas or characters or symbols.

To ask which of these is the right way to treat it is useless, not only because we cannot suppress our curiosity concerning literature but also because a book has many facets, can be seen in many perspectives. The purely " aesthetic " treatment is as legitimate as the historical or the psychological or the moral; nor do its conclusions contradict in any way the conclusions of the other kinds of treatment. There is no more contradiction between, let us say, the historical and the psychological treatment than there is contradiction between physics and chemistry. To impoverish human scholarship, and consequently human interests, is not to confer any benefit on human life, and the usual appeal to " purity " is simply an attempt to convince by the use of question-begging epithets.

It is one of the merits of these essays to utilize several methods of investigation at will. And the merit of this complex method is its demonstration of the richness and diversity, the many-sidedness of the books under study. Mr. Williamson, for instance, in his study of the *Divine Comedy* re-emphasizes the observation of De Sanctis that Dante utilized material that was commonplace in medieval literature, but that by putting himself into the poem, he welded the temporal and the eternal together, joining history and religion. But he does not merely harp upon this string. He also shows Dante's peculiar use of figures of speech which depend upon, or issue from, a new outlook on life and religion. Mr. Malone in his essay on *Beowulf* not only introduces the subject with an historical statement, he also interprets the fusion of Christian and Pagan elements in the poem aesthetically. Mr. Spitzer speaking of Rabelais points out the serious purpose of his buffoonery, a purpose which had previously been expounded as simply the protest of a learned man against traditional culture. Rabelais and his characters become the first of the moderns, men who are sensitive to the absurdity of the non-logical and yet rejoice in it. Mr. Lancaster presents us with a Molière who creates a new kind of comedy out of traditional characters, emphasizing his author's dramatic genius, his insight into human psychology which led him to give new life to the stock in trade of the dramatist. Since the writers of these essays were given a free hand to put down what they thought important, and since each is a free individual living in a society which is still free, it was to be expected that a variety of points of view would be expressed. There will be critics who will deplore this. They will take it for granted that there is only one proper approach to a work of art and they will look for it in these pages. When they find themselves unable to spot it, they will inevitably lament so multiple and diverse a manner of literary scholarship. But when one comes to think that authors are human beings like the rest of us, and do not write to make the task of critics easier, such heterogeneity is seen to be unavoidable. Let the essays which follow this brief introduction be evidence of the richness and complexity of Occidental literature as well as of the complexity of Johns Hopkins scholarship.

GEORGE BOAS

April 2, 1953

Literary Masterpieces

of the

Western World

I

The Bible

W. F. ALBRIGHT

THE BIBLE as we have it is a translation into our vernacular from Hebrew and Greek. The Old Testament was almost entirely written in Hebrew, with a little Aramaic; the New Testament was entirely written in Greek. The Old Testament represents the national religious literature of the people of Israel, with additions from the time after Israel had ceased to be an independent people and had become a religious group, while the New Testament contains the earliest records of Jesus and the apostolic period.

It must never be forgotten that the authors of the New Testament considered the Old Testament to be Scripture which they were supplementing, not displacing. They had no doubt about the importance of their own writings, which they considered as of first-class value and as binding on all true, believing Christians; yet to them the Old Testament was sacred Scripture, not a word of which could be discarded without serious, if not fatal, results to their faith. Until comparatively recent times all Christians and Jews were content to study and interpret the texts of their sacred books—that is, of the Old and New Testament for Christians, of the Hebrew Old Testament alone for Jews—on the basis of tradition, without dreaming of subjecting them to the same criteria by which secular literature could be judged.

It was not until the eighteenth century that modern philologians worked out any method of critical interpretation of ancient texts. Then a brilliant group of scholars—English, German, and French —established what we know today as literary or historical criticism, sometimes called higher criticism. This higher criticism

3

consists of an attempt to establish criteria or principles by which
to judge the date and authorship, the unity and character of
compositions from any period. Such criticism is named higher
criticism in contradistinction to lower criticism, which describes
and applies the criteria for establishing the original text as written
by the author of a given composition. Since, of course, compositions were formerly handed down by word of mouth or through
copies made by hand before the invention of printing, it stands
to reason that mistakes would creep in. The lower or textual
critic endeavors to recapture the original text by arranging the
manuscripts in groups or families according to the mistakes and
peculiarities of their scribes, etc. When the various families of
manuscripts have been classified, he can apply his method to
determining the exact text of the oldest group of manuscripts, in
so far as that can be determined. Very few, even of the most
conservative scholars, doubt the results of sound lower or textual
criticism, but a great many have doubted the results of higher
or literary-historical criticism.

Historical criticism was carried to very great lengths during the
nineteenth and twentieth centuries. There can be no doubt, however, that it won a great many triumphs. For example, it was
able to point to certain classes of material, called " documents,"
which share stylistic and other peculiarities of philological nature
in the Pentateuch. It was able to show that the Pentateuch grew
through many centuries before it reached the form with which
we are now familiar. Literary criticism was able to show that the
book of Mark is the oldest of the Gospels and that the book of
John is the latest, in agreement with early Christian tradition. It
was able to show that the book of Isaiah, for example, consists of
an anthology of oracles and sermons, mostly in verse, which were
composed on different occasions in different periods; we speak,
for example, of First and Second Isaiah. Of course, some scholars
go much further and divide the book into a great many fragments,
a method which has sometimes worked havoc with the books of
the Bible.

In general, it must be said that modern historical and literary criticism has gone much too far. Thus it is claimed by many scholars of today, both in Europe and in this country, that we do not know anything about the life of Moses, much less about his laws. These scholars would relegate almost the whole Pentateuch to very late times. Other scholars deal devastating blows at the tradition of the Exile and Restoration. Some distinguished scholars in England and America have maintained that there was no true Babylonian Exile, that there was, therefore, no true sojourn in Babylonia, and no true Restoration; that Ezekiel, if he existed, was a semi-legendary character and that he may never have existed at all; that Ezra was no more than a figment of the imagination of later scribes. We have all grades of higher criticism from very moderate literary-critical deductions to extremely radical conclusions. On the whole, radical criticism has been gaining ground in recent decades, so that present Biblical scholarship frequently goes beyond the great German scholar Julius Wellhausen, who in the latter part of the nineteenth century worked out a reconstruction of Old Testament history, literature, and religion, which has been considered standard by most liberal scholars until recently. In the New Testament, on the other hand, it is doubtful whether any scholars of today go as far as the Tübingen school in nineteenth century Germany. According to the Tübingen school, the epistles of Paul were either apocryphal or very late, and the Gospel of John, for example, was written as late as after A. D. 150.

Fifty years after the beginnings of serious higher criticism came the first hints of a new age in archaeology. The world of the Ancient East, in which Israel arose, came to maturity, and declined, was scarcely known a hundred years ago. We had, it is true, a few inklings of historical tradition preserved in Greek and Latin authors and there was a very little in the Bible—but that was virtually all. None of the records of the Egyptians, of the Babylonians and Assyrians, of the Hittites and Canaanites had survived; all had perished.

Then came in rapid succession the decipherment of Egyptian hieroglyphics, of the Persian and Assyrian cuneiform characters, of Phoenician and South Arabic, of Hittite and many other ancient scripts and languages. Strangely enough, for every script and language which has been read, new scripts and languages have turned up waiting to be deciphered. We now have more undeciphered scripts awaiting attention then were known to exist at the beginning of the decipherment of the ancient oriental systems of writing a century and a half ago. We obviously do not have time to go into detail with regard to the extraordinary results of archaeological research in the ancient Orient. Suffice it to say that, step by step, the forgotten scripts and languages have been read. We are now in the fortunate position of having hundreds of thousands of published inscriptions on clay, stone, papyrus, leather, wood, and other materials from these ancient countries. Egyptian history, literature, religion, and art are now well known and are treated in many authoritative works. The same is true of Babylonian and Assyrian literature, history, civilization, and religion. Since 1929 the long-lost literature of the ancient Canaanites, who preceded Israel in Palestine, has been recovered, thanks to the work of M. Schaeffer at Ugarit (Ras Shamra) on the coast of northern Syria.

In 1950 and 1951 we were engaged in recovering the long-lost civilization of ancient South Arabia, thanks to the excavations of the American Foundation Arabian Expedition, in which I have been taking an active part. Methods of dating unwritten documents such as pottery, ancient walls, and objects of human use, have been worked out until we can now date almost anything that is dug up in the Bible lands within narrow limits—two or three centuries in the case of most classes of objects. In short, we now have such a wealth of material that scholars working in these fields cannot begin to cover them adequately or to present the material clearly to the world of today.

Thanks to archaeology, the Hebrew Bible is no longer a book of seven seals with respect to its background. We know that it is not only a divine but also a human document and that we can understand it far better by reconstructing the life of the ages in which it arose. We now see that the literature of the Old Testament reflects a selection of the very best literature and thought produced by the ancient Orient, profoundly transformed by being passed through the refining crucible of Hebrew religion. Where the ancient Oriental documents are polytheistic and often extremely crude, the literature of Israel is monotheistic, glowing with an ethical purity in strange contrast to the savagery of much ancient Oriental literature. It is extremely interesting to contrast some of the finest products of the ancient Orient with corresponding products of Hebrew literary genius.

We must not, however, be surprised to note that, just as might be expected from the fact that Palestine was situated in the middle of the ancient Orient between Egypt, Assyria, Babylonia, Arabia, and other countries, the literature of Israel was influenced from all sides. We find in the Bible literary elements coming from surrounding lands: from Egypt, from Babylonia and Assyria, etc. In short, the Bible is a product of the entire ancient world in so far as its literary background is concerned.

Another thing which we must remember is that there are two stages in ancient literature. The first is oral. Most of the earlier traditions of Israel and most of the early poetry of Israel passed through an oral stage before it reached the written stage. Many poems, laws, and other ancient documents were composed by word of mouth and not put into writing at all until after a lapse of time; sometimes centuries were to pass before the original composition was put into writing. During this period these documents were learned by heart and recited by professional rhapsodists and narrators. They were recited around campfires; they were recited as part of the liturgies of tabernacle and temple; they were recited by lovers of literature. In short, they had their own history, which is not the same as the history of written documents. Scribes make mistakes in transmitting written documents. In transmitting oral documents there are other kinds of changes. Words are replaced by more modern words; sometimes whole verses are dropped out or added, and the order is often modified. However, oral transmission has certain advantages which written transmission lacks, and written transmission has advantages which oral transmission lacks.

It is important to note that the Israelites had always been acquainted with writing from before the time of Moses on down, as has been definitively established by modern archaeological discoveries. So the Israelites were never completely illiterate. There were periods during which writing was used only scantily, but it was well known so the traditions of Israel were never unprotected by a written literary background as modern higher critics have assumed. I stress the distinction between oral and written transmission of ancient poems, laws, and other documents, because recent scholars, particularly in Scandinavia, are becoming aware of its importance for correct understanding of the history of Hebrew literature. We cannot say that a document is not authentic because it was modified slightly in the process of oral transmission, because these ancient Orientals, like the Hindus of more modern times, and like orthodox Jews and Moslems of our own day, were given to learning things by heart and repeating them with extraordinary precision.

At its best, oral transmission could be as accurate as written transmission, or even more so. We must remember that verse usually came first in literature because the desire to sing seems to be as old as self-conscious mankind. There is no people so primitive that it does not have songs or chants, crude though they may appear to us. In the ancient world, these oral compositions often had a long history before they were reduced to writing. The study of our new archaeological evidence makes it increasingly clear that the same was true in Israel. The Israelites had a large body of inherited poetry before they began to write down any extensive part of our Hebrew Bible. In fact, most modern scholars are of the opinion that the oldest poems of the Bible are earlier than any other Biblical literature. While these texts are often short, it is not because early poems were necessarily shorter than later poems. Recent discoveries in Babylonia and Syria have proved conclusively that long before the time of Moses and even before that of Abraham, there were long compositions in verse, preserved on cuneiform tablets. However, as a rule these early compositions did not commend themselves to the canons of taste in later periods. Naturally some great masterpieces such as the *Iliad* and *Odyssey* or some of the old Babylonian poems were handed down to very late times. As a rule, however, early compositions died out and only fragments of them were preserved for historical and other reasons. One of the oldest is probably only a fragment of a much longer one, quoted to identify the longer composition, which was still handed down orally. It comes from the wilderness days of Israel, when Moses was leading the Israelites through the desert (Numbers 21 : 17–18) :

> *Spring up, O well,   Say ye to her—*
> *Well which the rulers have dug,*
> > *Which the chiefs of the people have cleared,*
> > *Carving it out with their staves!*

Until very recently, few Biblical scholars would admit that any of the longer poems from the time of Moses have survived in the Hebrew Bible. In fact, one can say with confidence—thanks to the discoveries at Ugarit, modern Ras Shamra on the Syrian coast, already mentioned—that the Song of Moses and the Oracles of Balaam must go back to that time, since they have so much in common with the language and style of the mythological epics of the Canaanites in the fourteenth century B. C., only a century earlier. Just to illustrate how close the similarity is, we may quote from the very ancient Psalm 92 : 10:

> *For behold Thine enemies, O Yahweh!*
> *For behold Thine enemies will perish,*
> > *All evil doers will be scattered!*

A similar passage in the famous Baal Epic of the Canaanites from the early fourteenth century B. C., recovered in the last two decades, runs as follows:

> *Behold thine enemies, O Baal!*
> *Behold thine enemies shalt thou smite,*
> > *Behold thou shalt crush thy foes!*

It will be observed that style, vocabulary, and even wording are the same, though in Israel we have a monotheistic point of view displacing the old Canaanite polytheism and a new morality much higher than that of the Canaanites.

The Song of Miriam in Exodus 15 contains so many close similarities to Canaanite verse in style, vocabulary, and turns of phrase, that it is no longer possible to doubt its early age. Of course, in oral transmission for perhaps three centuries, there were changes here and there in detail. But these changes were very minor and we can safely assume that the poem as a whole goes back to the Wilderness Wanderings very soon after the escape of Israel from Egypt in that famous event known as the Exodus. Now to render a few verses:

Let me sing to Yahweh,   *For greatly exalted is He,*
Horses and their chariots   *He cast into the sea.*
The chariots of Pharaoh   *He cast into the sea.*
And his choicest warriors   *Were drowned in the Reed Sea.*
The deeps covered them up,   *They went down to the bottom*
                                    [like stones.

Thy right arm, O Yahweh,   *Is mighty in strength,*
Thy right arm, O Yahweh,   *Doth shatter the foe!*

It is interesting to note that in Exodus 15 : 17 we have a reference to " the mountain of Thine inheritance," which has been attributed by almost all modern scholars either to the period after the building of the Temple on Mount Zion in Jerusalem or even to the post-exilic period. Now, however, we have almost identically the same phrase, " the mountain of mine inheritance," with the same word for " inheritance " in the Baal Epic from the early fourteenth century B. C. This resemblance shows in the clearest possible way that there is no need whatsoever to refer this verse to post-Solomonic, much less to post-exilic, times. It actually must go back to the time of Moses.

The Oracles of Balaam, perhaps a generation later than the Song of Miriam, are in a different style but their antiquity cannot be doubted after recent discoveries have proved in the clearest way both the age of the Balaam tradition and the antiquity of words, phrases, and stylistic elements in the poems. In Numbers 23–24 we read the beginning of one of Balaam's oracles:

From Syria hath Balak brought me,
  Moab's king from the Eastern Mountains:
" Go thou and curse for me Jacob,
  Go thou and tell Israel's doom! "
How can I curse what El hath not cursed,
  How can I doom what Yahweh hath not doomed?
For from the mountain peaks I see,
  From the hill-tops I behold—
Who can count the dust of Jacob,
  Or can number Israel's dust-clouds?

Another of these oracles begins:

So saith Balaam, Beor's son,
  And so saith the man whose eye is true;
So saith one hearing the words of El,
  And one knowing what Elyon knoweth;
One seeing the visions of Shaddai
  In a trance with eyes unveiled.

The names El, Elyon, and Shaddai are the old names of the highest Canaanite or Northwest Semitic god. These appellations, meaning " the Mighty One," " the Highest," " the God of the Mountains " were adopted from their precursors by the Israelites as appellations of the God of Israel, who was also the God of the whole universe.

Not long after the settlement of Israel in Canaan, when the Judges ruled in Israel, was composed the famous Song of Deborah, long believed to be the oldest poem of any length in the Bible. It shares style and point of view as well as many details of vocabulary with the Song of Miriam. Like the latter, it swarms with similarities to the Canaanite literature of the immediately preceding age. It begins,

When locks grew long in Israel,
  When the people responded (praise Yahweh),

Hear, O Kings   *Give ear, O princes,*
For I to Yahweh   *Even I will sing,*
I will sing to Yahweh *Unto Israel's God!*

Yahweh, when Thou didst rise from Seir,
When Thou didst march from Edom's land,

The earth was quaking,	*The heavens were shaking,*
The mountains were rocking	*Before Yahweh's face,*
Before the face of Yahweh,	*Of Israel's God.*

Further on in the poem, we read the poignant words of Sisera's mother,

Through the window there looked,
Through the lattice, Sisera's mother,

" Why do his chariots	*Tarry in coming,*
Why linger the hoofs	*Of his chariot horses? "*

Her wisest ladies reply,
She echoes her own words,

" Do they not find	*And divide the spoil?—*
A maiden, two maidens,	*For every warrior,*

Spoil of dyed work for Sisera,
Spoil of dyed work embroidered? "

This same early style survived in the Psalms and the Prophets in old, or rather in archaizing, passages. We find one of the most striking of these archaizing passages in the famous Psalm of Habakkuk in the Minor Prophets.

God approached from the Southland
And the Holy One from Mount Paran,
His glory covering heaven,
While earth was full of His praise.
. . . .
Before Him Pestilence marched,
And Plague went forth at His feet;
Standing He shook the earth,
Gazing He made nations tremble,
While everlasting mountains broke up,
Eternal hills collapsed,
Eternal orbits were shattered.

And again,

> *The mountains saw Thee and quaked,*
> *The Deep gave forth its voice;*
> *The clouds streamed with water,*
> *The rivers, which cleave the earth.*
> *The exalted one, Sun, raised his arms,*
> *Moon stood on his lordly dais;*
> *By the light of Thine arrows they move,*
> *By the lightning sheen of Thy spear!*
> *In anger dost Thou tread the earth,*
> *In wrath dost Thou thresh the nations,*
> *Going forth to save Thy people,*
> *To save the people of Thine Anointed.*

Most biblical poems are written in later style, especially in the Prophets and the Writings (Hagiographa), which form the latest poetical books of the Bible. To the later style belong many beautiful poems. I shall limit myself to quoting from Canticles 8 : 6–7, in the translation of my teacher, the late Professor Paul Haupt of the Johns Hopkins University, in collaboration with Horace Howard Furness, the noted Shakespearean scholar of Philadelphia:

> *Hang me close to thy heart like a signet,*
> *On thy hand like a ring do thou wear me.*
> *For love is strong as death*
> *And passion as Sheol unyielding;*
> *Its flames are flames of fire,*
> *Its flashes are flashes of lightning.*
> *Nothing is able to quench it,*
> *Neither can any streams drown it.*
> *If one should resign for it all his possessions,*
> *Could any man therefore contemn him?*

If we turn to early Hebrew prose, we find that it has two principal categories. The first is formed by the laws, both civil and cultic, which form a very large part of the Books of Moses. The laws are particularly interesting since they are couched in the same formulaic language that we find in the ancient law codes of the East, such as the Code of Hammurabi and other recently discovered earlier codes from Babylonia as well as somewhat later ones from Assyria and Asia Minor. Some of these laws follow a formula beginning with " if," while the subordinate clause is introduced by " provided that." Since this characteristic formulation is found in all the ancient Near Eastern laws of the second millennium B. C., it follows that there is no need whatever for the usual assumption of critical scholars that the oldest body of civil law in the Bible, the so-called Book of the Covenant in Exodus 21–24, dates from after the age of Moses in the late second millennium B. C. An increasingly large number of scholars are recognizing that the Book of the Covenant is either Mosaic, in the strict sense of the term, or else reflects the Hebrew law of the Mosaic period, which comes to nearly the same thing. Another source of early Hebrew prose is formed by the traditions of the Hebrew patriarchs and of early Israel, covering the Exodus, the Wandering in the Wilderness, the Conquest of Palestine, and some later episodes. There can be little doubt that the late Professor Umberto Cassuto of the Hebrew University in Jerusalem and others are correct in recognizing a poetic substratum; that is to say, these prose narratives are paraphrases of older poetic sagas which came down in oral transmission from extremely early times. The poetic origin of the prose narratives is clear from the often highly poetic diction, from the frequent use of parallelism, and from numerous poetic quotations which have survived, imbedded in the prose text. This phenomenon is found so characteristically in the Book of Ruth that it can almost be put back into its original poetic form.

Poetry and prose meet again in the prophets of Israel. The Israelite prophets were a body of men and an institution so unique as to have no real parallels in any subsequent history. There is no trace of any developed institution comparable to that of the Hebrew prophets in the whole ancient Orient. We have in them a group of devoted men, at best absolutely fearless reformers, at worst imitators of the true prophets, who delivered their oracles in poetry and prose. So in the prophets we have Hebrew prose and Hebrew poetry meeting on their highest level; in them we have fiery words, spoken from the heart, winged words which thrilled kings and priests, nobles and poor men, or caused them to bow their heads in shame. The earliest prophets do not seem, as a rule, to have spoken at length, but from the eighth century B. C. on we find the anthologies of the so-called writing prophets. Actually, these latter prophets composed their words orally and they were then taken down in writing by their hearers, probably after the lapse of some time. In those days of little reading, men's memories were frequently far better than they are in practice today. The two earliest of these so-called writing prophets, Amos and Hosea, were followed within a generation by Isaiah and Micah, and a century after them by Jeremiah and Ezekiel, all towering figures whose words have profoundly influenced all succeeding ages.

The so-called " Writings " of the Bible, termed Hagiographa in Greek, belong to many periods, but they were put into the Canon of the Hebrew Bible rather late, and so they reflect a long period of Biblical history. The Psalter, for example, contains Psalms which go back to Canaanite times before the Israelite conquest, though their original polytheism was replaced by ethical monotheism. The tenth century is well represented in the Psalter and there are many Psalms from the period of the Dual Monarchy of Israel and Judah. Some Psalms certainly come from the Exile and Restoration, and there is a body of liturgical Psalms which are hard to date, but which do seem to date in their present forms from the fifth or fourth centuries B. C. I do not believe that there is a single Psalm from the Hellenistic period, let alone from the Maccabean period in the second century B. C., as held by many modern critical scholars. We cannot here discuss the Proverbs or Job, that great dramatic poem which deals with the problem of theodicy, how to justify the ways of God to man, or even mention the minor jewels which we find in the Hagiographa.

However, before passing on to the New Testament, we must say a few words about the intervening age, frequently called the Intertestamental Period. This Intertestamental Period lasted, roughly, for about four hundred years, from the completion of the latest historical books of the Old Testament down to the beginning of the New Testament period in the second quarter of the first century A. D. There are a few Old Testament books, such as Ecclesiastes and Daniel, which belong to the Hellenistic period, especially the third century B. C. These three centuries are illustrated, however, by a great many books found today in the Apocrypha, which remains in the Roman Catholic Bible as well as in some Anglican and Lutheran Bibles but has been removed from the Bible by most Protestant bodies. These books were never admitted into the canon of the Hebrew Bible and, therefore, were not considered by Protestants as of equal value. The theory was, of course, that the Jews had remembered the original Hebrew canon and that the apocryphal books did not belong in it since they were not admitted by Jewish tradition.

Actually, there are additional reasons for omitting these books. The main part of the Hebrew canon was completed by the fourth century B. C. and the later books, though they might commend themselves by their contents, nearly always had something in them which was not satisfactory to the orthodox theological sentiments of the Pharisees or of the Rabbis of the period of the Mishnah. Moreover, there was nearly always a tradition of the late origin of the apocryphal and pseudepigraphical books which prevented the Rabbis from considering them as of equal canonical value with the older books of the Hebrew Bible. The books of the Pseudepigrapha are more extensive and, of course, much more problematical in origin than the books of the Apocrypha. Among them are such books as Enoch and Jubilees, used in the early Christian Church, discarded almost entirely by the Jews, and rediscovered since the late eighteenth century in Ethiopic translations preserved by Abyssinian monks in the convents of Ethiopia.

These books of the Pseudepigrapha and others like them, such as the Testaments of the Twelve Patriarchs, contain so much puzzling material that scholars have been in serious doubt with regard to their date. Now, however, we have a very important new source of information in the Scrolls found since 1947 in a cave south of Jericho at the northwest corner of the Dead Sea. The Bedouin who first discovered these Scrolls sold them to the Monastery of St. Mark in Jerusalem and to the Hebrew University. The Archbishop Athanasius Joshua Samuel, who was here in Baltimore in connection with the exhibition of these Scrolls at the Walters Art Gallery in 1949, has generously allowed the American Schools of Oriental Research to publish the Scrolls in his possession, and the late Professor E. L. Sukenik began before his ill-timed death to publish the Scrolls which he had purchased for the Hebrew University. (Between the delivery of this lecture and the correction of galley proof, a wealth of additional data has been recovered from the Dead Sea valley south of Jericho. Thousands of additional manuscripts and fragments have been discovered in different caves by the Bedouin and by foreign excavators. It can already be said that this new material dwarfs the rich finds of 1947 in importance for our knowledge of the Jewish literature of the last two centuries B. C. and the first century and a half A. D.)

The Dead Sea Scrolls became known to the outside world in 1948, and in early 1949 the cave itself was rediscovered and excavated by two first-class archaeologists who were able to recover many hundreds of additional scroll fragments as well as over forty jars, nearly all badly broken, which had held a much more extensive library than would be indicated by the Scrolls which were preserved intact. The fragments of the linen wrappings which were used to wrap up the Scrolls have been subjected to the chronological test of radiocarbon (carbon isotope 14). They turn out to be over nineteen hundred years old, plus or minus two hundred years; that is to say, the linen was manufactured somewhere between about 200 B. C. and A. D. 200. Thanks to the study of the pottery chronology illustrated by the vases found in the cave and to careful comparison of the scripts of the material from the cave with other Hebrew scripts of the immediately preceding, contemporary, and following periods, it is possible to fix the date at which the latest manuscripts found in the cave were deposited as not far from the time of Christ. There is some occasion for uncertainty here, and there are still many scholars remote from ceramic chronology and palaeography who are skeptical about the antiquity of the Scrolls. There are even persons who insist on dating them in the Middle Ages, though this is rendered impossible by the radiocarbon dating. Fortunately the radiocarbon dating will convince a great many people who respect physics even when they are skeptical about such mysterious subjects as palaeography.

These Scrolls include, in part, manuscripts and fragments of the books of the Old Testament, in part, new books belonging to Jewish sectarians, probably Essenes. They also include fragments of the books of Enoch, Jubilees, and to judge from the extraordinary resemblance in content, the Testaments of the Twelve Patriarchs. We therefore know with certainty that the latter books belong to this sect and its related groups, and that they must be dated in the last two centuries B. C. This was already the opinion of the best scholars, such as the late R. H. Charles, but it was not held by everyone. For our understanding of the history of Jewish literature these new discoveries are thus of very great significance.

Turning now to the New Testament we note, first and foremost, that although the New Testament is very great literature, it is not literature in the same formal sense that much of the Old Testament is. Much of the Old Testament was written and polished by skilled literary craftsmen, and their works continued in favor partly because of their literary excellence. The books of the New Testament were not written by literary craftsmen though they sometimes reach a high level of literary excellence. They must always stand high from a literary point of view because of the matchless simplicity and beauty of the Gospel narrative and because of the incredible fervor and deep poetic feeling of the Apostle Paul.

The date of the Gospels has been questioned by many critical scholars of today and even in the most recent journals of Biblical literature and theology there are articles by prominent New Testament scholars, insisting that the Gospels were deeply influenced by contemporary—or supposedly contemporary—Gnosticism and that they are therefore to be dated as late as the end of the first century and the early second century A. D. The Gospel of John has been a particular target for higher critics ever since it was first dated in the late second century by the German members of the so-called Tübingen school, followed by the Dutch school of Loman and Van Manen. According to them, the Gospel of John was not composed by the Apostle John but by a much later writer and it reflects the Gnosticism of that period. This is the view, for example, of Professor Robert M. Grant in a recent number of the *Journal of Biblical Literature*. Actually, however, the Dead Sea Scrolls now make this position untenable. It has already been maintained by historians of religions and ideas, such as Professor Erwin Goodenough of Yale University—who is no conservative—that the Gospel of John precedes the beginnings of Gnosticism around the fifties of the first century A. D. and thus reflects a pre-Gnostic conceptual background. That is to say, the ideas and the wording of the Gospel of John are not influenced in any way by the atmosphere of Gnosticism but reflect the atmosphere of late pre-Christian Judaism. The Scrolls confirm this view in the most striking way. Here we have over and over again expressions and combinations of words which remind us of the Gospels, in particular that of St. John. We have the same contrast of light and darkness, good and evil, truth and falsehood, as well as terms common to John and to the conceptual imagery and ideology of our Jewish sectarians in the last pre-Christian period. Contemporary Biblical scholars are inclined to oppose the antiquity and authenticity of the Scrolls precisely because their radical hypotheses are controverted.

A great deal of light has been shed on New Testament Greek through the discovery of the Greek papyri of Egypt during the last seventy-five years or so, especially in the last half century. These Egyptian papyri exhibit a form of Greek, called the *Koiné*, which was spoken all over the Mediterranean basin and was characteristic of the period in which the New Testament arose.

This fact proves most clearly that the authors of the New Testament were not interested in couching their writings in literary Greek but they tried to be understood by the common people, who spoke *Koiné* Greek. On the other hand, being Jews, their *Koiné* is impregnated by Hebraisms, that is by Hebrew words and expressions which go back to early Rabbinic times. St. Paul's letters were not written by a literary man anxious to impress his contemporaries by the beauty of his style; they were written by a man in deadly earnest who had the soul of a poet and in whom poetic inspiration vies with religious fervor. I will quote just one selection from First Corinthians 13, a very famous passage which illustrates most vividly what marvelous literature Paul could produce when he was carried away by his own inspired genius: " If I speak in the tongue of men and angels, but have not love, I am an echoing bronze or a clashing cymbal. And if I have prophetic power and understand all secrets and all knowledge, and if I have all faith, so as to remove mountains, but have not love, I am nothing. If I give away all my possessions, and if I hand over my body to be burned, but have not love, I have no advantage. Love is patient and kind; love is not envious or conceited; it is not arrogant or bad-mannered. Love does not seek its own way; it is not irritable; it thinks no evil; it does not rejoice over wrong-doing but rejoices in the truth; love bears all things, believes all things, hopes all things, endures all things. Love never fails; but prophecy will be nullified, tongues will cease, knowledge will pass away. For our knowledge is imperfect and our prophecy is imperfect; but when what is perfect comes, what is imperfect will pass away. When I was a child, I spoke like a child, I understood like a child, I thought like a child; when I became a man, I gave up childish ways. For now we see in a mirror obscurely, but then face to face. Now I know in part; then I shall know fully, even as I am fully known. Now there remain faith, hope, love, these three; but the greatest of these is love." *

---

* All unacknowledged translations are the writer's own.

II

The Iliad of Homer

HENRY T. ROWELL

THE ACTION of the *Iliad* begins in the tenth year of the Trojan war and covers a period of only a few weeks. Homer tells us all we need to know about the cause of this war and the events which preceded the landing of the Greek punitive expedition on Trojan soil in bits of information scattered throughout his poem. But we hear very little of what has taken place during the nine long years of siege and fighting.

On a visit to Sparta, Paris, a son of Priam, King of Troy, persuaded Helen, the wife of Menelaus, King of Sparta, to abandon her husband and home and to return with him to Troy. There she lived openly with him as his wife. This outrage to hospitality and its flagrant conclusion called for satisfaction in the eyes of the injured husband and his relatives and friends. The restitution of Helen was demanded, but the Trojans, although they were not all of one mind, refused. So Agamemnon, king of Mycenae and brother of Menelaus, moved to balance the account by force. He sent out chieftains of acknowledged authority and eloquence who were in his confidence—such as Nestor of Pylos and Odysseus of Ithaca—to persuade other chieftains to join an expedition against Troy or to send their sons. Achilles, the son of Peleus, and Patroclus, the son of Menoetius, were recruited in this way.

The expedition assembled at Aulis on the Greek mainland and set sail for Troy. As we have said above, Homer tells us very little of the nine years which followed the landing. We hear of

21

sallies into the surrounding country and attacks upon neighboring islands. Otherwise we must imagine the Greeks living in the encampment close to their beached ships where we find them at the beginning of the *Iliad* or in combat on the plain which separted Troy from the sea.

As compensation for the unparalleled monotony of camp life and the desultory periods of actual fighting, there had been booty taken in raids and battles: armor, male captives who could be held for ransom, and women who could be kept for pleasure and solace. But most of these spoils had gone to the chieftains and lieutenants, the heroes of the poem, for Homer's world belongs to nobility and prowess, and he is not interested in the common soldiers as individuals. They meet in assemblies to hear the proposals of their leaders and fill the background of the battle scenes with their shouting and clashing and nameless dying. In the foreground, the noble and excellent perform their valorous deeds and we learn their names and the names of their fathers even if they appear upon the scene only to be struck down and sent into oblivion by a mightier hero.

At the beginning of the *Iliad*, the rank and file are ready to go home at a word from their leaders. But they will remain and continue to fight and fight well so long as they are properly commanded. The leaders, on the whole, are still loyal to their commander-in-chief and determined to carry on the war until Troy is destroyed. Several of them are far greater warriors than Agamemnon and several have keener wits, better judgment, and finer perceptions. For the sake of the success of the expedition, they are willing to take second place—all of them except Achilles, the leader of the Myrmidons.

Although it is the quarrel between Agamemnon and Achilles in the first book of the *Iliad* which determines the course of the action or story, directly or indirectly, until the end of the poem with the twenty-fourth book, we learn from the words exchanged in the quarrel itself that Achilles had long been dissatisfied with the conduct of the war by Agamemnon as it affects him personally. In a bitter attack upon Agamemnon, Achilles complains that he has been bearing the brunt of the fighting for Agamemnon's perpetual enrichment. What is he doing before Troy, he asks, since the Trojans have never injured him? He joined the expedition and others with him to please Agamemnon and Menelaus. Since this is not appreciated, since his part in the war is not duly rewarded, he will go home.

It is clear that Achilles was ready to bring matters to a head and give vent to his feelings at the proper opportunity. It was provided by a stupid act of Agamemnon in the course of the first event described by Homer.

Chryses, priest of Apollo, comes to the Greek camp holding the symbols of his priestly office in order to ransom his daughter who is a captive of Agamemnon. He asks that the ransom be accepted out of reverence for the god, and the Greeks in a body approve his request. But Agamemnon ignores the wishes of his army and packs the priest off rudely with a threat. The priest prays to his god that the Greeks be made to atone for the injury, and Apollo in compliance visits the Greek camp with a plague. The pyres burn incessantly as they consume the corpses.

On the ninth day Achilles calls the Greeks into assembly. It is worth noting that Agamemnon, who should have acted first in the grim emergency, allows Achilles to take the initiative. The plan of the latter is simple and direct: to ascertain from some prophet or priest why Apollo is angry and to make atonement. Chalcas can best advise the assembly since by the gift of Apollo he knows past, present, and future, but he fears Agamemnon's reaction to the truth. Consequently, he bids Achilles swear to protect him and Achilles states that no man while he is alive will lay hands on Chalcas, not even if he mentions Agamemnon " who claims to be by far the greatest of the Greeks."

Encouraged by the oath, Chalcas proclaims the cause of the plague already known to the reader and infuriates Agamemnon, who assuages his own guilt by reviling Chalcas. Nevertheless, Agamemnon will give up the daughter of Chryses but the Greeks must prepare a suitable prize to take her place. It is unseemly that Agamemnon, alone of the Greeks, should be without a prize.

Achilles answers with harsh words and some hard facts: Agamemnon is " most acquisitive "; there is no common pool of property from which he can be compensated; for the moment all booty has been distributed; a redistribution would be unseemly; let him give back the girl; if Troy is taken, the Greeks will make threefold and fourfold compensation.

But Agamemnon cannot wait, for he feels himself challenged in his authority before his army and his pride compels him to force the issue from an untenable position. He will not have Achilles keep his prize while he, Agamemnon, surrenders his; if the Greeks will find him one to his taste, well and good; if not, he will personally take away the prize of Achilles or Ajax or Odysseus; in the meantime Chryseis will be returned to her father so that Apollo may be propitiated.

Ajax and Odysseus do not answer, for they do not feel themselves threatened. It is apparent to all that Agamemnon is addressing Achilles alone and that a personal quarrel of long standing is coming to a head. We have already noticed Achilles' answer culminating in the statement that he is returning home. These last words are taken up by Agamemnon and twisted into an unforgivable insult. " Flee, if you wish," he says to the man who has never turned his back on toil or peril; " I shall not beg you to remain for my sake." And to this insult, he adds the threat of unbearable injury. If he, Agamemnon, must surrender Chryseis, he will come personally to Achilles' quarters and take away his woman, Briseis, so that Achilles may know well that Agamemnon is the better man and others will be deterred from thinking themselves the equals of their commander.

This is too much for Achilles. His impulse is to fling himself upon Agamemnon with drawn sword. As he hesitates, hand on hilt, the goddess Athena appears to him, commands him to curb his intended violence, and promises him abundant compensation in the future for the outrage. She permits him, however, to assail Agamemnon with words, and this he does as he thrusts his sword back into its sheath. His tirade ends with a prophetic oath: the day will come when all the Greeks will miss him. When many fall at the hands of Hector, Agamemnon will not be able to help them and his heart will be torn because he did not show due honor to the " best of the Greeks."

After the assembly disbands, Achilles returns to his quarters by the sea while Agamemnon prepares to return Chryseis to her father. He does not carry out his threat to Achilles in person, but sends heralds with instructions to bring Briseis to him. Achilles treats the heralds courteously and allows them to take Briseis. But this arrogant deed fixes an enduring wrath in the heart of Achilles against Agamemnon—a deed for which all the Greeks will pay.

" Sing, goddess, of the destructive wrath of Achilles, the son of Peleus, which brought countless woes upon the Greeks and sent countless brave souls of heroes to Hades—." These are the words with which Homer begins his poem, and the word " wrath " is the first word in the first line. We have seen with what rapidity and sensitive psychological understanding Homer reveals the pre-existing kernel of bitterness, its development into a passionate quarrel, and its culmination in an implacable anger. It is chiefly through speech and action that Homer gives us insight into the characters of his men and women, and we are hardly through the middle of the first book before we have learned a great deal about Achilles and Agamemnon.

At the very beginning Homer has not only told us that the subject of his poem will be the wrath of Achilles but also what the result of this wrath will be: the destruction of countless heroes. It is clear now that the Greeks will suffer heavy losses because anger has caused their greatest fighter to withdraw from combat. But Homer does not let the matter rest here, for he adds: " and the will of Zeus was fulfilled." This is our first glimpse of divine purpose and plan. It is now time for us to learn more about this aspect of the story.

When Briseis has been led away, Thetis, the mother of Achilles, a sea goddess, hears her son despairing and comes to him to find out the reason for his tears. He explains to her all that happened and asks her to beg Zeus to take the side of the Trojans and to allow them to drive the Greeks back against their ships in a murderous onslaught, so that the Greeks may have " full enjoyment " of their king and Agamemnon himself recognize his madness in having failed to honor the " best of the Greeks."

There is a particular pathos in this scene between mother and son, because we learn here for the first time from Thetis' answer that Achilles is fated to die before long. The mother feels out of her desparate love that the short space of life still allotted to her son should be free of woe and tears. Although helpless against fate, she will attempt to achieve his immediate desire. In the meantime, he is to persist in his anger and refrain from warfare completely.

In a charming scene of persuasion which takes place in Olympus, Thetis explains to Zeus how her son has been dishonored and begs the father of gods and men to honor him by giving strength to the Trojans until the Greeks have learned their lesson and made due restitution of honor to Achilles. Zeus hesitates. The granting of the request will put him at odds with his wife, Hera, who already scolds him incessantly on the grounds that he is helping the Trojans. This is sorry business, but he will consider how the matter can be accomplished. And in solemn witness that his promise will be carried out, he bows his head in assent.

The result of Achilles' wrath has now become a part of the ineluctable will of Zeus. We have learned from the beginning of the poem what this result will be: the death of countless Greek soldiers. We now know that these deaths will be inflicted by Trojans in a rout of the Greek army. But Zeus has promised to support the Trojan victory only until due amends have been made to Achilles. We do not know whether they will be made in time to save the Greeks from utter disaster or how; or, in other words, we know in general what will happen up to a certain point but not where that point will be or what lies beyond it. There is still ample room for surprise and suspense.

From a well-motivated quarrel between two men, Homer has led us skillfully to a crystallization of anger and hatred which on the human level alone was very likely to have serious consequences.

With equal skill, he has established the inevitability of these consequences and increased their effect by giving them a divine universality within the compass of his story. Achilles' wrath is now truly fateful, for its consequences have become a law of the cosmos in which the action of the *Iliad* takes place. We have been prepared for a development of more vast and tragic scope than that to which a purely human quarrel would lead of itself.

The general background of the opening action and the contents of book 1 have been described in some detail because book 1 contains the main-spring of the plot or story and almost everything which follows is directly or indirectly a consequence of Achilles' wrath. Now we must move more quickly and in handling the subsequent books, it will be convenient to consider as two groups the books in which Achilles appears in person and those in which he is absent. But before we do so, let us glance at affairs in Troy.

In the tenth year of a siege of which she had been the initial cause, we might well expect Helen to be surrounded by loathing and abomination, especially on the part of the royal house, with the exception of Paris, which would lose the most if Troy fell. Priam, the ruling monarch, and Hector, his son, who has borne the brunt of the fighting, had just cause to consider Helen a plague visited on their heads. But as Priam and Helen meet on the city walls, it is the old king who calls her " dear child " and tells her gently that the gods, not she, are to blame for the war in his eyes. And later when Helen leads the funeral lament over Hector's corpse, she speaks of him as the dearest of all her husband's brothers and states that she has never heard an ugly word from him since first she came to Troy.

The attitude of Priam and Hector toward Helen springs from their innate nobility and generosity. Both know that Helen, by this time, rues the day on which she abandoned her husband and home and that she is a prey to bitter remorse. Now she is with them, and so long as Paris will not give her up, spite and insult are unworthy and out of place. Resentment against Paris, who could not keep his hands off another man's wife, is another thing. Hector, more than once, throws ugly words into the teeth of Paris, blaming him for the war. Yet he will not compel his brother to give up Helen nor will he support Trojans, such as Antenor, who are urging this course of action.

So the Trojans fight on in defense of their city. They are outnumbered and the plan of the elders has been to fight a defensive war, although Hector has stood for taking the offensive. But skirmishes and combat did take place on the plain and could be watched from the walls by the mothers and wives of the Trojan fighters. We see them gathering around Hector at the Scaean gate when he returns from the battle field, inquiring about their men. "For many," as Homer puts it simply, "sorrows were in store."

Hector is the acknowledged leader of the Trojans chiefly because of his excellence as a fighter. He is the best man in the Trojan forces. In character, he is the antithesis of Achilles. His bravery is a moral obligation which he has shouldered voluntarily. He must fight to the utmost to defend Troy not only in order to protect his most valuable possessions, his wife and child, but because his fellow Trojans expect it of him, and he would be ashamed to fail them. He has the usual characteristics of an Homeric hero, a thirst for glory, an appreciation of self, an impulse to what we would call unnecessary cruelty in the heat of battle. But still we feel him to be the symbol of ordered living, a man who is subject to moral law, caught in the ties which a community and a family weave about a man—a patriot, a good husband and father. It is by necessity as well as by inherent ability that Hector, the citizen, has become a splendid fighter.

In his relations with his wife, Andromache, we find the reverse of the elements which dominate the fighting: tenderness, reason, sympathy and love. The scene in which she recalls the destruction of her family and makes Hector realize that he is all that she has, and begs him to have pity on her and to remain within the protection of the gate " so that you will not make your child an orphan and your wife a widow," is almost unique in its overwhelming pathos. But Hector must go. He knows that the day will come when Troy will fall and Priam and Priam's people will perish. It will then be Andromache's fate to ply the loom and carry water as a captive handmaid in far-off Greece. "But may earth be heaped over my dead body before I hear your cry as you are dragged off into captivity."

Here in the love of Hector and Andromache is the contrast to the sensuous infatuation of Helen and Paris which was the seed of the war. We see the latter together in Paris' house in Troy. Her reason has learned to despise him, but her body has long been accustomed to his caresses. Thus she can taunt him with his inferiority to Menelaus in battle and a few moments later cede to the importunity of his physical desire. In view of this situation, which is humiliating to her self-respect, it is no wonder that she flings reproaches at herself, wishes she had perished on the day of her birth, then adds if these things had to be, by the will of the gods, then, at least, she might have gotten a better man. Paris is unstable and has a lordly indifference to what men say about him. But Homer does not make him a coward.

So in Troy, we see the best and worst of men and women within a relatively normal civilized society. Life in a city under siege cannot, of course, be called normal; but in comparison with an armed camp, where the only women are captive concubines, or the slaughter and madness of the battle field, it is fair to say that Troy, to a large extent, represents the normal circumstances under which men and women live together in families forming a community. The scenes in Troy furnish relief and contrast to the activity of warfare which occupies the plain and the camp.

After Thetis has left Achilles in book 1, he does not appear again until book 9. At this point the Trojans, aided by Zeus, have moved into the plain in force and are preparing an attack on the Greek camp. The situation for the Greeks is precarious and, at the suggestion of Nestor, Agamemnon sends an embassy to Achilles with the purpose of placating him and persuading him to do battle. Among the gifts and honors which he offers Achilles is marriage with one of his daughters who will bring him a dowry of several cities. The embassy is composed of Odysseus, Ajax, and Phoenix.

They find Achilles in his quarters. He greets them courteously as friends and entertains them with food and drink. When they have had their fill and toasted their host, Odysseus comes to the point. The Greeks are in a critical situation; Achilles must help them now before it is too late; he must remember his father's parting instructions and curb his pride; the Greeks will admire him the more for putting aside his anger; Agamemnon offers just compensation; indeed, this is an opportunity for Achilles to win great glory by meeting Hector, who thinks that no Greek is his equal, face to face in battle.

The speech is well reasoned. It comes appropriately from the mouth of the chieftain who combines the skill and virtue of an able soldier with a lively intelligence, profound shrewdness in the use of it, and persuasive eloquence. The mention of Hector is clearly calculated to arouse Achilles' love of glory and prick his self-esteem.

Achilles speaks out baldly in return, since a man who says one thing and thinks another is as hateful to him as the gates of Hades. He then enumerates the grievances with which we are already familiar, but now he sweeps through them, piling detail upon detail until the cumulative effect is crushing. No, the Greeks will have to look out for themselves without him. As for the gifts of compensation, he would not accept them if they were as numerous as the sands of the sea. He needs no daughter of Agamemnon to wife; he has his choice of suitable maidens at home. Material things, the wealth of cattle and herds can be taken or bought; when a man's breath has left his body it cannot be recovered. His divine mother Thetis has shown him two paths which he may travel on the way to his grave. If he remains fighting at Troy, he will never return home but his glory will be eternal; if he returns now, he will lose the glory, but his life on earth will be a long one. This is his message to the Greeks. Phoenix will spend the night in his quarters and set sail in the morning with him if he wishes to do so.

It is now the turn of Phoenix, who was Achilles' tutor and performed for him those countless little acts of care and affection which rivet a man's devotion to those who have brought him up in kindness. In testimony of his love, he recalls scenes from Achilles' helpless infancy. But his loftiest and most moving words are reserved for the Prayers who are the daughters of Zeus. They follow limping and wrinkled upon man's folly and make amends for it. The man who respects their approach is helped by them and they hear his wishes. But to the man who denies them, they beg Zeus to send folly and infatuation so that he may be harmed and pay his penalty in turn. Let Achilles learn from the story of Meleager who remained inflexible too long. The gifts of Agamemnon are honorable; they should be accepted while they are offered. But Achilles is still adamant.

Ajax sees that all pleading is useless. Yet he cannot refrain from adding a few bitter words regarding Achilles' savage lack of feeling for his companions. A man will accept a blood price for the slaying of a brother or a child; but Achilles is implacable for the sake of a single girl—a single girl, although Agamemnon is offering him seven of unusual loveliness. Achilles must relent. These are his dearest friends who are speaking to him under his roof. They wish to remain so.

This is soldier speaking to soldier professionally. What counts for Ajax, the best man in combat after Achilles, is the brotherhood in arms which Achilles is betraying. In his bluntness of feeling, he sees the situation as a simple matter of fact: seven girls are better than one; honorable compensation has been offered; Achilles should accept it. He is a world removed from the psychology underlying the situation. Achilles is not untouched by the words of his fellow warrior, but his anger will not let him act otherwise. It will be time enough to stop Hector when he has slaughtered his way to the ships and quarters of the Myrmidons. This is his final message to Agamemnon.

The speeches in this ninth book show plainly why many Greeks of later periods considered Homer the supreme master of the art of eloquence. They are masterpieces of language and content and are founded on a profound understanding of the characters of the several speakers and the situation. But superb as they are, the book as a whole has a larger importance when viewed as a part of the entire epic, for it contains the act of fatal obstinacy in Achilles himself which will make his personal tragedy inevitable. By his refusal to permit reason to overcome the passion which possesses him, he lays the foundation for the crushing sorrow which will come to him in the death of Patroclus and compel him to reverse his stand. Achilles has now made himself responsible for future events.

But he is too noble to leave Troy for the long life which awaits him at home. Thus when the Trojans have broken into the Greek camp and are setting fire to the ships, he is still in his quarters by the sea. Patroclus, his dearest friend and comrade, finds him there in the sixteenth book and begs him, since he will not enter combat himself, to lend him his armor in order that he and the rest of the Myrmidons can come to the rescue of the hard-pressed Greeks. All the best fighters on the Greek side have been wounded and Ajax alone is attempting to stem Hector and the Trojan tide. Is Achilles pitiless, he asks, or does he know of some prophecy which restrains him from fighting?

It is only his anger, Achilles replies, which forbids him to fight. Patroclus may have his armor and the command of the Myrmidons. But he must keep this in mind: he may drive the Trojans away from the ships toward the city but then he must return, for too great a success would deprive Achilles of honor. And he must not lead an attack upon Troy itself for fear that one of the immortals might come against him. As Patroclus goes forth to do battle, Achilles prays to Zeus to give him glory and a brave heart and to bring him back unwounded with his armor and companions. Zeus hears his prayer, as Homer tells us, but grants one part of it alone.

Here again Achilles' obstinate anger is the cause of his friend's death. It is tragic irony that Achilles, of all men, should have been the one to send Patroclus to his doom. The instructions to be prudent and not diminish Achilles' own glory have a particular irony, for Homer has told us previously that Patroclus is destined to die in the forthcoming battle. And he does die by the final thrust of Hector who strips his body of Achilles' armor. The body itself is defended by the Greeks in stormy fighting in which Menelaus distinguishes himself.

News of Patroclus' death is brought to Achilles at the beginning of the eighteenth book. From then on he dominates the scene. His wild sorrow at the loss of his friend and his sense of guilt for the part he has played in it kindle a new wrath directed at Hector. Hector must be killed to atone for the death of Patroclus; and when new armor has been made for Achilles by Hephaestus at Thetis' request and a reconciliation with Agamemnon has been effected, Achilles strides into battle.

For two brilliant books we watch Achilles, the incomparable warrior, in action. In valor and consummate skill in arms, he is everything that he himself and all others have said him to be. The best of the Trojans fall before his savage attack. His killing is vast, calculated, and ruthless. He pits himself against the Scamander, the son of a sea goddess against a river god, and the great Olympians, Hera and Athena, support him. Hector alone stands up to him.

From the battlements Hector's father and mother have begged him to take refuge within the walls. This he cannot do, for it would be a betrayal of the city and himself. He is frightened at the thought of the coming encounter and toys with the idea of throwing himself unarmed on Achilles' mercy. Then his reason asserts itself: he will have to fight it out.

But Achilles approaches and the reality of his presence again terrifies Hector. He succombs to sheer physical terror and flees before his enemy. It is the flight of the horror of a dream: " As in a dream a man is unable to overtake another fleeing before him, yet the pursued cannot escape or the pursuer overtake him, so Achilles was not able to catch him in his running or Hector to escape him." In his flight Hector might have been brought down by one of a dozen Greek spears. But Achilles insists that vengeance is his alone. When finally Hector makes a stand,

Achilles kills him. With his death, Troy is doomed—but so is Achilles, for he is fated to die soon after Hector. Achilles has known this all the time, but now, since the loss of Patroclus, he will accept what comes with indifference, provided that Patroclus is avenged.

With Hector's death, the rest of the Greeks run up and plunge their spears into the body of the dead hero. Achilles further mutilates it by cutting holes beneath the tendons near the heels. He passes straps through them and attaches them to the rear of the chariot. Then laying on his horses with the whip, he drags off the corpse. At the moment of death, Hector had beseeched Achilles to give back his body to his parents against ransom, so that he might be honorably buried. But Achilles in his fury answered him that it would be the prey of dogs and birds. Priam and Hecuba, Hector's father and mother, have witnessed the killing and mutilation; Andromache, his widow, reaches the battlements in time to see the body dragged away. It raises the dust of that plain where Hector had fought so long and so bravely for all the Trojans.

We need not dwell on the funeral games held in honor of Patroclus. Even after the ashes of his beloved friend are laid away, Achilles' anger is unabated and daily he drags Hector's corpse three times around the tomb of Patroclus. But the gods protect it against defilement or decay, and when Zeus wills that it shall be finally returned to Priam, Hermes is sent to guide the old king in safety through the Greek camp to the quarters of Achilles. As Priam slips in unnoticed and throws himself at the knees of Achilles and kisses " the terrible, murderous hands which had killed many of his sons," Homer teaches us an unforgetable lesson in human anguish and a father's love. Priam reminds Achilles that he too has a father on the grim threshold of old age, a father who rejoices because his son is alive and hopes for his return from Troy. But Hector was the last of Priam's fifty sons, the one who protected the city. Now he is gone and Achilles must remember his own father and respect the gods. He must have pity.

Achilles is touched. He thinks of his own father and Patroclus, and in comforting Priam his mind turns to the sorrow that can come to any man from Zeus. It was not to be expected that his consuming anger would be extinguished at once by a flood of compassion. It flares again for a moment in the course of the scene. But the innate generosity of Achilles is now the moving force. The ransom offered by Priam is accepted and the body of Hector surrendered. It is decently burnt by his fellow Trojans as the poem ends.

This, then, is the story of Achilles in the books of the *Iliad* in which he appears. It is the tragedy of a noble man whose passionate concentration upon himself and obstinate refusal to be moved by just consideration for those whom he was morally obligated to consider, his friends and companions-in-arms, brought him to disaster. He lost his dearest friend and to avenge his death, he was obliged to perform the act by which his own destruction was hastened. But by his refusal to take any of the steps by which his own life could have been prolonged, he preserved his own soul.

As we have already seen, there are a number of books of the *Iliad* in which Achilles does not appear. To a certain extent, it is his very absence which makes them possible. They are filled with the exploits of other heroes, both Greek and Trojan, and contain the account of battles sweeping back and forth across the plain. But more than battle scenes are contained in these other books. The encounters of Priam and Helen, Helen and Paris, and Hector and Andromache appear in them. We observe the Trojan women in a vain attempt to appease Athena, and the treachery of Pandarus, who breaks a truce between Greeks and Trojans. We hear of Nestor's deeds of valor when he was young and learn of Patroclus' pity for the hard-pressed Greeks.

It would not be right to say that we have Achilles in mind when we read these parts of the poem which have an immediacy of their own. Nor do the other major heroes lack distinct personalities which make them interesting in themselves. It is rather that the *Iliad* acquires its organic unity in relation to Achilles and his actions, both positive and negative. The master plan of Zeus is slow to be achieved, but we are not allowed to forget that it was established to honor Achilles. The tragedy of Hector is the tragedy of the constant and upright man who dies fighting for his country against superior odds in a war which he has done nothing to bring on—a war, in fact, the original cause of which he feels to be indefensible. By its very nature, it is the tragedy of many men and we feel an instinctive sympathy for Hector, for any of us could have been in his position. The tragedy of Achilles is personal. It belongs to him alone and, unlike Hector's, it could have been avoided. It springs from a particular flaw in the character of an individual under certain fixed circumstances. Its lesson is universal, but it has itself a life of its own in which we cannot share through the identification of common experience. It is the true tragedy of the *Iliad* and raises the poem far above a brilliant account of warfare in the epic style. Achilles gives the *Iliad* its incomparable greatness.

Throughout the long period which begins with the earliest mention of Homer's name at the end of the sixth century B. C. and ends with the collapse of classical culture in the West with the disintegration of the Roman Empire about 1100 years later, the men and women of Greece and Rome believed that a man named Homer had existed. This man was the poet who alone had composed the entire *Iliad* and the entire *Odyssey*. In this vast consensus of opinion, there were scholars, to be sure, who argued that the two epics were composed by different authors, or that lines, passages, or even considerable parts of the poems were later additions to the original texts. But there is no evidence that any one of them questioned the reality of Homer as a person. We have many references to " Homer's *Iliad* " and " Homer's *Odyssey* " in Greek and Latin literature. The writers of these phrases were expressing the same relationship between work and author that we express today in speaking of " Shakespeare's *Hamlet* " or " Shakespeare's *Macbeth*."

This belief in Homer as a historical person led to efforts on the part of Greek historians and chronographers to establish the period in which he lived. Since Homer says nothing about himself in his epics, but speaks of his heroes as belonging to an earlier and better generation, it was natural to assume that he had lived after the Trojan war. Deductions could also be made from geneologies, apparent reflections in his poetry of such events as the Dorian invasion and the Ionic migration and the report that he had contended with Hesiod in a poetic contest at Chalcis in Euboea. Unfortunately, the date of Hesiod was as uncertain as that of Homer, and as for the data furnished by the poems, they could be interpreted in several ways. Consequently our ancient sources give us many different periods for Homer's life and the problem is further complicated, when Homer is dated in relation to the fall of Troy, by the fact that ancient historians often differed in regard to the date of that event. To summarize briefly, we have one Homer who lived a hundred years after a fall of Troy which was dated in 1183 B. C. and another who lived around 900 B. C. and was a contemporary of the Spartan law-giver Lycurgus. The latest date for Homer in an ancient source is the twenty-third Olympiad or about 688 B. C., while the earliest makes him a contemporary of the war which he described. The historian Herodotus held that Homer lived not more than four hundred years before his own time, a reckoning which places Homer in the middle of the ninth century. These are but a few of the conflicting opinions of the ancients regarding the period in which Homer lived.

The ancient reader could turn away from this confusion to the ancient biographies of Homer. Some nine of them have come down to us and all of them betray the marks of a relatively late origin (first century A. D. or after). They contain many conflicting details, but underlying almost all of them is a core of agreement which probably goes back to a *Life of Homer* which was in circulation as early as the sixth century B. C. The points on which most of the extant biographies agree are these.

Homer was born in Smyrna. He was first named Melesigenes because he was born near the river Meles or the river god Meles was his father. He later acquired the name Homer because he served as a hostage in a war between Smyrna and Colophon and the word *homeros* means hostage in Greek. Or else, since *homeros* meant blind in the Aeolic dialect, Homer was so named when he was afflicted with blindness. He spent the first part of his life teaching school, then turned to poetry and traveled over much of the Greek world. He was particularly active on the island of Chios and died and was buried in Ios. He was blind, poor, and unappreciated. His contest with Hesiod we have already mentioned.

Of all this data, there is very little which cannot be explained away today as pure fiction. The wanderings of Homer reflect those of the historical rhapsode or professional reciter of epic poetry who moved from city to city to display his skill or compete for prizes. The blindness is a trait of the bards described in the *Odyssey*. The association with Chios comes from the fact that there was a clan or family of Homeridae on that island. The name Melesigenes recalled the river Meles which is located near Smyrna and the name Homer lent itself to the invention of a hostage Homer. Thus we can discern how the biographical legend grew up or was put together. Yet it in no way eliminates the possibility that a poet called Homer once existed.

To the Greeks, Homer was " the poet " and his two epics were generally acknowledged to be the supreme literary achievements of Hellenic culture. Unfortunately, we cannot dwell here on the part which he played in the formation of the Greek character— there were those, as Plato tells us, who praised Homer as the poet who had educated Greece—and the influence which he exercised on almost all aspects of subsequent Greek literature and art. Any discussion of Homer's place in classical culture would also have to deal with his influence on Roman education and literature and this subject would fill an interesting chapter by itself. Rather we must content ourselves with saying that Homer's supremacy as a poet was recognized by Greeks and Romans alike for over a thousand years until the dark ages when a knowledge of Greek all but disappeared in the West and Vergil alone was left as the classical poet *par excellence*.

With the recovery of Greek literature in the Renaissance,
Homer again became known to Europeans. But his supremacy
as a poet in a world which was steeped in a classicism based on
Latin authors was not readily accepted. In fact, he seemed to
many critics and authors to suffer in comparison with " our
Vergil " who was held to be the model of poetic elegance and taste.
Moreover, new works of great artistic merit were being composed
in Italian and French which, reflecting the taste of the times,
were readily appreciated and, consequently, seemed in the judgment of some superior to a poetry, the spirit of which was alien
and not profoundly felt. Much of the criticism then leveled at
Homer now seems ridiculous. But the critical attitude from which
it sprang was the forerunner in a different guise of the Homeric
criticism which was yet to come.

At the same time, scholars were collecting notices in classical
literature which appeared to support the view that the *Iliad* was
composed of a number of shorter songs or lays which had circulated separately before being united in a single poem. No one in
antiquity, to be sure, had doubted that Homer was the author of
these parts of the greater whole. But it was not a long step for
one who believed that the *Iliad* had come into being in this way
to assume a number of different authors and thus to account
for the errors of taste, inconsistencies, and discrepancies which
hostile critics had been marshalling against Homer since the
fifteenth century.

In the year 1715 a book was published anonymously entitled
Conjectures académiques ou dissertation sur l'Iliade. Its author,
the Abbé d'Aubignac, had died some forty years before. His
thesis was that the *Iliad* represented a number of different poems
by different authors which had been worked into the large epic
that we have today, by additions, subtractions and the insertion
of passages of transition, arranged to give the impression of a
single integral work. Hence for the first time in history Homer,
the person and poet, completely disappeared and his place was
taken by several nameless poets and an equally nameless rhapsode
who was the final compiler. D'Aubignac held that the latter

entitled his compilation " Homer's Rhapsody " because Homer meant " blind " and the poems had been recited by blind men; without writing, so large a poem could never have been handed down; originally it must have been poems, not a poem, which were memorized and transmitted orally. Moreover, with the elimination of a single author, the flaws also vanished, for they were not such in reality, if they were considered only in relation to the respective smaller poems in which they occurred.

By proposing his theory of multiple authorship, d'Aubignac created " the Homeric question." In its simplest form it is this: were the Homeric poems composed by a single author or are they a conflation of a number of smaller poems composed by different authors at different times and later put together into the epics which we have? Moreover, if the latter is so, what position is held by the person Homer in relation to the genesis of the poetry? D'Aubignac had posed the crucial problem which was destined to preoccupy Homeric scholarship for generations.

For many years after its publication d'Aubignac's treatise lay virtually unnoticed. It was completely overshadowed in the nineteenth century by the *Prolegomena ad Homerum* of the German scholar Friedrich August Wolf, which was published in 1795 and gave birth to the " higher criticism " in Homeric studies. Wolf's master idea was that writing was unknown to the Greeks at the time when the Homeric epics were being developed. He therefore thought it impossible that a single poet could have composed them in their present extent by memory alone. On the other hand, a single man could have begun the poems and established their fundamental lines. As they were passed on from generation to generation by professional reciters, additions and modifications were made until the poems were written down and thus received a firm organization in the sixth century B. C. In Wolf's opinion the original author was Homer, but he maintained also that it could not be proved where Homer's work leaves off and that of a successor begins. In making this concession, Wolf honestly expressed his feeling for the artistic unity of the poems in their present state.

The studies which followed the *Prolegomena* were chiefly directed towards explaining the genesis of the Homeric epics by breaking them down into their component parts. The basic assumption on which the work was conducted was that the two epics as we have them represent a conflation of a number of shorter poems composed at various times by different poets. The main task was to discover the joinings and strata within the epics themselves. Contradictions, inconsistencies, and discrepancies could be made to serve as indications of lack of unity and where it lay. Moreover, the rapid development of the disciplines of archaeology and comparative linguistics raised high hopes that they might be used to distinguish older and newer strata. But it is precisely in this regard that they proved to be most disappointing. So scholars had to fall back again on the poems themselves.

It is not an exaggeration to state that every book, passage, and verse of the *Iliad* has been scrutinized for an indication of the stratum or part to which it belongs. In the studies of the Analysts, we are often told exactly where one stratum ends and another begins, and the length of interpolations and transitional passages are given with precise figures. On the basis of such calculations, many theories regarding the composition of the poem as a whole were advanced. In them we find every possible concept, from D'Aubignac's patchwork in which there is no place for a poet Homer, to the conflation of several large epics by a master poet who was able to work them into an artistically organic whole by making modifications and adding passages of his own creation.

Such disagreement could not fail to elicit a strong reaction. It was not only felt that the method of the Analysts was mechanical and preoccupied with the splitting of hairs, but also that a grave injustice had been done to the poetry itself. When a part of the *Iliad* which had been considered by generations of literary critics to be of the highest order was dismissed as a late botch, many scholars thought that the time had come to call a halt. It was not difficult to demonstrate how the individual Analysts who could not agree with each other had abused or misinterpreted the evidence. It was another task to gain some idea of the intrinsic nature of Homeric poetry and to move from there to a concept of how the *Iliad* was composed. A great step forward in this direction was taken by an American scholar, Milman Parry, in his study, published in 1928, of the traditional epithet in Homer. Parry's investigation not only gave impetus to studying the way in which Homer wrote and what it signifies, but to comparing the Homeric epics as forms of poetic expression with the epics of other lands and languages, a field in which Parry himself was active with good results.

This new direction in Homeric studies has led to what might be called a moderate Unitarianism. In general, it does not extend as far as holding that the *Iliad* and the *Odyssey* were composed by the same poet, but it does see the master hand of a very great poetic genius in each poem. It is recognized that he worked from traditional material, but credit is given him for selecting and fashioning this material into an organic whole. Greater justice is now being done to the poems and the poetry and an aesthetic and humanistic approach is giving us a new appreciation of Homer's art. At the same time, research is constantly pressing forward with the help of comparative literature, archaeology, and linguistics toward clearer conceptions of how the Homeric poems developed, not as mechanical compilations, but as the results of a long tradition of oral poetry.

It is hazardous to speak of any general agreement on the Homeric problem at the present time. New books and articles on Homer are flowing from the presses without interruption, and they present many interpretations and opinions. But in the course of Homeric scholarship since Wolf, a residuum of agreement has gradually been built up around certain essential points and although the reader must be warned that much remains to be settled—and possibly never will be settled for lack of evidence—views on the following points are not likely to be changed radically in the immediate future.

The origins of Homeric poetry go back to the Mycenaean period, that is roughly from 1600 to 1100 B. C., on the mainland of Greece. This is shown by archaeology in the description of objects belonging to Mycenaean civilization, linguistics in the Aeolic and Arcado-Cypriote strain in the Homeric language, and the contents of the poems, especially in their relation to the heroes from the Greek mainland. During this period the great deeds of outstanding nobles were recounted in songs for the delight and instruction of succeeding generations, and as the accounts passed from mouth to mouth, they were expanded and embellished to the point where the original kernel of historic fact was often distorted beyond recognition or deeply buried. Stories about the gods were developed out of superstition or religious experience in much the same way.

These songs were delivered in the palaces of the Nobles by professional singers who accompanied their recitations on a stringed instrument. They were aristocratic in character and contained no criticism of the nobility. In fact, the singer might be singing of the great deeds of an ancestor of the lord before whom he was performing. The singer did not pretend to sing of things which he had seen. They were things of which he had heard and he called upon his Muse to stand by and remind him. The singer enjoyed a certain freedom in treating his material, but the main lines were already known to his audience and it is not likely that he could have given a familiar and popular account a radically new turn. He could, of course, add, embellish and modify. The tendency in poetry of this sort is to add, not to subtract, to the traditional material.

Thus in its earliest stage, Homeric poetry was composed and delivered orally. It is filled with devices which made this kind of composition possible, such as combinations of adjective and noun which could be used in a given metrical position in any verse and formulaic lines which could be repeated in introducing a specific situation or describing a specific event—for example, in introducing a speech or in describing the fall of a warrior in battle and the clatter of his armor as he falls.

There are also recurring themes such as a banquet or sacrifice which the poet was equipped to describe with a set of standard descriptions. These he might use *verbatim* or vary slightly. He could also repeat passages of some length which were not thematic. For example, we have a number of speeches in the *Iliad* which are delivered to a person and then repeated by that person to another in the self-same words, except for a change in the personal pronoun. These devices eased the strain of original composition or facilitated the delivery of poems which had been memorized.

While the Mycenaean kingdom was enjoying its greatest prosperity in the fourteenth century B. C., Mycenaean settlers were pushing out from the Greek mainland to other parts of the Mediterranean world. With the destruction of Cnossus about 1400, the Mycenaeans were free to move beyond their own boundaries. We find Mycenaean pottery at Troy and in Egypt, Sicily, and south of Italy. Mycenaean settlers were in Rhodes and Cyprus by the beginning of the fourteenth century. Our Hittite texts speak of a country of the Ahhiyawa who can be identified with the Achaeans of Homer (the historic Mycenaeans) with considerable probability. If the identification is correct, the Mycenaeans had established a principality in Asia Minor by the middle of the same century.

As pressure from the Dorian invaders increased on the mainland and the Mycenaean kingdom began to disintegrate into cities which were cut off from each other and hence had to prepare to defend themselves individually, sporadic emigration from the constant perils of life on the mainland to securer places overseas must have taken place, followed by organized colonization around 900 B. C. Both in this period and in the earlier periods of settling abroad, we may assume that the settlers brought their traditional poetry and their bards with them. In the part of Asia Minor known as Ionia, this Mycenaean poetry continued to flourish and develop with the greatest vigor. For let us remember that we are still dealing with oral poetry—that is, poetry within a state of flux and not yet frozen by the written word.

It was in Ionia too that this poetry underwent its last great linguistic change. It was recast in the dialect of the region (Old Ionic), although many of the original words and phrases were left unaltered. The result was the language which we call the Homeric dialect, created by generations of bards from old and new material. It was a language which lent itself admirably to oral composition and the memorizing of old material. It had the dignity of its ancient forms and the sanctity of being a thing apart, the possession of the bards and their Muses.

We do not have to assume that much time elapsed between the period when the Greeks first began to adopt the Phoenician alphabet in order to be able to record words in writing and that when the professional reciters used the new device to aid themselves in the exercise of their profession. By this, I do not mean that we should imagine them reciting from a text to their audiences, for centuries later when texts had been established and widely circulated, it was still the tradition that the rhapsode should speak from memory. Rather, we may assume that written material played a part in the training of new reciters and made it easier for all to add to their repertories.

Now the *Iliad* has two qualities among others, which have made a profound impression on poets and scholars who have been willing to enjoy and study the poem as a whole: a vast complexity yet a clear unity of design. That these disparate elements could have been wedded so felicitously without the device of writing seems unlikely, if not impossible, to many students of Homer of whom the present writer is one. It is one thing for a professional reciter to produce some fifteen thousand verses of oral poetry on a traditional epic theme or a number of themes with the help of memory and improvisation. It is another to weave dozens of threads together so that a single clear and ordered web is the result, in which the parts are intrinsic to the whole and the whole has the vitality and integrity of the consummate work of art.

No one will deny that the threads were gathered from many places and that there are places where the interweaving shows diverse origin. The important thing is the poetic genius (no smaller word will do) by which the artistic whole was created. To put it in a different way, the composer of the *Iliad* worked to create a single complete poem and achieved his goal. With the

Iliad we have come far beyond the consistency or design which any professional reciter could impose upon an episode or two sung for an evening's entertainment and have reached a masterpiece of literature planned and executed on a large scale. Its composition as we have it demands a poet who was steeped in the traditional material, language, and techniques of the epic art. It also demands a poet of the highest genius who could make of these traditional elements the first and greatest single poem of Western literature.

For want of a better name, we can call this poet Homer. We cannot tell what he added himself to his traditional material, what he changed or modified or omitted. As I have said above, it does not seem likely that he could have done what he did without the art of writing, and we do not know when he wrote. But we shall not be very far wrong if we assume that the *Iliad* in the essential form in which we have it was fixed in writing by 750 B. C.

In my description of the *Iliad* at the beginning of this chapter, I touched upon some of its great poetic qualities: the nobility of its rhetoric, the profound understanding with which its chief characters are delineated, the almost unbearable tragedy and pathos of some of its scenes. In closing, a few more words about Homer's approach to his subject may not be superfluous. The *Iliad* is primarily a poem of warfare and Homer presents us with all its aspects. We are told not only what men are killed, but how. We see the spear passing through the mouth, the arm chopped off, the entrails pouring forth upon the ground, the head severed from the body and rolling away in the dust. These are facts which Homer does not dwell on unduly or avoid. Like eating and drinking and sleeping, they are part of the physical picture.

But Homer knows well that there is more to warfare than the mechanics of slaughter. Those who kill or are killed are human beings, and again and again the poet reminds us of the tragedy for parents and friends which lies in someone's death. Moreover, he has a way of presenting an obscure hero with a few sympathetic words regarding his earlier life, so that we ourselves cannot help but feel peculiarly touched when he is cut down. He may be a young man who had a bride at home, could hope well of the future and deserved a better fate; or Axylus, a rich man and a friend of mankind, who lived in Arisbe and entertained all who came to his house. We feel the pity of it when death shrouds the eyes of such men in utter darkness.

Homer understands men under the pressure of battle. He never makes the cheap and common error of mistaking fear or prudence for cowardice. He recognizes that some men are by nature worse fighters than others and that it is best to put them between superior soldiers where they will have to make a stand. But he also knows that panic can seize the bravest man and that it is the common sense of some to withdraw before two enemies each one of whom alone would be a fair match. He is acquainted with others, too, whose appetite for battle makes them face up to all comers, regardless of the consequences. In spite of the strong and consistent personalities which Homer's heroes possess, they have certain common traits which reflect their world and their society. Ancestry is a priceless possession. A man is what he is not only because of his excellence, but that too of his forbears. There is no hesitancy in speaking at length about lineage, and to talk of self with complacency, to rehearse past achievements and predict new glories, is as natural to the Homeric hero as breathing. It is a hospitable society for those who belong to it. The guest receives the best in entertainment which the household can afford and the splendid gift is given not only as a token of the giver's affluence, but also from the heart. There is pride in material possession, whether in precious metals, animals, acres, or works of art. But there is no place in the *Iliad* where a man sells his soul for material gain.

On Homer's battlefield, there is a code of behavior and as on all battlefields, it is violated under the stress of blinding fury. Homeric heroes act wholeheartedly under the surge of violent emotion, both in peace and in war. There is taunting and vilification, cruelty and mutilation, and a savage satisfaction in inflicting the final penalty of death upon an enemy. At the same

time and within the same books we find exquisite courtesy, a
sensitive respect for ties of hospitality and blood, unshakable
loyalty, and a generosity of mind and spirit which is truly noble.
Homer's women are not easily forgotten. They occupy a
position of dignity and respect within their families and society
and enjoy a freedom of action which might well have aroused
the envy of the secluded woman of fifth century Athens. Their
sufferings are the sufferings of all women whose husbands and
sons and brothers are daily facing death. But they will have even
more to suffer in captivity if their city falls. Homer feels the
pity in their position. The man may win his moment of glory
in the excitement of battle; it is the woman's lot to pray, to
entreat, and to continue to love in an anguish of apprehension.

Homer knows the small detail which illuminates the larger
scene with poetic feeling. Hector turns to embrace his son a final
time before going forth to battle. The boy cowers screaming in
the bosom of his nurse, frightened by the bronze of his father's
helmet and its trembling crest of horse-hair. The father and
mother laugh at his terror and Hector removes the helmet, so
that the boy may again find the familiar image that means his
father to him. This exact observation of a natural reaction on
the part of a child brings us the pleasure of recognition. Its place
in a scene in which the wife and mother has been beseeching her
husband not to take the step which may make the child an orphan
increases our compassion for this ill-fated family of which even
the most innocent is doomed. Examples of this sure poetic touch,
in which contrast, sympathy, irony, and suggestion are blended
to move the heart and give the reader pause are many in the *Iliad*.

The divine element in the *Iliad* is probably the least attractive
to the modern reader. In general, the gods will appear to be far
below the mortals morally in their wanton indulgence in man's
baser appetites. They have their quarrels and jealousies, are
unscrupulous in the use of their powers, and are restrained only
by the superior force of Zeus which they spend much of their
time in thwarting. The lady goddesses, in particular, who rarely
act like ladies, are put to shame by the human women of Troy.

Family life on Mount Olympus has its serene moments, but on the whole, the scheming, taunting, selfish atmosphere is not designed to make us think very highly of the Homeric pantheon.

The chief gods and goddesses have their human favorites. They stand by them in battle, give them advice, and trick their opponents into unfavorable positions. They cannot kill each other for they are immortals, but they can wound and hurt each other and they do. Very old and often very primitive ideas and concepts can be discerned behind their anthropomorphic forms. Occasionally, they have a psychological quality and represent what a man would have said to himself upon reflection, as when Athena restrains Achilles' impulse to attack Agamemnon with his sword. On the whole, however, they act as human beings who lack the restraint placed upon the heroes by their own code of nobility.

The rapidity of the Homeric hexameter and the skill with which it is manipulated, the richness and color of the vocabulary, the contrast between the traditional epithets and lines and the passages in which the poet is working more independently—all these qualities are difficult to discern even in the best translations. But the general sense and feeling of Homer can be caught in the medium of another language effectively and the reader will not be left in doubt regarding the greatness of the *Iliad* as literature.

Homer presents his moral lessons not only by implication or a passing observation; he uses old stories or myths as illustrations. He handles them as individual short poems and they lend variety and interest to the whole. The same can be said of his similes where an action in the poem is given vividness and immediacy by being compared to something which his audience has witnessed or experienced: scenes from nature or the common pursuits of hunting and herding. With the similes we enter the world in which Homer lived when he was composing his poetry.

The *Iliad* is the monumental gate through which we enter into the literature of Western civilization. It is a mature poem which represents the culmination of centuries of poetic endeavor. It is epic poetry at its noblest and a commentary on all mankind. It stirs our emotions, invites us to reflection and entertains us with the variety, richness and movement of the parts. It has withstood every kind of analysis and criticism. It has inspired many poets of all generations and tongues and brought to countless readers one of the purest and deepest of pleasures, that of participating in the revelation of life which is the gift of the masterpiece of literature. The unique experience of reading the *Iliad* from beginning to end for the first time is available to all. Those who will do so, will not need to be urged to return to it again, for the spell which it casts is enduring.

III

Vergil's Aeneid

HENRY T. ROWELL

PUBLIUS Vergilius Maro was born in the village of Andes not far from Mantua on October 15th of the year 70 B. C. His parents did not belong to the kind of provincial family which had important connections in Rome and was part of the local aristocracy. The father was a self-made man in a society in which forbears and inherited social position were of recognized importance. He appears to have accumulated considerable land in the territories of Mantua and Cremona before his death, and his wife, the daughter of a minor municipal official, may have brought him as her dowry the modest capital with which he laid the foundation of his fortune. But be that as it may, there was money enough to send young Vergil away to school in other towns of the Po Valley and later to Rome. There is no indication that Vergil was not financially comfortable throughout his life and he had no need either of a Maecenas or the gift of a Sabine farm to assure him of a leisure which he could devote to writing.

Vergil grew up as a country boy. The scenes and activities of his youth are reflected in the *Bucolics* and *Georgics*, and his love of Italy as a whole in its countless manifestations of natural beauty inspired some of his finest poetry. He is the first great Italian poet in his interest in all parts of Italy and its past. About a century and a half before, Cato the Censor had seen that there was more to a history of Italy than a history of Rome and had included the origin of other Italian towns in his *Origins* written in Latin prose. In Latin poetry, we look in vain for any similar appreciation until we come to Vergil. It is not likely that this width of comprehension and depth of feeling for all Italy and its countryside would have developed as strongly as it did in a boy who had grown up within sight of the Roman forum and whose idea of the country was the hills of Latium pleasantly dotted with the country estates of the richer Romans.

The first elements of education were probably acquired at home: reading, writing, and the calculation of simple sums. At Cremona where Vergil was sent before his fifteenth year and later at Milan, we can assume that he devoted himself to the traditional literary studies of the period. They included the detailed examination of Greek and Latin authors from many points of view. The contents of the books furnished lessons in mythology, geography, and history; stylistic, poetic, and metrical elements were analyzed; and the text at hand furnished the example and starting point for original compositions and the development of an ability to speak and write correctly. Such studies were thought to furnish a firm foundation for the training in rhetoric which normally followed. Provincial parents who could do so provided the means by which a son might obtain this training in Rome.

In the first place, the best formal instruction was available there. But, the fact that the student would be at the heart of Italy's political life where he could listen to the greatest orators of his time played no small part in deciding on a Roman education. An influential provincial family might manage to place their son under the tutelage of men of political distinction and thus give him at an early age the connections and support which were almost indispensable for a successful career within the Roman government. A more modest family could hope that their son would develop his oratorical talents, profit from the cultural advantages of the great city, and make some useful friends before returning home to attend to family affairs and to participate in the public life of his native town. We can assume that hopes such as these were entertained by Vergil's parents when they sent him to Rome.

They were not destined to be realized. When Vergil reached Rome, he had already begun to experiment with the poetic forms which were fashionable at the period, and during his first stay there, if not before, he felt himself attracted by the study of philosophy. He was not an orator by nature and a shyness which seems to have remained with him throughout his life created further aversion to public speaking. The pedantic atmosphere of the rhetorical schools with their emphasis on formal distinctions and routine devices was distasteful to a mind which was discovering the wider horizons of poetry and philosophy, while the fame, wealth, or political success to which the accomplished orator might attain in the council chamber, market place, or courts of law meant little to him. We are told that he pleaded only once in court.

In Naples, the philosopher Siro had gathered together a group of men to study Epicurean philosophy under his direction. It included such literary personalities as the epic poet and dramatist Varius Rufus and the critic Quintilius Varus. Here was an environment in which Vergil could breathe fully and peacefully. Since the year 49 B. c. when Julius Caesar crossed the Rubicon and set off a chain of civil wars, Rome had been in constant turmoil and change. To be sure the decisive battles had been fought outside of Italy in Thessaly, Africa, and Spain; but an atmosphere of revolution prevailed and living must have seemed an uneasy adventure into perpetual change. Vergil was not a man to thrive under the excitement and tensions of such a period. Relative seclusion and the opportunity to meditate upon a philosophy which counseled a tranquil indifference to the stormy world outside the soul must have seemed irresistibly attractive. He joined Siro's group, probably around the year 45 B. c.

Vergil fell in love with the old Greek city of Naples and its incomparably beautiful surroundings. He acquired property and became a familiar figure to the Neapolitans, who gave him the name of Parthenias in reference to the virginal purity of his character and the name of the city which he had made his own. For Naples was also called Parthenope. It is there that we find him finishing his *Georgics* in the summer of 29 B. c and there that his bones were entombed ten years later. He also kept a house in Rome near the gardens of Maecenas on the Esquiline, but he avoided the city insofar as he could and shrank from the notoriety to which he was subjected on its public streets. We also have passing mention of a retreat in Sicily.

The civil war which broke out shortly after the assassination of Caesar in 44 B. C. had a direct effect upon Vergil's fortunes. Following the defeat of Brutus and Cassius at Philippi in the fall of the year 42, it was decided that the soldiers on the winning side should receive land, which would be confiscated from Italian towns that had sided with the losers, as a bonus. Mantua was among them, and Vergil's property—or that of his family—was in danger of passing into the hands of a veteran. Vergil appears to have travelled north in an effort to stave off the disaster. In his *Bucolics* he addresses a number of the men whom we know to have been connected officially with the land distributions: Asinius Pollio, Alfenus Varus, and Cornelius Gallus. The details of the negotiations are far from clear since they are chiefly known to us from the poetry of the *Bucolics*, and it is always difficult and often impossible to find the sober fact under the poetic coloring and the element of the fictitious. Suffice it to say what is generally held: Vergil managed to bring his case before Octavian, the later Emperor Augustus, who was the most powerful person in Italy at the time, and recovered his property.

The *Bucolics* caught the attention of Maecenas, who was anxious to include the most promising poets of the period within his circle of friends. Some he could help financially as he helped Horace, others he could encourage and advise. The group was "nationally" minded in the sense that they stood firmly for Rome, Italy, and Octavian against Antony and the Hellenistic east. Vergil knew Maecenas well enough by 38 B. c to introduce Horace to him. He began to write his *Georgics* a few years later and they were dedicated to Maecenas.

Vergil appears to have begun his final and greatest work, the *Aeneid*, in 29 B. C., as soon as the *Georgics* were published. He labored with it for ten years and then decided on a three year sojourn in Greece and Asia Minor during which he would put the poem into final form. At the beginning of his trip, he met Augustus in Athens and decided to return to Rome with him. On an excursion to Megara, he fell ill but pressed on with his journey home. He reached Brindisi in a serious condition and died there a few days later on the twenty-first of September of the year 19. His bones were brought to Naples and placed in a tomb outside the city walls. He had written his own epitaph:

> *Mantua me genuit, Calabri rapuere, tenet nunc*
> *Parthenope; cecini pascua, rura duces.*

The reader who has read the previous chapter on Homer will be struck immediately by the difference in what we know about the two greatest epic poets of classical antiquity. The short biography of Vergil which has just been presented is based on reliable information which was collected not long after the poet's death. Vergil lived in an age which is well known to us from documents of every sort, and the *Aeneid* was written in the full light of history. Whereas Homer's existence as a person and his relation to the *Iliad* had to be deduced from the nature of the *Iliad* itself and some general considerations of an external nature, we could here start with the man Vergil as the author of the *Aeneid*.

For Vergil was its author in the sense in which we use the word today. He alone was responsible for his poem in the last analysis and its creation and permanence would have been impossible without the art of writing. This does not mean that Vergil was not influenced by earlier works including the Homeric epics. But he was influenced by them as works which were frozen in writing, a far different situation to that of Homer, if we have analyzed it correctly, who stood in the midst of a vast and changing flow of oral poetry, parts of which he organized into the *Iliad* through his own poetic genius and the relatively new device of writing. Whatever Homer himself may have added he had to compose in the manner of the material which he had inherited, that is, in the manner of oral poetry. Vergil was free to make his own approach, limited only by the respect which he would be expected to show for the tradition established by the writings of his predecessors.

In the *Aeneid*, we are taken back to the world of Homer after the fall of Troy and, at the same time, to the events which led to the founding of Rome. In book 20 of the *Iliad*, Poseidon prophesied that the Trojan hero Aeneas and his descendants were fated to rule over the Trojans. Accordingly, later authors were compelled to make Aeneas escape the destruction of Troy. A Sicilian poet, Stesichorus, seems to have been the first to bring him to Italy and the Greek historian Hellanicus (last half of the fifth century B.C.) made him the founder of Rome which he named after one of the women in his expedition. We need not dwell on the many forms which the legend received at the hands of the fourth and third century Greeks. Most of them, in one way or another, brought Aeneas together with the Roman legend that Romulus and Remus had founded Rome, by making the latter descendants of the Trojan hero within a few generations.

The Romans, however, were establishing their own chronology in the third century B.C., and by working backward from the founding to the Republic through the period of kings they had reached the middle of the eighth century (*c.* 750 B.C.) as the time when Rome was founded. Since the date for the fall of Troy was now fixed in the first part of the twelfth century, it was impossible for the Romans to make Romulus and Remus direct descendants of Aeneas. A long period of time had to be filled in with historical events if Aeneas was to be kept as part of the legend, and the Romans were not inclined to remove him. Therefore, a line of kings was invented which descended from Aeneas and a Latin wife and who ruled over the Latin city of Alba Longa. Romulus and Remus were made the last of this line.

In the last century of the Roman Republic, many distinguished Roman families began to trace their origin back to the Trojans who had settled in Italy after the fall of Troy. The Julian family claimed to be descended from the son of Aeneas and grandson of Venus who had changed his original name of Ascanius to that of Iulus on coming to Italy. Thus, Julius Caesar and his adopted son who later became the emperor Augustus could boast of divine ancestry and direct descent from the hero who had founded the Roman people. A poem celebrating Aeneas would not only celebrate the distant origins of this people, but also those of the Julian family.

At the time when Vergil wrote the *Aeneid*, Augustus, a Julian, had made himself the master of the Roman world. The opportunity to deal with material which was pertinent to Rome and its emperor while falling within the orbit of Homeric tradition and the legendary history of early Italy was not lost upon Vergil. We know that he once contemplated writing an epic on the historical achievements of Augustus. He wisely abandoned his plan for a field in which his creative imagination and poetic genius would have a far wider scope. The details of legendary material lack rigidity and are usually refashioned from generation to generation. Vergil had found a medium in which his poetic genius could move more freely than among contemporary events.

In dividing the *Aeneid* into two even parts, books 1 to 6 and 7 to 12, we are following in Vergil's footsteps. At the beginning of book 7, he informs us that he is engaging upon a greater work; and, it may be observed in passing, that this is precisely the part of the *Aeneid* which is the least well known to the modern reader. It was also noted by the ancients that the first six books reflect the *Odyssey* while the last reflect the *Iliad*. This is true to a certain degree, but the comparison must not be pressed too closely.

The first book of the *Aeneid*, like that of the *Iliad*, provides us with a key to the entire poem. We soon learn that we shall be confronted with such traditional epic elements as Olympian gods and their intervention in human affairs, characters of heroic stature, nobility of diction, and even such devices as the simile. But we learn also that we are dealing with a poem in which the traditional material has been reworked to serve far different ends, that much is present of which Homer could not have dreamed, and that the poetry is no pale imitation of the Homeric but carries the stamp of the originality of a master poet.

In the very first lines of the first book, Aeneas is characterized as a man who is distinguished for his *pietas*. Our word " piety " with its predominantly religious sense renders only one connotation of the many which are contained in the Latin word. To the Roman a man who was *pius* was one who had a strong sense of moral obligation. His actions were governed not only by respect for divine authority but also by his sense of duty towards his fellow men and the society and country to which he belonged. By this very word, *pietas*, Aeneas is removed from the world of the Homeric hero with its rather primitive morality and placed within the orbit of Roman ethics. The first great transfer has been made.

Moreover, we are told in the same introductory passage that Aeneas, because of the relentless wrath of Juno, will suffer hardships on land and sea before he is safely settled in Italy and can start the historical process which will lead to the founding of Rome. Hence, we are to have a story in which a man of high moral character is often tried by misfortune, and no less a power than the queen of the gods is determined to thwart him in his mission. Here too is a different Juno. To be sure, she still nurses the old grievances which made her take the part of the Greeks in the Trojan war, but she pursues the Trojans cruelly in their defeat primarily because she is aware that the descendants of the Trojans in Italy, the Romans, are fated to overthrow Carthage, a city dear to her heart. The historical fact of the final outcome of the Punic wars is thus made a reason for Juno's continuing wrath.

When we first see Aeneas and his band of Trojans, they are caught on the open sea between Sicily and the bay of Naples by a tempest which Juno has raised. Aeneas is facing death and has the normal physical reaction of terror to the situation. But his mind turns to Troy and his first words are of the good fortune of those Trojans who were able to die fighting at the foot of its walls. These are appropriate words of *pietas* regarding his lost country, where he would have died (as Vergil will make clear to us later) if the divine will had permitted him to do so. But we must also respect the fortitude of a man who could feel the chill of fear and still wrench his mind to conditions under which he would have died more nobly. Aeneas and his band survive the storm, however, and when he has landed safely with some of his ships on the shore of north Africa, we see in him the competent captain who first looks after his men's physical needs and later raises their fallen spirits, while hiding his own dejection.

His divine mother, Venus, has been shaken by her son's plight and addresses reproaches to Jupiter who has been looking down from heaven upon affairs on earth. He has already promised that the Romans, the descendants of the Trojans, would be the lords of the earth. Has he changed his mind? In answer, the father of gods and men reassures Venus by revealing to her the secrets of the Fates: Aeneas will reach Latium, overcome the opposition of the local tribes, and found a city; his son Ascanius will establish the long line of rulers which will end in Romulus, the founder of Rome. There will be no limit in time or place to the power of the Romans and Juno herself will repent of her anger and cherish them. Augustus, a descendant of Ascanius who will have the new name of Iulus, will stand at the peak of Rome's destiny. After great and successful wars, he will establish a new order of virtue, law, and the gentler arts. The gates of the temple of Janus will be closed and the *pax Augusta* will reign.

Jupiter's words give us the master design and moral purpose of the whole poem. Rome's greatness and her dominion over the Mediterranean world is a matter of divine will and, consequently, is divinely justified. It must all come to pass, but what has just happened to Aeneas reminds us that it will not come to pass easily and that human valor, endurance, and effort will play their due parts. Aeneas, as founder of the Roman people, must demonstrate the very virtues which will make his descendants worthy of the gifts which Fate has in store for them. As the epic proceeds, we are allowed to forget not Aeneas' mission, the divine character of which is increasingly impressed upon him, but the fact that the mission must turn out successfully at the end. When Aeneas faces adversity and must make difficult decisions, we feel that the action which he takes is determined freely by his own sense of moral obligation and that we are witnessing the old conflict between the world and a man who would serve god and save his own soul. Disaster is visited upon Aeneas from on high; at times he is divinely reminded of the action he should take; but the final decision is always his to make.

Thus we have an epic, the morality of which is expounded on two planes, divine and human. Aeneas is the agent through whom the initial and crucial step in the execution of the divine plan for Rome's future greatness is carried out. The final result of the plan will be the historical situation in which the first Romans to read the *Aeneid* found themselves. They are reminded that their supremacy was founded by human virtue, labor, and determination as well as by divine authority. They must continue to show the same qualities as Aeneas in order to enjoy continuing favor from on high.

Unlike the *Iliad*, the *Aeneid* is not rich in characterization. Apart from Aeneas, there are only a handful of characters who have the vitality and completeness of individuals. Of these, a woman, Dido, is drawn with the finest lines and most profound sympathy. Her tragedy comes from no fatal flaw within herself but from the warmth and generosity of a noble heart impelled by circumstances, some of which are divinely contrived. When we first meet her, she is in the course of organizing an expedition to found a new kingdom, Carthage. Aeneas who has been sent to her by his divine mother Venus watches her first actions. Venus has already told Aeneas and the reader of the grim circumstances which compelled her to abandon Tyre—the death of a beloved husband at the hands of her brother—and kindled admiration for her strength and enterprise.

She is not only a very beautiful woman, as Vergil tells us expressly, but her first actions also proclaim her to be a great ruler. She is in complete command of the complicated task of founding a new kingdom. When Ilioneus and other Trojans who had been separated from Vergil by the storm and had landed on another part of the coast arrive to beg her protection and aid, she treats them with immediate kindness, offering to help them on their way or to take them into her new city on the same footing as that of the original colonists. On witnessing this scene Aeneas comes forth from the mist which has surrounded him and in an eloquent speech pledges his eternal gratitude. He prays that the gods may reward Dido for her benevolence and swears that he will never forget her. This is not the only passage in the *Aeneid* where Vergil makes full use of anticipatory irony.

Dido is immediately impressed by the appearance of Aeneas and her heart is moved by the tragedy which he has suffered. She herself has passed through cruel events and learned to help the unfortunate. She invites him to be her guest, and he sends for his son Ascanius and suitable gifts. But Venus fears some treachery and substitutes Cupid for Ascanius. He is instructed to inspire love in Dido, so that she may do no harm to Aeneas, and in the guise of Ascanius, he fulfills his mother's wish. Unhappy Dido. From this moment, she must love. But the nature of her love will be determined by her own great character and it will be a love which will find in death alone a liberation from the intolerable circumstances which have impaired its nobility.

It is at a banquet in Dido's palace that Aeneas, at Dido's request, describes the fall of Troy and his wanderings. The second book is devoted to the fall and is an epic in itself. It is the story of the last fatal night of Troy's existence when the Greek warriors sallied forth from the wooden horse to unbar the gates to their companions in arms who had pretended to sail away. We witness scene after scene of violent action as we move through the dark streets with Aeneas in his desperate attempt to stem the tide. We feel pity for the helpless, the women who will be carried off as captives, and for aged Priam, butchered on an altar in the center of his palace by the ruthless son of Achilles. Around us the flames are mounting and buildings are crashing to the ground. There is confusion and pillage, the rattle of arms, and the corpses of the dead. It is a night of horror.

In making Aeneas escape final destruction, Vergil was confronted by an ethical problem. A hero and particularly the founder of the Roman people should have died fighting to protect his city. Hector had done so with many another Trojan, and Rome would have expected the same course of action from any of her soldiers. Aeneas must be compelled to abandon Troy by a force which it would be a greater fault to disobey. Hector first appears to him in a vision and informs him that all is lost. Aeneas must save Troy's household gods and create a new home for them across the sea. But Aeneas follows his first instinct. He seizes his weapons and dashes into the fray.

Aeneas fights valiantly, but he and the little band which he has collected cannot manage to turn the tide. Nevertheless, it is Venus alone who can make him desist from further resistence by appearing in person to him and showing him that the great gods themselves, including Jupiter, are taking an active part in the destruction of the city and inspiring the Greeks to victory. Aeneas now has divine authority for leaving the city, for a pious man will not pit himself against the gods. But his father Anchises, old and crippled, refuses to leave and again the rightness of fleeing is confirmed by omens from on high. In the confusion of flight, Creusa, Aeneas' wife, is lost, but when he returns into the burning city to seek her, her shade appears to him and informs him that it was not the will of the gods that he should carry her away. After many wanderings, she continues, he is destined to find a new kingdom and a queenly bride in the western land by the Tiber. His future is part of a divine plan.

The wanderings are described in the third book. Aeneas and his companions set out in the spring and their voyage to Sicily takes them about a year to complete. In spite of Creusa's mention of Italy as Aeneas' goal, he does not appear to remember her words. This is not the only matter in which book 3 does not accord with the rest of the poem and we shall come to the reason below. It is enough to say here that Aeneas' destination is gradually revealed to him by oracles and other prophetic utterances in the course of the book. He sails from Troy to Thrace, Delos, Crete, and places on the west coast of Greece. From there, he crosses the Adriatic, lands on the heel of Italy and pushes on across the Gulf of Tarentum and around the lower part of Sicily to its western tip. The description of these movements might have been mechanical and monotonous in the hands of another author. Vergil fills it with a great variety of incidents which holds the reader's interest: in Thrace we hear the pitiful story of the murder of Polydorus; in Crete, we witness a devastating pestilence; there is the encounter with the obscene Harpies in the Strophades and the reunion with Helenus and Andromache at Buthrotum; we share in the Trojan's excitement in seeing Italy at last, and in Sicily we are exposed to the elemental fury of Aetna and the brutality of the Cyclops. On reaching Drepanum on the western tip of Sicily, Aeneas is hospitably received by another group of escaped Trojans. But there he loses his father Anchises who has been the solace of his anxieties and his counselor in difficulty. Aeneas will have to face the future without the comfort of his immediate presence. Very soon, as we shall see, he will need his guiding spirit.

Let us recall here that Aeneas has described the fall of Troy and his wanderings to Dido in the first person at the banquet which took place at the end of book 1. The storm which opens the same book occurred after the Trojans had left Sicily on their way to the Bay of Naples. Hence in books 2 and 3 we have the events which led up to book 1.

In a Hellenistic poem Dido would have fallen in love with Aeneas at first sight with or without the direct intervention of Cupid. But Dido is not an inexperienced young girl to be over-come by a sudden flare of emotion at the apparition of the handsome and gallant young man of whom she has been vaguely dreaming. She is not a Medea or an Ariadne but a mature widow who has already experienced a profound love in her first husband Sychaeus. She has vowed to be true to him beyond the grave, and she is not one to treat such a vow lightly. Moreover, her innate modesty and self-respect, her *pudor*, would alone have restrained her from intimacies which, she felt, should belong to only one relationship, a relationship which she had had and was now forever past. The memory of Sychaeus had to be effaced and this was the task of Cupid; human persuasion through a reasonable presentation of practical considerations was undertaken by her sister Anna; and Aeneas had to show himself a person who could attract and deserve her love.

He does so in his account of the events in books 2 and 3. The bravery of his behavior, the nobility of his bearing, and the vicissitudes to which he has been subjected by Fate arouse an admiration and sympathy in Dido which she recognizes as the traces of an old fire. Urged on by her sister who sees every advantage in a remarriage with Aeneas, Dido consults the omens under a false pretence. She places herself in a proximity to Aeneas which cannot fail to stir up her emotions. And yet divine intervention is required for the final, irrevocable step.

Juno proposes to Venus that they lay down their enmity. Dido, now deeply in love, will serve a Trojan husband and both goddesses will rule over the new kingdom. Venus discerns Juno's scheme to prevent Aeneas in this way from reaching Italy and founding the Roman people. But she acquiesces, pretending an uncertainty regarding Jupiter's will, while being certain that he will not allow a permanent fusion of Carthaginians and Romans. By a union with Dido, Aeneas, at least, will have complete protection for the meantime.

A hunting party is organized by Dido. It has the color, pomp, and brilliance of the preparations for a royal wedding. Juno sends a storm which forces Dido and Aeneas to take refuge in a cave away from the rest of the party. While the elements rage ominously without, the union is consummated and Dido seals her own disaster. Thereafter, she is too big a person to conduct a clandestine affair. She calls their union "marriage," but it is not a legal marriage in the eyes of men and Aeneas knows it.

For the moment, however, he seems to have forgotten his mission. Adored by a beautiful and intelligent woman and living in comfort and peace, he had every reason to put departure from his mind. He is even participating in the building of Carthage when Jupiter sends Mercury to order him on.

It does not occur to Aeneas to disobey and he makes immediate preparations to depart. But he is only too human when faced with the awkward predicament of telling Dido that he must abandon her. Like any man he procrastinates, waiting for just the right moment to approach her with the news, hoping with the traditional optimism of the male in such circumstances that there can be a right moment to tell an adoring woman that something is going to be done which will break her heart. But Dido has heard of his plans and is the first to speak. She reproaches him with treachery, recalls their love, appeals to his gratitude and pity. He admits his indebtedness, corrects her in her concept of their "marriage," patiently explains his feeling for Troy (to which he would return if he could) and the order of Jupiter that he must return to Italy. His cold reasoning fills her with horror, and she heaps scorn upon him before she flees. But she still loves him and engages her sister to persuade him to remain, if only for a short time. This too he refuses to do.

It is clear to her now that death by her own hand is the only atonement which she can make for the guilt with which she has tarnished herself and the only liberation from her humiliation. She can and does prepare this end, but hopelessness confirmed by more than words must bring it about. Again Mercury urges Aeneas to hasten his departure. This time there is no delay and Dido sees his fleet pulling out to sea. Her suicide occurs on the pyre which she had pretended to erect to burn all the objects which might remind her of Aeneas.

The episode of Dido and Aeneas is probably the most absorbing part of the whole epic to the modern reader. It is a story of romantic love handled with deep psychological insight, and it is a true tragedy because of the nobility of Dido who is here the chief actor. Today our sympathies are likely to lie entirely with her. Vergil makes it clear that Aeneas was never moved by the kind of devastating passion by which Dido had been uprooted from her principles, and it can be plausibly argued that he felt no more than gratitude and affection, although he was quite willing to allow her to delude herself into believing that her love was returned in equal measure and to shower pleasures and comforts upon him. We feel it to be his fault that he allowed their relationship to progress to the point where his departure would cause her suicide.

To be sure, Aeneas seems to have forgotten his divine mission until he is reminded of it by Mercury. But why, we ask, if he thought he could live on in Carthage, did he not call for a marriage into which Dido would have been only too glad to enter? The impression of a man who has hit upon a golden opportunity which he cannot bring himself to forego by weighing the consequences of its exploitation is difficult to dispel. The coldness with which he answers Dido's entreaties alienates our sympathies. We understand that he cannot disobey the express command of Jupiter, but we scorn the alacrity with which he complies. Dido's lofty character, her ability to love completely, and the nobility of her death place her among the great heroines. Vergil has shown his hero to be a man subject to human frailty and this we accept. But it is a just cause for resentment that the kind of frailty which Aeneas shows causes the destruction of so much that is fine. Granted that the gods conspired against Dido, Aeneas could have avoided the part which he played in making their conspiracy result in her death.

The Trojans return to Sicily, celebrate funeral games in honor of Anchises, and push on to Cumae near the bay of Naples. An entrance to the underworld is situated there and Aeneas, protected by the golden bough and guided by the Sibyl, Apollo's prophetic priestess, descends. We are reminded of Odysseus' visit to the underworld in Book 11 of the Odyssey, for Vergil's underworld has many of the elements which were traditional since Homer. But the Latin poet uses the Homeric example for a far different purpose at the end of the book. Then Anchises who has joined the Sibyl as guide shows Aeneas the impressive spectacle of the men who will achieve Rome's future greatness. To Aeneas, they are souls yet to be born; to the Roman reader of the *Aeneid*, they were the illustrious dead who had raised Rome from a settlement of shepherd's huts on the Palatine to the great city which was the mistress of the Mediterranean world.

Vergil was here emphasizing what every Roman knew from his poets and historians and from word-of-mouth tradition: Rome's greatness was an achievement of men and character. But there is more to the lesson than this reminder. In a memorable passage Vergil, through Anchises, explains to all Romans the nature of Rome's political mission: to rule the peoples of the earth and to impose the ways of peace; to spare those who have submitted and to vanquish the defiant by force of arms. It is a program of political supremacy through power which we would call imperialism today. But Rome's supremacy must be responsible. It must justify itself by bringing peace and equitable treatment to all men. For Vergil's time, this was a lofty concept, nor has it lost its moral validity wherever, in our world, such supremacy through power is still exercised.

The last six books are chiefly devoted to events in Latium, the country around Rome. Here Aeneas must overcome armed opposition on the part of the native inhabitants in order to establish himself in the fated land and to win a Latin bride. His chief antagonist in the drama is a native prince, Turnus, whose anger against Aeneas is aroused when the hand of the Latin princess Lavinia whom he had expected to marry is given to Aeneas by her father Latinus in accordance with divine instructions. Juno still pursues the Trojans relentlessly and is instrumental in arousing the Latins and protecting Turnus until his inevitable death at the hands of Aeneas.

Much of these last six books is devoted to descriptions of combat, but when they threaten to become monotonous, Vergil renews the reader's interest with scenes of a different nature. Also, his presentation of fighting is more varied than that of Homer. There are lengthy episodes of great charm such as Aeneas' visit to the site of Rome, then no more than the rustic village of the Arcadian Evander, and episodes of moving heroism such as the loyalty to the death of the two young Trojans, Euryalus and Nisus. We are moved by the extinction of youthful nobility and beauty in Pallas, the son of Evander, and Camilla, the virgin warrior. We are led into the wonderful old Italy of local myths and legends in which the settings and landscapes are those which Vergil knew and loved.

Finally, we have in Turnus a character whose very flaws are readily forgivable when they are considered against the background of his temperament and valor and the circumstances in which he is placed. As Aeneas grows in moral perfection before our eyes, as his actions become more and more the results of right reason, as he becomes harder and surer of himself in righteousness, we look with increasing sympathy on the humanness of Turnus. Ardent, obstinate, fearless, he fights on to the end against superior human odds and destiny itself. He can be accused of ignoring the express will of the gods, of putting his honor before the welfare of a whole people, and of lacking self-control. But he remains true to himself and his concept of honor and will not suffer himself to fall in his own esteem at any cost. His death like that of Dido makes us feel that something of great human value has been destroyed. Aeneas overcomes him with the help of one of the furies, who is sent by Jupiter. She transforms herself into an obscene bird which flutters back and forth before Turnus' face to confuse and terrify him. It is not the clean end which he deserved. With his death at Aeneas' sword, the epic is finished. The first great obstacles on the path to Rome's historical greatness under the descendants of Aeneas have been overcome.

The *Aeneid* as we have it today is an unfinished poem. We not only know this from Vergil's biographers but from the state of the poem itself. It contains unfinished lines, contradictions, and discrepancies which would not have appeared in the final draft. Scholars have used them as evidence in attempting to discover the order in which the individual books were written. We know, again from biographical sources, that Vergil made prose summaries of the contents of each book and then worked on episodes as the spirit moved him. It is fairly certain that books 1, 4, and 6 were composed more or less in that order. Book 5 was certainly written after them, and 3, which has many passages which cannot be made to accord with the rest of the epic, was probably the earliest to be written and would have had to be thoroughly revised.

These imperfections, however, do little to detract from the perfection of the *Aeneid* as a whole or the quality of its poetry. Whether a book be considered early or late, it shows the same sustained poetic excellence which appears in all parts of the work. The meter of the classical epic, the dactylic hexameter, had been established by Homer and was adapted to the Latin language early in the history of Latin literature. But it was not a meter which could be bent to the Latin tongue with ease, and it is no small achievement of Vergil's genius that he developed it to its greatest perfection in Latin.

The gigantic shadow of Homer fell across Vergil's path in many other ways. We have already mentioned his adoption of such Homeric elements as the Olympian gods and we have also seen how this element was reworked to serve a moral and political purpose: the divine justification of Rome's hegemony. But in this very regard, a Jupiter could not be accepted who ruled Olympus like Homer's Zeus through sheer superior strength and the terror which he could inspire in the other gods. Hence, in the *Aeneid* the will of Jupiter and Fate are virtually equivalent and the god rules by reason, persuasion, and his acknowledged position as the head of the Olympian household. He is a Roman *pater familias*, not without his family troubles, but quite able to cope with them without resorting to force. And his family is infinitely more civilized.

We see Vergil on many occasions taking a passage or even a book of Homer as his starting point and refashioning it so that it is entirely his own. As an artist Vergil, when he is dealing with material of the same nature, is great enough to keep within the tradition which his Greek predecessor established without betraying the slightest servility. A comparison of the funeral games held in honor of Patroclus in book 25 of the *Iliad* and in honor of Anchises in book 5 of the *Aeneid* is instructive. Homer gives us one long and brilliant description of the main event, the chariot race, which is incomparable in its excitement and portrayal of character. The other events are brushed over in a rather pedestrian fashion. Vergil substitutes Trojan ships for Homeric chariots and thus gives himself the opportunity to create an entirely different setting within which the same kind of incidents that befall the Homeric charioteers are transformed and given a new life of their own, although their kinship with Homer's examples is never intentionally concealed. In the three contests which also appear in the *Iliad* Vergil shows greater detail, variety, and interest. He is more of a craftsman than Homer, not only in handling each one of them individually, but also in placing them in an ordered relation to each other and to the ship race so that an artistic unity of the whole is achieved.

But admirably as Vergil has handled Homeric elements, it is not in his relation to Homer that he is great. He created an epic that is fundamentally his own in its spirit and poetic feeling. There is a brooding compassion which accompanies the men and women of the *Aeneid* who must live and die under the inexorable laws of fate. There is tenderness for the young and gentleness for the old and a place for the tears of our common mortality. The touch is always sure, for it is directed by the large qualities of genius and an understanding heart. We feel what we must feel in the presence of any truly great poem; that its author knows more about mankind than even he can tell. The *Aeneid* as a work of art deserves the lofty place which it has occupied in the literature of Western Europe for almost two thousand years.

IV

Beowulf

KEMP MALONE

THE LITERARY history of England falls into two great divisions, commonly called medieval and modern but better named in terms of the Protestant Reformation, an upheaval which had revolutionary effects not only on English religious life but also on English literature, as indeed on every aspect of English civilization. The works of literary art which have come down to us from the England of pre-Reformation times vary markedly, of course, in many ways, but they go together at bottom: they are rooted and grounded in the Latin Christianity which dominated the culture of western Europe from the post-classical period to the sixteenth century. The Church, however, had grown up and taken form in the midst of a powerful pagan culture, the civilization of classical antiquity, and the Roman and Irish missions of the sixth and seventh centuries planted the Church of England in the midst of another pagan culture, that of the ancient Germanic peoples. The new religion did not scorn the literary tradition either of classical or of Germanic paganism. Aldhelm, the first Englishman to compose religious verse in Latin, and Cædmon, the first Englishman to compose religious verse in English, were contemporaries, and both followed essentially the same procedure. Each sang the praises of the Christian God in an artistic medium inherited from paganism. Each poured new wine into old bottles.

In one respect, nevertheless, the two pioneers differed greatly. Christian literature in the Latin tongue was no novelty when

Aldhelm and Cædmon began to sing. On the contrary, by the seventh century a large body of Latin Christian prose and verse had come into being, and Aldhelm had many Christian as well as pagan literary models at his disposal; that is to say, his task was one of imitation rather than of innovation. Cædmon, on the other hand, showed great originality, an originality which deserves the name of genius, when he seized upon the inherited native English way of composing poetry and used it in making poems Christian in theme and spirit. Nothing of the kind had ever been thought of before, so far as we know. Cædmon himself, indeed, had had no thought of such a thing in his waking hours; his inspiration came to him in sleep, and took the form of a dream, in which a messenger of God made a poet of him and told him what to sing. It took a miracle to show Cædmon and his fellows that the native English poetical technique was worthy of use in serving God. One is reminded of St. Peter's vision at Joppa, when he

saw heaven opened, and a certain vessel descending unto him, as it had been a great sheet knit at the four corners, and let down to the earth: wherein were all manner of four-footed beasts of the earth, and wild beasts, and creeping things, and fowls of the air. And there came a voice to him, Rise, Peter, kill, and eat. But Peter said, Not so, Lord; for I have never eaten any thing that is common or unclean. And the voice spake unto him again the second time, What God hath cleansed, that call not thou common. [Acts 10 : 11-15].

In the seventh century and for many centuries thereafter, Latin was the language of the Church of England. The Latin tongue was the tongue of God, the natural and proper medium for high and holy thoughts. English was associated with worldly matters, and the English way of making poetry in particular could hardly have been turned to religious purposes without a specific revelation from on high.

This revelation came to Cædmon, and its authenticity was duly accepted by the Church. In consequence, English poetry, from the earliest times of which we have record down to the Protestant

Reformation, was predominantly religious poetry, and throughout Old English times this predominance was overwhelming. Or perhaps it would be safer to say that only a small part of the Old English verse which survives to us can be reckoned purely secular. The custom of using the vernacular, alongside Latin, for religious poetical purposes, spread to the Continent in the eighth century, thanks to the English missionaries who in that century converted the Germans to Christianity and reformed the Gallican Church. Cædmon, then, may be looked upon as the father, not only of English religious poetry, but also of the religious poetry in the vernaculars of continental Europe.

Here we are primarily concerned not with Old English religious poetry in general but with a particular poem: *Beowulf*. This poem holds a unique place in the literature of Europe. Its fundamentally Christian orientation is now widely recognized, and needs no discussion in this paper. Nevertheless, one cannot properly classify it as a religious poem in any strict or narrow sense. The action of the poem takes place in a part of ancient Germania and at a time thought of by the poet as ancient and therefore pagan. The characters are not Christians and know nothing of Christianity. The hero is a virtuous pagan. He is made as Christ-like as the setting permits, but all his virtues can be explained quite naturally as growing out of the heroic ideals of conduct traditional among the English as among the other Germanic peoples.

The monkish author, devout Christian though he is, finds much to admire in the pagan cultural tradition which, as an Englishman, he inherited from ancient Germania. It is his purpose to glorify this heroic heritage, this spiritual heirloom, this precious birthright of his nation. He accomplishes his purpose by laying stress upon those things in Germanic tradition which agree with Christianity or at any rate do not clash seriously with the Christian faith. In particular, his hero in all he says and does shows himself high-minded, gentle, and virtuous, a man dedicated to the heroic life, and the poet presents this life in terms of service: Beowulf serves his lord, his people, and all mankind, and in so doing he does not

shrink from hardship, danger, and death itself. In many passages
the poet's own Christianity comes to the surface, most notably,
perhaps, in the so-called sermon of the aged King Hrothgar, who
out of the fulness of his wisdom warns the youthful hero against
the sin of pride. But even here the king's words, though obviously
based on Christian teaching, are not put in specifically Christian
terms, and most of the time the author keeps his Christianity
below the surface. Nor does he falsify Germanic paganism by
leaving out those features of it inconsistent with the Christian
faith. Thus he puts in the mouth of Beowulf himself the following
piece of pagan wisdom:

it is better for every man
to avenge his friend than to mourn much [1384b-1385]

The poet's picture of the Germanic past is idealized but not
distorted. The devil-worship of the Danes (as the medieval
Christians conceived it to be) is mentioned with perfect frankness
in a famous passage (lines 175 ff.). Anachronisms are fewer and
less serious than one would expect in a poem of the eighth century.
Indeed, perhaps the most remarkable though not the most important feature of the poem is the relatively high standard of historical accuracy which it maintains. The author was clearly a man
learned in the traditional lore of his people, and concerned to tell
the truth as he saw it.

We have seen that the earliest Christian poets of England,
whether they composed in Latin or in English, took over the
poetical manner traditional for the language of composition (and
pagan in origin) but supplied their own matter: namely, Christian
story or Christian teaching. For the matter handed down in the
old pagan poetry they had no use; indeed, they objected strongly
to what the old poets had to say, much though they admired and
imitated their way of saying it. For illustration, I shall have to
limit myself to two utterances of Alcuin, an Englishman of the
eighth century best known for the help he gave Charlemagne in
the so-called Carolingian revival of learning. In one of his poems,

Alcuin compares the Song of Songs most favorably with the poetry of Vergil, saying,

I urge you, young man, to learn these canticles by heart. They are better by far than the songs of mendacious Vergil. They sing to you the precepts of life eternal; he in his wickedness will fill your ears with worthless lies.

Alcuin condemns with equal severity the stock of traditional story drawn upon by the English scops of his day. In a letter of his he has this to say about one of these stories:

What has Ingeld to do with Christ? Narrow is the room, and it cannot hold both. The heavenly king will have nothing to do with so-called kings, heathen and damned, because that king reigns in heaven, world without end, but the heathen one, damned, laments in hell.

This attitude toward pagan literature prevailed, on the whole, down to the rise of humanism in fourteenth-century Italy. The humanists, however, found admirable in, say, Cicero, not only his artistic skill as a writer of Latin prose, but also his philosophy of life. This widening of interest served to accentuate, in the humanists, the reverence for classical antiquity so characteristic of the Middle Ages in general. The new movement brought the cult of classicism to the verge of idolatry, and humanistic thinking may be looked upon as the last and most extreme phase of medieval idealization of classical culture.

Let us now go back to the *Beowulf* poet. It would hardly do to think of him as an eighth-century humanist, six hundred years before his time, since his interest lay, not in the philosophy of life of classical antiquity but in that of Germanic antiquity. Nevertheless his case is not unlike Petrarch's in that both authors, Christians though they were, sought and found spiritual as well as stylistic values in a pagan literary culture: each in the particular culture which was his own by inheritance. In this matter the *Beowulf* poet did not stand alone. The author of *Deor* taught the virtue of patience under affliction by exempla drawn from pagan Germanic story, and the author of *Maldon* sang of a Christian lord and dright who fought and died for the faith, inspired and sustained by the same heroic ideals that their heathen forefathers had cherished. These ideals held their own to the very end of Old English times, and made many a man a hero in life and death not merely by force of ordinary tradition but also, and in large measure, by force of poetic tradition. The scops kept the old ideals strong by singing the heroes of the past. The very attack which Alcuin made on heroic story tells us that in his day the old songs were still sung even in the citadels of English Christian piety: the monasteries. Such performances became impossible, of course, after the monastic reform in the latter part of the tenth century, a reform which swept western Europe and established a more rigorous pattern of monkish life wherever it went. But the English monk of that same century who composed the poem on the Battle of Maldon still knew and loved the traditional poetry of his people, and we may be sure that he was one of many.[1]

The complex and sophisticated art of the *Beowulf* poet calls for a correspondingly elaborate analysis, an analysis which we cannot make at this time. We shall have to content ourselves here with a mere glance at the main fable or plot, before going on to a somewhat narrower study of the episodes. The action of the poem falls into two main parts. In part one, the hero Beowulf, then young, goes from his homeland to Heorot, the hall of the Danish king Hrothgar, in order to cleanse it of Grendel, a troll who for years had haunted it at night; he overcomes Grendel single-handed and afterward slays Grendel's mother, who sought to avenge her son. In part two, the hero, now grown old, goes out to defend his own kingdom against the ravages of a dragon; with the help of a faithful young kinsman he kills the dragon but himself falls in the fight. About two thirds of the poem are devoted to part one; about one third is devoted to part two. The

---

[1] For further discussion, see " The Old English Period," Chapter V, in Baugh, Brooke, Chew, Malone, and Sherburn, *A Literary History of England* (New York, 1948).

course of events in part one takes six days; in part two, one day (excluding preliminaries in both cases). Between the two parts there is an interval of many years.

It will be seen that the poet deals in detail with two chapters only of the hero's life, and that these two chapters stand in sharp contrast. In the first, the hero is young; he is represented as an ideal retainer; he undertakes a task which he is not in duty bound to perform; full of the generous spirit of youth, he goes out of his way to do good; he fights single-handed against two foes (taken one at a time); he wins, and goes home in triumph. In the contrasting chapter, the hero is old; he is represented as an ideal king; the task he undertakes is one which he cannot avoid without failing in his duty to his own people; sad at heart, he meets the issue without flinching; he fights, with a helper beside him, against a single foe; he wins, but at the cost of his own life.

The two chapters, however, have one feature in common: in both, Beowulf fights as the champion of mankind, against monstrous embodiments of the forces of evil, adversaries so formidable that only the greatest of heroes could possibly cope with them. Our Christian poet makes much of the hero as monster-queller, not only because a fight with a monster in the nature of the case is more dangerous and therefore more heroic than a fight with another man, but also, and chiefly, because the struggle between hero and monster symbolizes the struggle between good and evil in our earthly life. Mere man-to-man fighting lends itself far less readily to treatment in terms of right and wrong, and the poet accordingly makes little of his hero's military career. Here our author goes his own way, the way of a Christian moralist, departing deliberately and radically from the practice usual in heroic story, where the hero's exploits in battle get plenty of attention.

The poet's neglect of Beowulf's deeds of valor in ordinary warfare must have been deliberate. Certainly he was well informed about them. He tells us himself, though with the utmost brevity, about one of the many battles which his hero had survived with honor. In this particular battle, fought in the Low Countries,

Beowulf had covered himself with glory: he had killed no less
than thirty of the enemy in hand-to-hand conflict; one of them,
the Frankish champion Dæghrefn, he slew with his bare hands.
The poet informs us further that Beowulf was the only man on
his side to survive the battle. His own triumph over the enemy
was so complete that, though his fellows all lay dead, he held the
field alone and stripped from the bodies of the thirty men he
had slain the armor to which his victory over them gave him
honorable title, the surviving Franks not daring to interfere and
allowing him to fall back to the sea unmolested. The story of
King Hygelac's ill-fated expedition to the Netherlands, and in
particular the story of the last stand of the doomed army, the fall
of Hygelac, and the death of man after man of the king's devoted
dright, until at the end Beowulf stood alone—this was surely
a fight worthy of celebration in song. The *Beowulf* poet, in four
scattered passages, has something to say about the expedition
and its outcome. But he fails to make even an episode of it,
much less a major part of the poem. Some poets would have
thought it enough for a whole epic.

But I do not wish to blame the poet for what he left undone.
He knew what he was about. Hygelac's expedition had no high
moral purpose. The king and his men were out for booty, and
our pious poet, though he loved a good fight as well as anybody,
chose for extended treatment tasks undertaken and carried
through by the hero for the benefit of mankind.

One exploit of Beowulf's remains to be considered: his swimming
match with Breca. This match makes a clean-cut episode, to
which more than one hundred lines are devoted. The story of the
match is not told as such, however. It is set in a frame: the
fliting between Unferth and Beowulf. The integration of frame
and story is beautifully complete: the swimming match is the
subject of the fliting, each contender in the war of words giving
us his own version of the story of the match. In consequence,
this story is told twice. The repetition is characteristic of the
Beowulf poet, who loves to tell a story more than once. We have
already seen that Hygelac's expedition up the Rhine is spoken of

no less than four times. The most elaborate piece of repetition in
the poem, of course, is Beowulf's report to Hygelac when he comes
back from Denmark; this report amounts to a retelling of the
story of the fight with Grendel and Grendel's mother. Many
other cases of repetition occur in the course of the narrative. The
poet repeats himself in a masterly fashion; the device as he
employs it not only emphasizes and clarifies but also gives
esthetic pleasure. When we come to a given repetition we know
what to expect in a general way, but we always find novelty
enough in word and thought. The two versions of the swimming
match differ markedly, of course, in point of view, and therefore
are highly differentiated, much more so than is the case with the
other repetitions in the poem.

But why does the poet make so much of the swimming match?
It comes under the head of the hero's *enfances,* or exploits of
boyhood, a familiar feature of heroic story, but one fundamentally
trivial in character. Beowulf mentions some other boyish feats
of his when he first addresses King Hrothgar. His speech begins,

Be thou hale, Hrothgar! I am Hygelac's kinsman and retainer. I did
many glorious deeds when I was a boy [lines 407-409a].

This is pretty vague, of course, but later on in the speech he tells
Hrothgar, more specifically, that he had been a giant-killer, that
he had taken five giants captive, that he had slain sea-monsters
by night, and that he had fought with success against certain
unnamed foes of his own people. Obviously if Beowulf fought
monsters as well as that in his boyhood he ought to be able to
cope with Grendel now that he has become a full-grown man.
In other words, Beowulf's catalogue of his early exploits is meant
to convince the king that here at last is the man he needs. The
catalogue serves also to instruct the reader or hearers of the poem;
they learn out of Beowulf's own mouth—that is, from the most
authoritative source possible—that he is a redoubtable champion;
in particular, that he is a monster-queller. This device of self-
characterization is familiar in literary art. One finds it in Shake-

speare, for example. The *Beowulf* poet's use of it is, in all likelihood, highly traditional and conventional.

Beowulf's mention of sea-monsters which he had slain by night takes us back to the swimming match with Breca, one detail of which is precisely this monster-quelling on the part of the hero. The quelling, as Beowulf himself points out, is of benefit to mankind, and may be taken for a kind of prelude to the more important quelling which is to follow at the Danish court. But after all, the two boys, when they agreed and vowed to swim to sea, had no thought of rendering a service to their fellow men. They risked their lives in this swimming match on the high seas in a spirit of recklessness. They were showing off. In Beowulf's story of the swim we catch the apologetic note: " we were both still in our boyhood " [536b-537a], he says. The implication is clear that the Beowulf who had reached young manhood would not have undertaken such a match. One should not risk one's life in vain.

It now becomes clearer why the poet makes a good deal of the swimming match. The story of the match gives us a short but vivid view of the adolescent hero in action. We get other glimpses of him as a boy, but nowhere else is any event of his boyhood told in detail. The poet reserves the main fable for his hero as a young man and as an old man, but in one episode he presents him in his immaturity. Here the future champion of mankind against the world of monsters is already a monster-queller, though not yet informed with a high moral purpose. He plays with the heroic life to which, later on, he will dedicate himself in earnest.

Most of the episodic matter in the poem, however, is concerned not with the hero himself but with his setting. The author, as we have seen, was not only a Christian moralist. He was also an Englishman; that is, a man of Germanic stock and traditions. He chose a hero of his own race, and gave him for setting the golden age of ancient Germania, that glorious period of migration when the Germanic tribes overran the Roman Empire and made its provinces into Germanic kingdoms. A well-known American scholar, after remarking upon the intense patriotism characteristic of the English, adds,

It is very surprising, then, in turning to the oldest English epic, to find that there is nothing patriotic about it at all. We call it an English poem, and rightly. It was written on English soil, for Englishmen, and in the English tongue. . . . Yet the epic deals neither with English people nor with English heroes. . . . The peoples whom it celebrates are foreigners, Scandinavians. . . . In short, *Beowulf* is a story dealing with foreign subject-matter, borrowed from an alien and even hostile people, with no trace of English patriotism about it. How is this strange situation to be explained? [2]

Our answer must be that the question is ill conceived, arising as it does out of a mistaken view of eighth-century England. In those days the English, so far as their culture was concerned, still belonged, in part, to a commonwealth of nations, the Germania of their Continental forefathers. Within that commonwealth they were at home, and felt the Goth, the Swede, the Langobard alike to be cultural fellow-countrymen. The *Beowulf* poet was intensely patriotic; his poem shows at every turn the warmth of his love for his native culture and his native race. But his patriotism embraced Germania as a whole; it was no narrowly English affair. It is particularly significant, I think, that his hero lived and died in southern Scandinavia, the heart of the old Germanic homeland, the cradle of the race, the region least affected by foreign influences. Moreover, it was from the Jutland peninsula, a part of this very region, that the English themselves had come, in their great migration to Britain. We must not forget that England in its earliest centuries was still colonial territory. The stream of settlers from the Germanic motherland had probably stopped flowing by the time of the *Beowulf* poet, but the English had not forgotten their origin nor yet the source of their cultural traditions. Above all, *Beowulf* is a poem of the past, of a past thought of by the poet as remote. The action of such a poem obviously

[2] W. W. Lawrence, *Medieval Story*, p. 30.

must take place in the homeland, not in a colony of recent foundation.

It may be worth our while, however, to speculate about the poet's reasons for not making King Offa the hero of his poem. Offa is the only English king of the Continental period about whom we have much information. We learn of him both in *Beowulf* and in *Widsith*. The *Beowulf* poet calls him the best of all mankind, and adds that he was held in high esteem far and wide because of his generosity and his success in warfare. The poet also tells us that Offa ruled his country with wisdom. In *Widsith* we get more specific information about Offa's achievements: while still a boy he overthrew " with single sword " (that is, by his own efforts, without help from others) the kingdom of the Myrgings, and dictated a boundary between his own kingdom and theirs, a boundary which his successors were able to keep. Moreover, we have reason to think that Offa was the first English king whose realm included western as well as eastern Sleswick. As I have said elsewhere,

The extension of the English king's authority to the North Sea coast of Sleswick made possible the later migration of the Angles to Britain, a migration which obviously would never have taken place had the English holdings remained strictly Baltic. Offa's war with the Myrgings, then, must be reckoned one of the great turning-points of English history. . . .

It seems clear that Offa was a man eminently suitable for celebration in song. An English poet in particular might be expected to make Offa the hero of a poem set in the Germania of the migration period, the heroic age of the Germanic peoples. Why did our poet choose Beowulf instead? The answer, I think, is simple. Beowulf was famous chiefly as a queller of monsters, whereas Offa won his fame as a queller of men. The poet, pious Christian that he was, found spiritual values in Beowulf's monster-quelling which he could not find in Offa's man-quelling. Nevertheless he did not like to leave Offa out of his poem altogether. The great hero of his own tribe must be brought in somehow. The episode in which

Offa figures I describe elsewhere as having been introduced by a *tour de force*, and this may well be a correct statement of the case. But the poet's technique of linkage here has a parallel in at least one other episode. I will take up Offa first.

King Offa is introduced not directly but by way of his wife, Queen Thrytho, and most of the episode is devoted to the lady, whose unorthodox behavior makes her more interesting than her pattern of a husband. The introduction of a husband through his wife, however, is certainly no *tour de force*. It is the introduction of Thrytho herself which makes trouble for modern readers. The poet gets her in by contrasting her with Hygd, wife of King Hygelac. Beowulf has come back home after his Grendel adventure and is approaching Hygelac's hall to make his report of the journey. The author stops at this point to comment on the hall, the king, and the king's wife. But he disposes of hall and king in a line and a half; Queen Hygd is the one he gives most of his attention to. She is characterized in accordance with the etymology of her name. *Hygd* means ' thought ' and the queen is represented as thoughtful indeed: wise, well behaved, and mindful of other people's wishes and feelings. The poet explains Hygd's exemplary conduct as the fruit of deliberation, study, mental activity. He says,

The good queen of the people [i. e., Hygd] bore in mind (wæg) the haughtiness, the terrible violence of Thrytho [lines 1931b–1932].

In other words, Hygd took warning by the example of Thrytho. She took care to behave differently. This brings the poet to Thrytho's own behavior, which was certainly not very encouraging to would-be suitors, for she objected so strongly to the attentions of men that if one of them so much as looked at her she had him put to death. The poet goes on to say, " that is no way for a lady to do." We learn, however, that Thrytho turned over a new leaf after her marriage to Offa, whom she loved dearly. King Offa, it would seem, proved master of the situation at home as well as on the field of battle.

Linkage by contrast also serves to bring in the second Heremod passage (lines 1709-1722), a part of the so-called sermon of Hrothgar. The aged king after praising Beowulf speaks of Heremod as Beowulf's antithesis. He brings the passage to an end by exhorting Beowulf to profit by the evil example that Heremod has set. The sad fate of Heremod should be a lesson to the young hero. The same device of contrast is used in the first Heremod passage (lines 901-915), but here this type of linkage comes at the end of the passage; the poet, by contrasting Heremod with Beowulf, brings the narrative back to his hero. This passage about Heremod is introduced by the use of a different device: sequence in time. The poet has been speaking of the famous hero Sigemund, the dragon-slayer. He shifts to Heremod very simply, saying that Sigemund flourished after Heremod had had his day. We get no hint that the two men are connected in any other way, and the device which serves to link them in the poem strikes us as artificial enough. In this case, however, the Scandinavian evidence makes it clear that Sigemund and Heremod were traditionally associated, though just what the association was we are unable to make out. This information, gained from a study of Icelandic poetry, forces us to revise our opinion of the artistic technique of the *Beowulf* poet. We now see that the true linkage between Sigemund and Heremod was left unexpressed and needed no expression, since it was already firmly fixed by tradition in the minds of the poet's audience, to be evoked at will by a mere mention of the names. It is our misfortune, but not the poet's fault, that we in our ignorance miss the true link and have to depend altogether on that sequence in time which the poet uses, as an external device only, in proceeding from the one member of the heroic pair to the other.

The device of contrast, too, now begins to have a different look. One may well suspect, though one certainly cannot prove, that the coupling of Beowulf and Heremod, and of Hygd and Thrytho, belong to tradition and have their roots deep in Germanic story. If so, the English poet took up these characters together, not as a mere device for changing the subject, but because they went together in the songs that had come down to him, the sources he drew upon for the tale he had to tell.

What functions do the episodes have in the economy of the poem? I have already said that most of them bring out the setting in which the hero lived and died. This setting was ancient Germania; more particularly, the Scandinavia of the fifth and sixth centuries of our era. The story of Scyld, mythical founder of the Danish royal house, gives us a taste of an old legend, and the description of his funeral takes us back to pagan rites dim with antiquity. The tale of Ecgtheow's feud with the avengers of Heatholaf makes the father of the hero more than a name to us and links him with the Wulfing tribe, famous in heroic story from Iceland to the Mediterranean. When Hrothgar's scop, after singing Beowulf's praises, goes on to the exploits of Sigemund, he puts our hero side by side with a hero of Frankish legend, one of the chief figures of Germanic story. That night the scop sang once more; this time he told the tale of Finn, an ancient story very welcome at the Danish court, since it ends with a Danish victory. The tale of Ingeld the English poet puts in the mouth of Beowulf himself, as part of his report to Hygelac on the state of Denmark. All these passages serve to make our hero part and parcel of the heroic age of Germanic antiquity.

It is possible, however, to make a distinction here between those episodes which have been drawn into the narrative and those that remain external to it. Examples of the former are the passages about Scyld, Ecgtheow, and the swimming match; examples of the latter are the passages about Sigemund, Finn, and Ingeld. In part two of the poem the integration of the historical passages into the story of the dragon fight has been done in such a way as to disturb many modern readers. Thus, Klaeber says (*Beowulf*, 3d ed., p. liv),

The facts of Geatish history, it cannot be denied, are a little too much in evidence and retard the narrative . . . rather seriously.

This verdict does less than justice to the narrative art of the poet, who in part two tells the story of his hero's tribe: past, present and future. The attack of the dragon on that tribe, and Beowulf's counter-attack, ending in the death both of the hero and of his monstrous antagonist, make part of the tribal story, a part which we may call the present crisis (present, that is, from the point of view of the hero). The poet gives us his account of this crisis not continuously but in sections, sections which alternate with accounts of earlier crises in the tribe's history. The death of the dragon ends the present crisis, but the messenger of Wiglaf foresees disaster for the tribe in the future, now that they have lost their great king. He justifies his forebodings by reminding his hearers of certain events of the past, events which in due course will lead to ruin, want, and exile. The poet himself adds that the messenger's fears are fully justified. The poem ends in the present, with the funeral of the hero.

It will be seen that the author of *Beowulf* in part two of his poem uses a technique of alternation between events of the present and events of the past. He restricts himself throughout to his hero's own tribe, in marked contrast to his procedure in part one, where he ranges widely over Germania. The unity of part two, in theme and form alike, is noteworthy. As for the technique of alternation which the poet uses to drive home this unity, it is a technique very familiar today, especially in the narrative art of screen and novel. Many recent screen plays follow this method of shifting repeatedly from present to past. In Hollywood they have a name for the shift backwards in time: they call it a flashback. A recent novel, *Raintree County*, by Ross Lockridge, makes systematic use of the flashback technique. In the novel, just as in part two of *Beowulf*, the action is restricted to one day, but the flashbacks take us deep into the past. It is not likely that the novelists and scenario writers of today learned this technique by studying *Beowulf*, but theirs is the technique of the *Beowulf* poet none the less.

The shift from present to past occurs three times in the narrative of part two. The poet makes the transition in a different way each time. In all three cases he manages the shift with great skill. The second transition is of special interest, as an example of the poet's craftsmanship. Beowulf and his little band of men had reached the immediate neighborhood of the dragon's lair. Beowulf was to go forward alone from that point. He sat down on the headland, and bade his followers goodbye. The aged king fell to thinking about his childhood and youth, and began to talk. His reminiscences take up nearly one hundred lines of verse. The technique seems almost realistic here. What could be more natural than for an old man to talk about old times?

One may now ask whether the three long passages on the history of the Geatas incorporated in part two should really be looked upon as episodic. Without them the story of the dragon fight would remain, but would lose greatly in spiritual quality, since we should not know as we do the people for whom Beowulf was giving his life. As the poem stands, the fate of the hero and the fate of the tribe are bound together in such a way that each lends weight and worth to the other. We mourn for the Geatas as well as for their king, and this double mourning deepens as well as widens the sweep of the tragic march of events. One cannot doubt that the poet meant it so. For him, Beowulf would not have been a hero if he had not had a people to die for. The *Beowulf* poet was above all a patriotic poet.

We end as we began, with a look at the poem taken in the large. As we have seen, *Beowulf* falls into two parts, devoted respectively to the hero in young manhood and the hero in old age. Part one is predominantly cheerful in tone, as befits a period of youth. When one reads the Sigemund episode, for instance, one feels that it is good to be alive in a world made for heroic adventure. Even the Finn episode has a happy ending if one sides with the Danes, as our poet does. Now and then the shadows of feuds that are to come darken the picture of the Danish court, and the aged Hrothgar is fond of talking about his own troubles and those of others, but the hero takes all this in his stride and goes home in triumph, leaving a cleansed and happy Heorot behind him.

Utterly different is the tone of part two. Old age has come, and death is near at hand from the start. No longer does the hero leave home, to fight the good fight in other lands. He stands strictly on the defensive. He is sad at heart; his breast surges with dark thoughts. But there is one thought which he does not have. It does not occur to him to give up. Great though the odds against him, he takes the field and fights to the last. In this world defeat and death are sure to come in the end. The hero is he who, like Beowulf, faces the worst without flinching and dies that others may live.

V

Dante's Divine Comedy

EDWARD WILLIAMSON

IT IS NATURAL that a chapter on Dante should follow closely one on Virgil. The most striking experience of Aeneas is his journey to the other world, and the *Divine Comedy* is but the story of Dante's journey to the other world. Moreover, Dante chooses Virgil as a guide, and gives us to understand that Virgil not only conducted him through the nether world but acted in a guiding capacity in shaping the poem: *tu se' lo mio maestro e 'l mio autore* —" you are my teacher and my writer "—he remarks (*Inf.* I, 85) to the Roman poet when they meet in the dark wood from which the journey starts. This is biographically true: Dante knew the *Aeneid* by heart; but even if we had no other evidence, we could tell by the text of the *Comedy* itself how deeply Virgil's words had penetrated the very texture of Dante's mind.

Notice that I have used the phrase *tu se' lo mio maestro e 'l mio autore* in an ambiguous way, a way intended to represent the intersection of two separate relationships; for there are two Dantes and two Virgils. The first Dante is the protagonist of the poem, he is a character in it, a personage making a journey through supernatural realms; the first Virgil is his guide, and like him a character in the poem; this Dante and this Virgil do not exist in any world outside the poem. The second Dante is the author of the poem, a man born in Florence and living in exile, whose physical fingers at some historically real moment set down the words we now read; even as the second Virgil is the man who lived in the reign of Augustus and wrote the poem which Dante had studied. It was, of course, the first Dante who made the remark to the first Virgil; but it was the second Dante's mind which had been struck into response by the second Virgil's words.

It is important to keep separate in one's mind the two pairs, and equally important to sense the web of relationships which the poem creates between them, as in the simple phrase "you are my teacher and my writer." If we do not keep the character separate from the person, we fall into two errors: first, we stop reading the poem as a poem and begin to use it as a document to establish biographical facts about the historical Dante, and from there it is but a step to converting it into a document to set up little biographies for the other people mentioned: Boniface, Francesca, Ugolino, Manfred. Second, we try to control the poem by references to history, deciding that since so and so is known to be true, that is what the poem must mean even though it quite plainly says the contrary. On the other hand, if we do not keep in mind the currents of relationship which continually flow between the pairs of poles, we shut our attention against a circulation of forces which gives a particular quality to the poem and is, indeed, essential to its structure.

Dante's use of Virgil's work is not echo but counterpoint: a list of the phrases which occur in both the *Aeneid* and the *Divine Comedy* would tell you nothing; the whole significance lies in the way Dante uses them as against the way Virgil had used them. In the Earthly Paradise at the top of Mount Purgatory, Beatrice appears to Dante, a woman clothed in flowing drapery, standing upon the chariot of the church, surrounded by a miraculous rain of flowers, while heavenly voices chant *Manibus o date lilia plenis!* (Purg. XXX, 21). It is a moment of overwhelming joy, and its supreme expression is in the cry, " Oh, give lilies with full hands! " But these were words which Virgil had used, though in how different a context. In the Elysian meadows Anchises was pointing out to Aeneas the procession of their descendants, who were to be kings and conquerors of Italy, joyfully reckoning the glory of each of these heroes as they passed one by one before him, until, at the end, there came a youth of exceptional beauty, strong and upstanding in his armor, with all about him an air of promise. Aeneas asked, " Father, who is he? " Then Anchises, the tears starting to his eyes, began, " Oh, my son, do not ask about the deep sorrow of your people. The fates will but show this boy to the earth and not suffer him to stay. No young man of our stock shall give such promise, but alas! he who could be the greatest of our line must die in youth. Give me lilies with full hands; let me scatter purple flowers; let me heap over my offspring's shade at least these gifts, though I perform a useless service."

> *manibus date lilia plenis,*
> *purpureos spargam flores animamque nepotis*
> *his saltem accumulem donis et fungar inani*
> *munere.*   (*Aeneid*, VI, 883)

A moment of overwhelming grief, finding expression in the cry, " Give me lilies with full hands "; and it is the memory of this sorrow which Dante evokes at a moment of great joy. A cry of anguish for a boy doomed to die in youth—and of Beatrice we know only this, that Dante loved her and that she died in her twenty-fourth year. By thus casting our glance back from life in heaven to death on earth Dante effects a mighty synthesis: this blessed spirit surrounded by the elders of the church and hymned by choirs of angels, above whose head stream rainbow fires from seven candlesticks and about whose chariot wheels rejoice the seven virtues, is the woman whom Dante loved and lost on earth. The Virgilian echo catches up into Dante's heavenly joy the grief he had felt on earth, and because of it the moment is humanly moving and Beatrice a human rather than an apocalyptic figure.

There is in the same scene another reminiscence of the *Aeneid.* Across the terrible wasteland of Hell and up the arduous ledges of Purgatory, Dante had been sustained and drawn on by the promise that, if he overcame the intervening dangers and difficulties, he would see Beatrice. When he doubted that he should set out on the journey at all, Virgil quieted his fear with the assurance that Beatrice had ordered it (*Inf.* II, 70) ; when he was weary, the mention of her name sufficed to make him say, " Let us go faster, for now I am not tired as I was before " (*Purg.* VI, 46); and when at the end he was afraid to cross the ring of fire which guards the summit of Purgatory, Virgil said, " Between you and Beatrice is this wall," and at once he plunged into it (*Purg.* XXVII, 36). And all this time it was the Beatrice he had loved who beckoned him on; he expected to find again the woman he had lost. The reader shares this expectation. By little touches here and there the poet gives the impression that there will be a reunion of lovers: thus Virgil speaks (*Purg.* VI, 46) of " Beatrice whom you will see at the summit of this mountain, happy and smiling "; within the fire he encourages Dante by saying, " I seem already to see her eyes " (*Purg.* XXVII, 54); and afterward, when they have gained Eden, he tells Dante he may rest " until the beautiful eyes come rejoicing " (*Purg.* XXVII, 136). In us, as in Dante, there has grown a great desire to see these smiling eyes, so long promised, so long withheld.

But when Beatrice at last appears her face is covered with a veil; we would not know her, but Dante does. The moment the draped and veiled figure appears, something happens within him: " not a drop of my blood but trembles; I recognize the signs of the old fire."

> *Men che dramma*
> *di sangue m'è rimaso che non tremi;*
> *conosco i segni dell'antica fiamma.*
>
> (*Purg.* XXX, 46)

These were the words of Dido when she met Aeneas, and realized that in her heart had waked again what she once felt for Sychaeus: *agnosco veteris vestigia flammae* (*Aeneid*, IV, 23). It is a beautiful and moving reference to a great human love, and by it Dante tells us that he was expecting the woman who held his heart in human love.

But a terrible surprise awaits him: Beatrice begins to speak, and she is no longer his Beatrice; she is the messenger of heaven, and standing like an admiral upon a deck (*Purg.* XXX, 58) she indicts Dante for his sins. It is a moment of extreme importance for the poem, the moment when earthly standards are replaced by heavenly, the moment when it is first brought home to Dante that his love of Beatrice must change its nature and become a love of Beatrice in God. The triumph of that new love will be sung in cantos of great power at the poem's close; here we are at the moment of humiliation from which it rises, the moment of the crushing of the old love; and that moment is made poignant by an echo from the *Aeneid*.

Manibus o date lilia plenis;

. . . .

conosco i segni dell'antica fiamma.

What a rich counterpoint of sentiments is added to the simple narrative by these Virgilian overtones; what a multiplicity of deliberately clashing feelings is aroused within us as we recognize the old words in a new setting. In this sense, and not in any manner of simple copying, was Virgil Dante's *maestro e autore*.

And yet, having said so much of Dante's debt to the *Aeneid*, it remains for me to add that if you would understand the *Divine Comedy*, you must cast your mind back, not to Virgil, but to Homer. In his *Defence of Poetry* Shelley remarked, "Homer was the first and Dante the second epic poet: that is, the second poet, the series of whose creations bore a defined and intelligible relation to the knowledge and sentiment and religion of the age in which he lived. . . ." The *Iliad* contains the whole of a culture, so does the *Comedy*; but while the *Iliad* captured a primitive society, the *Comedy* caught a civilization: when Dante came to write, Gothic architecture had reached its perfection; the painting of Simone Martini, of Duccio, and of Giotto was to be seen; a complex canon of lyric poetry had been established by the troubadours and longer works included masterpieces as diverse as the *Roman de la rose* and the tales of Crestien de Troyes; scholastic philosophy had attained its culminating position; and the conflict between church and temporal power was in its final crisis. This medieval European world is as completely mirrored in the *Divine Comedy* as the early Greek world is in Homer; in this sense it is proper to speak of the *Comedy* as an epic, and because of it Shelley was justified in saying, " The poetry of Dante may be considered as the bridge thrown over the stream of time, which unites the modern and ancient world."

But the ideas which we find in Dante may also be found in Brunetto Latini, in Albertus Magnus, and in the legends of the time. The material of the *Comedy* is not new; the Middle Ages teem with traditions of supernatural appearances in which the prevailing elements were the terrible, the fantastic, and the demoniacal. In this lore there are a hundred descriptions of the three realms forming the scheme of the *Comedy*; often the punishments of the damned, the scenery, and the inhabiting beings are identical with those found in the poem. In what way has Dante reworked this material and made a coherent world of it? This is the core of the critical problem, for the pre-existent materials did not create the *Comedy*, they were only its antecedents; the jumble of legend and truth did not of itself become poetry.

One of the means by which Dante was enabled to take possession of this world was the device of putting himself into the poem: this furnished the necessary dramatic element. The older stories of the supernatural perished at their birth because there were in them no living men, no conflict of character, no free will. This was pointed out some ninety years ago by Francesco De Sanctis in a series of lectures on the *Comedy* which he gave at Turin. " Dante," he said, " has managed to weld together two apparently hostile themes (history, which ties man to earth, and religion, which carries him beyond humanity) by assuming himself a part in the development. He, a living mortal, enters the realm of shades while retaining all his human and political passions, and thereby makes even the still vaults of heaven resound with the echoes of earthly things. Thus the dramatic element is restored and time reappears in eternity."

The device by which Dante gives his world coherence is allegory. He himself stated the nature of this allegory in a letter to Can Grande della Scala, " The subject of the work, taken in the literal sense, is the state of the soul after death; but if the work is taken allegorically, its subject is how man by the exercise of his free will justly merits reward or punishment." Dante's phrase is, more precisely, " rewarding or punishing justice " (*iustitiae praemiandi et puniendi*), and he means to emphasize that in this life, as in the life after death, a man receives what he has himself elected and that both rewards and punishments are administered with perfect justice. This establishes the Dantean universe as a reasonable universe. Dante admired reason and believed in its power; he did not conceive that reason was opposed to faith, but on the contrary that it was an essential part of man's journey to God: reason leads man to the Earthly Paradise and from there he ascends to the Heavenly one. Dante's belief in reason was the basis of his political views. In order to reach the Earthly Paradise (that is, the blessedness of this life) from which to mount to Heaven, man must exercise his reason; to do this, he must have peace; peace is possible only if the world has a single ruler; therefore, the whole world should be under the governance of one emperor, and this emperor must maintain justice in temporal matters as God maintains it in the spiritual world.

Justice is the measure of the distance between the primitive epic and the *Divine Comedy*: Juno may kill a dozen people out of wounded vanity, but a God whose punishments are whim would be unthinkable to Dante; unless its rewards and punishments are established by justice his universe becomes a chaos. Justice requires that punishment shall be proportionate to sin; Dante goes beyond this concept and makes the sin itself the punishment. This is easily the most striking and original feature of Dante's Inferno.

Astonishment is sometimes expressed nowadays at the emphasis on the moment of death: if a man dies at peace with God he is saved, if he dies at odds with God he is punished through all eternity. Dante did not invent this idea, nor is it a sort of gamble on the time of death; he took it from prior religious writers, and the thought which underlies it is this: if a man unrepentantly sins up to the very moment of his death, he may be said to have fixed his end in sin and to have willed to sin forever.

Medieval theologians had envisaged the punishments incurred by such sinners as horrible tortures, in themselves irrelevant to the type of sin committed. Dante applies his concept of justice to achieve a more satisfying balance. As the man who dies unrepentant has willed to sin forever, he shall have, says Dante, exactly what he willed, and his punishment shall be only that he continue in his sin forever, but conscious of its true nature. Thus, throughout Dante's journey across Hell, the punishments which he sees the sinners undergoing, however fantastic in their literal details, will be in their true meaning only a picture of the sin as it really is.

Before Dante reaches Hell itself, he and Virgil cross a sort of vestibule or ante-inferno; here are the souls who never declared themselves for good or bad—Laodiceans neither cold nor hot—who are neither in Heaven nor in Hell. As in their lives they chose no cause, but shifted with fluctuating opinion and fortune, so here they rush to and fro after aimless and heterogeneous banners. Beyond them is Limbus, which holds the souls, otherwise pure, of those who were not members of the community of Christ; their only punishment is that they live in darkness and long now to enter the presence of God. The first group of people who had committed overt acts of sin is that of the incontinent: people who fell into excess or insufficiency with respect to a quality which rightly exists as a golden mean. Among them are the lustful, blown about by gusts of wind, just as in life they had been at the mercy of the buffets of passion; the gluttonous, who lie exposed to a cold, dirty rain; and the avaricious and prodigal, who heave great round stones with their shoulders along a circular track, the avaricious in one direction, the prodigal in the opposite, so that they meet with a shock in the middle and then retrace the futile course until they bump again on the other side. Like all the people in the poem who have concerned themselves too much with money, their human expression has been so debased that they cannot be recognized from their faces.

The treatment of the gluttons admirably illustrates the advance of Dante's concept of appropriate punishment over previous imaginings of Hell. The medieval representations frequently showed demons stuffing frogs, snakes, and filth down the throats of gluttons; sometimes hot oil was funneled into them; but these punishments have only a picturesque and superficial relation to the sin. Dante looks to the essence: gluttony is the abuse of the fruits of the earth, the perversion to a wrong end of the fructifying rain. Consequently what should have been a life-giving shower turns over them into a chill, vile substance; and as gluttony is the most monotonous of sins, so does the perpetual beat of the rain embody that monotony in punishment.

Across a marsh where the angry lie immersed, Dante is ferried to a wall surrounding the city of Dis. Within it the heretics lie in burning sepulchres, and a little below them are confined the violent. The tyrants, highwaymen, and other aggressors who had been violent against their neighbors stand in a river of boiling blood; the suicides, who were violent against themselves, exist in the shape of thorn trees, and after the Last Judgment when all other souls put on their flesh again, these will drag their bodies hither and hang them from a dry branch, for as they have rejected them they shall not have them again; those who had been violent against God are on a desert over which falls in slow flakes a rain of fire.

Far down a steep cliff from the violent are the fraudulent, distributed in ten ditches. Among them are the grafters, who are submerged in a lake of pitch; the hypocrites, who walk around and around with a decorum induced by their mantles, beautifully gilded, but of heavy lead, and typifying how burdensome it is forever to pretend to causes in which one does not believe and to be nice to people whom one hates. Down another cliff from the fraudulent are the treacherous, those who betrayed some special trust. Here is Cain, who betrayed his brother, and Antenor, who betrayed his guests. With all other traitors they are encased in a great plain of ice, apt symbol of the cold and treacherous heart. At the center stands the betrayer of God, Satan, once Lucifer, now as ugly as he once was beautiful; in his three mouths he crushes and mauls Judas, who betrayed the Church, and Brutus and Cassius, who betrayed the Empire.

As you see, the unrepentant sinners in Hell are grouped according to the overt acts which they committed. In Purgatory the repentant sinners are grouped in accordance with inner tendencies which cause sin. After a man has sincerely repented his evil ways and determined to do better, there is a considerable period during which the old habit or urge persists. The penance which the church imposed on a forgiven wrong-doer was intended to be, not a punishment, but a discipline which would help him combat the residual tendency to sin. In practice, of course, the penances imposed were often irrelevant to the purpose, and no doubt a great mass of the lesser clergy failed to grasp the psychological reality which underlay the sacrament; but the learned—and Dante was one of the most learned men of his age—clearly understood that penance was corrective and not punitive.

The theologians had divided into seven the tendencies to sin, and Dante adopts the sevenfold classification. Any one tendency could cause a variety of overt sins: thus envy might cause a man to steal, to murder, or to betray. In Hell he would be classed and punished according to the worst act he had committed, in this case treachery; in Purgatory he would be among those sharing the same cause of sin—envy—though in them it might have urged toward quite different acts. This is because the punishments of Hell are retributive, while the disciplines of Purgatory are remedial. This difference of purpose leads to a difference in the nature of the pain experienced: in Hell it is the sin itself; in Purgatory it is the opposite of the sin.

Dante imagines Purgatory as a series of terraces halfway up a mountain. On the lowest ledge are the proud; they totter about, bent, almost face to earth, by heavy stones which they carry on their backs; and this bending under a load voluntarily maintained is, of course, the outward sign of the humility which inwardly corrects pride. On the ledge above them are the envious; their eyes are wired shut and they lean one against another; for the outward calculating eye must be turned inward, and the self which sought to harm its neighbors must sustain them, till that discipline become a habit, and the habit become the soul's fixed will; then the soul is pure and rises to Paradise.

The last discipline of Purgatory clearly illustrates the difference between the principles of Hell and Purgatory. At the top of Purgatory proper, separating it from the Earthly Paradise which crowns the mountain, is a great ring of fire, in which the lustful purge away their excess of desire. The flame of passion is an old and well-worn symbol; had we found the lustful in Hell plunged into a bath of flame, it would have figured forth appropriately the nature of their sin. But here lust cannot be purged by lust, but by its opposite, which is *caritas*. In a fourteenth-century manuscript of homilies there is one beginning:

> *This fir call I charite*
> *That brinnand in us au to be.*
> *It clenses man of sinful lust,*
> *As fire cleanses iren of rust. . . .*

Something of the same idea underlies the lines of T. S. Eliot in Part IV of *Little Gidding*:

> *The dove descending breaks the air*
> *With flame of incandescent terror*
> *Of which the tongues declare*
> *The one discharge from sin and error.*
> *The only hope, or else despair*
>   *Lies in the choice of pyre or pyre—*
>   *To be redeemed from fire by fire.*

> *Who then devised the torment? Love.*
> *Love is the unfamiliar Name*
> *Behind the hands that wove*
> *The intolerable shirt of flame*
> *Which human power cannot remove.*
>   *We only live, only suspire*
>   *Consumed by either fire or fire.*

Eliot speaks of love and I have spoken of justice. They are, in Dante's view, inseparable, and each permeates his universe. On the gate of Hell were inscribed the words:

> *Giustizia mosse il mio alto fattore;*
> *Fecemi la divina potestate,*
> *La somma sapienza, e 'l primo amore.*

(Inf. III, 4)

" Justice moved God to create me; divine power, highest wisdom, and primal love made me." So that love entered even into the ordering of Hell. It is not that justice and love are co-operating and compensating principles; they are one. Justice is love and love is justice, aspects of a single unity. But it is easier to grasp the nature of the unity if we consider it in its aspects, and so there is in the *Comedy* a sort of progression of dominance from justice to love. Hell is most easily understood as the realm of justice; justice and love together give the rule of Purgatory; and Paradise is the kingdom of love. Here dwell the blessed in a realm of light, enjoying and reflecting the love which streams from God in greater or lesser degree according to their capacities. But Dante is careful to show us that the allotment of differing capacities is just.

It is in Paradise that we find unquestionably the finest section of the poem. Here we follow Dante as, now under the guidance of Beatrice, he rises through the spheres of the planets to the Empyrean, which is the seat of God. In his *Storia della letteratura italiana*, De Sanctis described it thus: " The stages are shown entirely by light. We have not, as in Hell and Purgatory, qualitative differences, but only quantitative, a more or a less. At first the light is not so brilliant as to eclipse the human face; the higher we go, the more the soul's form is hidden by light as by a sanctuary. And the smile of Beatrice is a crescendo beyond determination, as the light is. Rightly the poet dedicates the extreme of his powers to this part of the poem, conscious of the greatness and difficulty of the undertaking. He is roused by this world of Paradise, by the novelty and wonders of its phenomena; the poetic images spring forth alive and moving. Ascending ever higher and higher, he soars to unimagined heights, serene and ecstatic. The difficulty seems to fascinate him, the novelty to strengthen him, the infinitude to exalt him."

This is the skeleton of the work—but it does not correspond to anything in the poem. What I have given is a series of abstractions: I have said " the lustful," " the avaricious," " the envious," " the proud "; but Dante nowhere uses such general terms. Within the wall of Dis we meet not " the heretics," but Farinata, an individual with individual traits; on the shores of Purgatory we meet not " the tardily repentant," but Manfred, Casella, Sordello, and Belacqua—individuals, with individual personalities. It is important to remember this when you hear or say that the *Comedy* is an allegory. We have come, erroneously, to associate allegory with personified abstractions; and the word calls to mind works like the *Pilgrim's Progress* in which a character named Christian sets out from the City of Destruction and passes through the Slough of Despond and Vanity Fair, meeting such personages as Evangelist, Pliable, Faith, Pride, Shame, and Mr. Worldly Wiseman; or eighteenth-century poems in which Fame hovers over a general or Victory perches on his standard. The device was, at the time it entered poetry, very useful; it enabled writers to explore mental phenomena for which there were no descriptive terms. But for modern readers it has a great defect, which might be called misplaced emphasis. When you hear about a character called Talkative, the son of Say-well, who lives in Prating-row, you do not for a moment believe there is any such person, and what is more, you feel the author never meant you to believe it. His interest was not in the personification but in the abstraction, not in his character but in the vice or virtue which it represents.

Dante avoided this pitfall by adopting a method of presentation which is usually called symbolism, and which consists primarily in choosing or creating a personage who typifies an abstract quality. So, instead of putting into his story a character called Dictatorship, an author introduces Hitler, or instead of Egotism builds up Hedda Gabler; as, instead of Lust, Dante gave us Paolo and Francesca, and instead of Reason, Virgil. It is a subtler and altogether more satisfying way; it is, we now believe (though the belief may change), the only way compatible with poetry. And Dante's work is poetry.

The stress of Dante criticism in the twentieth century has been upon the poetic quality of his work, with a correlative disregard of the intellectual content, which reached its extreme in the criticism of Croce, who actually discarded the plot as irrelevant. Croce found the poetry of the *Comedy* to lie exclusively in certain lyric passages; the journey through the other world he termed " an ethico-politico-theological novel," a structure unrelated to the poetry. " The structure of the Comedy," he said in his *Poesia di Dante*, " might be regarded as a framework upon which a luxuriant vegetation is clambering, decorating it with flowers; but its relation with the poetry is simply that which exists between a didactic novel and the lyric which continually interrupts it." Such a view is untenable. It was valuable that critics should bring us back to realize that the *Comedy* is a poem, and is to be understood in poetic terms and by reference to poetic standards; their work corrects a tendency of the late nineteenth century to concern itself with historical identification, and of several centuries to focus on moral and theological implications and reduce the work to a treatise. But our new appreciation of Dante's technique must not blind us to his content. Dante, endowed beyond all other poets with visual imagination, created individuals; but we wrong him if we consider them simply as a gallery of portraits. They are individuals raised to the power of a symbol.

The greatness of Dante lies in his achieving the moment of poetic fusion when the doctrine becomes image, when the word is made flesh. He responds to Francesca as to a lady, lovely and lost, but he also sees a fragment of soulhood set in a vaster circle of existence and eternity. This existence and this eternity are not, for Dante, a conceptual trellis to support frail lyric flowers; the vision of eternal glory moves through the whole poem, as necessary to it as sap to a vine. Thomas Aquinas worked out a doctrine logically; Dante saw salvation and clothed it in raiment white and glistering. From the moment we leave the dark wood and turn toward the fainter gloom of Limbo and the murky glimmering of Dis, there is an ever-growing light, an ever-mounting flame, which carries us at last to bliss. It is not some instantaneous inspiration, some flash of lyric, which gives beauty to the close, but the grandeur of the completed cycle, the fruit brought forth upon the vine which had its roots in the *oscura selva*. It is the fact that—with the poet—we have risen from the dead, that this corruption has put on incorruption and this mortality become immortal, that gives an exaltation, a more than ordinary meaning to the final lines: " O Light Eternal, abiding in Thyself, Thou alone knowest Thyself, and in Thyself both known and knowing, smilest on Thyself in love. . . . Here power failed the soaring imagination, but now my desire and my will, like a wheel that turns with equal motion, were revolving with the Love that moves the sun and other stars."

> *O Luce Eterna, che sola in te sidi,*
> *Sola t'intendi, e, da te intelletta*
> *Ed intendente te, ami ed arridi!*
>
> . . . .
>
> *All'alta fantasia qui mancò possa;*
> *Ma già volgeva il mio disio e il velle,*
> *Sì come ruota ch'igualmente è mossa,*
> *L'Amor che muove il sole e l'altre stelle.*

A NOTE ON DANTE'S LIFE

Dante's biography does not explain his poem, but one has a natural curiosity to know something about the man who wrote so great a work. Dante Alighieri was born in Florence in May, 1265, of a family which, though noble, was neither wealthy nor important. He probably had some formal education, as he learned to write Latin, and he taught himself the science of metrics by reading the Provençal and Italian poets. While still quite young he gained a reputation as a lyric poet, and he knew the other Florentine poets, especially Guido Cavalcanti, whom he called " my first friend."

The most important fact of his youth was his love for Beatrice
Portinari, whom he celebrated in many lyrics. After Beatrice
died in 1290, Dante selected a number of these lyrics and wove
them into a prose account of his love, which he called the *Vita
Nuova*. This love, it cannot be too much emphasized, had its
existence within Dante's mind; with the actual Beatrice, who
was married, he probably had only a casual acquaintance, and
his story is not a romance.

The most striking of the outward events are that he saw
Beatrice when they were both eight; that he saw her again nine
years later and that she then greeted him; that she later heard
something about him which caused her thereafter to deny him
greeting; and that she died at twenty-four. There is no suggestion
of any conversation between them or of any sign of mutual
affection, but about these negligible facts is developed one of the
most intense psychological dramas ever recorded; Dante's love
for Beatrice was real, it was different from any love that any other
person has ever described, and it was a continuing force throughout Dante's life. Indeed, the change in the kind of love Dante felt
for Beatrice marks, in one sense, the difference between the *Vita
Nuova* and the *Divina Commedia*, and makes the former an
appropriate prologue to a reading of the *Comedy*. A few years
after Beatrice's death Dante married Gemma Donati and by her
had two sons and probably two daughters. After Dante's death
one of the sons wrote a commentary on the *Comedy*.

Dante was a Guelf, as were most of his friends; indeed, the
Ghibellines had been practically extinguished as a party in
Florence a few years before Dante was born. Toward the end of
the century, however, new factions arose, known as the Blacks
and the Whites. Dante was a White, although his wife was a
cousin of the leader of the Black party. The first open hostility
between the two groups occurred on May Day, 1300, when a
street brawl ended in one of the contestant's having his nose cut
off; thereafter there were several breaches of the peace.

In June, Dante was elected one of the priors of the city, and
with his colleagues voted to banish the leaders of both parties;

among them was Guido Cavalcanti, Dante's friend and a member of his own White party. The remedy was ineffectual, and when Dante's term of office ended in August the dissension was increasing. The Blacks invoked the aid of Pope Boniface VIII, and in 1301 he called upon Charles of Valois to enter the city and restore order. Because he promised to maintain peace between both sides, Charles was allowed to enter without resistance; but as soon as he was in control he simply turned the city over to the Blacks. Dante was away when Valois entered, and he prudently refrained from returning. He was ordered to appear before the Podestà, and because he did not, a sentence was passed in January, 1302, confiscating his property and banishing him for two years; in March the sentence was raised to death by burning if found in Florentine territory. Thereafter Dante never entered Florence; the remaining twenty years of his life were spent in exile and poverty.

Much has been made of the fact that his wife did not follow him into exile; it seems likely that she had means of support from her own property in Florence, where she could also receive help from her family, whereas Dante was a wanderer dependent on the charity of chance patrons and in no position to support a wife and children. For a time he joined the other exiles at Gargonza, but he soon fell out with them and formed, as he put it, a party of his own. He found a refuge with the Scaliger family in Verona for a time; then he was for a while the guest of Franceschino Malaspina at Sarzana. Thereafter his movements for some years are uncertain; the exact and intimate geographical details scattered through the *Comedy* make it seem likely that he wandered over much of Italy. About 1317 he was again with the Scaligers, this time at the invitation of Can Grande, and then he went to the court of Guido da Polenta at Ravenna, where he remained until his death in September 1321.

One of the consequences of Dante's unhappy political experience was that he changed from a Guelf into a Ghibelline; he wrote in Latin a treatise, the *Monarchia*, which argues that the papacy must confine itself to spiritual power, that all temporal power should reside in a single emperor, and that the Roman emperor is divinely appointed to this service. He supported the attempt of Henry VII to conquer the peninsula, and wrote letters to Florence and other cities of Italy, calling on them to receive their rightful emperor. The division of spiritual from temporal power and the necessity for harmonious co-operation between pope and emperor is a basic theme in the *Divine Comedy*, and it is true that unless he had had the experience which called into being the process of reasoning that ended in this conclusion, Dante could not have written the poem which he did write. During his exile Dante wrote other works, some of them unfinished, which are less intimately connected with the *Divine Comedy*: in Italian, the *Convivio*, and in Latin, the *De vulgari eloquentia*, the *Quaestio de aqua et terra*, and two eclogues. He called his poem simply *The Comedy*; the adjective *Divine* was first added by an editor in 1555 and meant "the excellent comedy" rather than "the comedy about divine things." After Dante's death Florence tried several times to get his remains, but Ravenna stubbornly resisted, and today Italy's greatest poet lies in the city which gave him refuge.

VI

The Works of Chaucer

KEMP MALONE

THE ENGLISH had a flourishing and extensive literature in the so-called Dark Ages, although most of that literature has not come down to us; only a very small part of it has withstood the tooth of time. Our earliest surviving verse goes back to the sixth century, and in the course of the seventh, eighth, ninth, tenth, and eleventh centuries a large number of poems and prose pieces were written, many of them admirable specimens of literary art, and at least one of them, *Beowulf*, a work of outstanding genius, one of the chief glories of English literature as a whole.

If such was the achievement of the Dark Ages in England, one might legitimately expect even greater things in the twelfth and thirteenth centuries, for these were the centuries in which medieval civilization reached its height and produced masterpieces unexcelled before or since. It was in the twelfth and thirteenth centuries that Gothic architecture took shape and flourished in western Europe. It was then that most of the masterpieces of medieval literature were composed, masterpieces like the *Divine Comedy* of Dante, the Icelandic sagas, the *Gesta Danorum* of Saxo Grammaticus, and the *Tristan* of Gottfried von Strassburg. The famous French epic, the *Song of Roland*, dates from the beginning of the twelfth century, and in that century and the next French literature got its start and grew great. But its elder sister, English literature, during the same period underwent a disastrous decline, almost to the point of extinction, and not until the fourteenth century, when the great days of the Middle Ages were over, do we again find vigorous and significant literary activity in English. The literary history of the English nation in the Middle Ages is unique. No other nation of western Christendom rose so high in the period from 700 to 1100; no other nation of western Christendom sank so low in the period from 1100 to 1350.

It was, of course, the Norman Conquest which brought about this tremendous, this catastrophic decline in English literary culture. The worst fate that can befall any nation is dominance by men of an alien tongue. In the nature of the case the speech of the rulers becomes the chief vehicle of culture, the medium in which the civilizing forces of the time are given expression, and the hapless subjects, few of whom ever succeed in mastering a language not their own, are cut off from the main stream of civilization and stand condemned, not only to physical serfdom but also to spiritual degradation. Such was the fate which loomed before the English nation when Harold fell at Hastings. And yet, in the second half of the fourteenth century, after three hundred years during which French remained the language of the upper classes in England, we find English culture not only still alive but come into its own again.

This survival and ultimate triumph in the face of conditions so adverse is one of the miracles of history. Or, rather, it bears eloquent witness to the strength of the English nationalism which King Alfred and his successors had built up. Here as always the fortress and citadel of the national culture was the national language, the English speech which not only set off the conquered from their French masters by an ever-present outward sign, but also served as the great vehicle of the national spirit, and the chief barrier against the constant progress of the French conquest, which, not stopping with political domination and economic exploitation, tended to wipe out all traces of English culture and to make the English people into low-grade Frenchmen. Thanks to its rich literary heritage, handed down from the days of freedom, the English language was able to maintain itself as a written as well as a spoken tongue. English monks and priests kept on writing in their native speech, clinging stubbornly to a tradition not at all characteristic of the medieval church in general but highly characteristic of the Church of England, and this in virtue of a practice centuries old and promoted by King Alfred himself, the father of English prose. Literature in English, prose and verse alike, continued to be cultivated to some degree in the darkest years of the French domination, and clergy joined hands with laity in maintaining the inherited verse forms alongside the rhymes and meters which in other Germanic countries (Iceland excepted) had won a complete victory. The old alliterative measure was not given up, indeed, until Tudor times, and has left its mark on our poetical tradition and practice to the present day. The great literary revival of the fourteenth century proves the vitality of English literary tradition.

But here we can make no study of this great literary revival as a whole. We must confine ourselves to its chief figure, Geoffrey Chaucer. This is the easier to do because Chaucer stands somewhat apart from the native literary movement which produced *Piers Plowman, Gawain and the Green Knight*, and other masterpieces of his day. These compositions were done in the old alliterative measure and carry on, directly, the literary tradition of Old English times. Chaucer knew alliterative verse; he refers to it in his writings. But he did not choose to follow it. Likewise he made no use of the old poetical vocabulary, the poetic diction inherited from Old English and still current in the metrical romances and alliterative poems of the fourteenth century. In meter and diction Chaucer was an innovator, so far as English was concerned. Let me hasten to add that he did not invent meters or words, so far as we know, although in a number of cases he seems to have been the first to use a given meter, or a given word, in English poetry. He took his meters from the international stock, and many of his words came from the same source.

For Chaucer was a citizen of the world. He was born and brought up in London, and from an early age was a member of the royal court. He kept these court connections all his life. He was a servant of the king, and of various princes, in many capacities. Such service in those days was not so highly specialized as it now is, and we search in vain for a modern label which will fit Chaucer's work. He was a diplomat, sent on missions to France and Italy. He was a civil servant, collecting customs duties and doing many other jobs that the king needed to have done. He was a soldier, fighting for the king in the French wars. All his life his associations were with the court, with the people who ruled England. He made his living not by writing but by serving the king at home and abroad. His work and his associations made him at home almost everywhere in western Europe. He knew at least three languages besides English: Latin, French, and Italian; and he was widely read in the literatures corresponding. When he wrote verse, it was easy and natural for him to use the meters then fashionable in western Europe generally, meters nearly all handed down from Greece and Rome, and embellished by a system of rhymes that had first become familiar in the Latin hymns of the church and gradually had been taken up in all the vernaculars, not only in French, Spanish, and Italian, but also in German, Scandinavian, and English verse.

Chaucer's diction, like his meters, came in part from the world of international affairs and of international culture in which he habitually moved. Chaucer knew lots of long words of foreign origin, and if such words were current in the English of his day he did not hesitate to use them in his verse. His willingness to do so may not seem very startling, but up to the fourteenth century English poets had steered pretty clear of foreign words, on the whole. A few such words had crept into use, but the poetic vocabulary had remained overwhelmingly native. Poetry is always much slower than prose to take alien elements, and this was very strikingly the case with traditional English poetry, which depended largely on a special poetic vocabulary for its effects.

Chaucer's practice in this matter may be described as follows. He rejected altogether the old words that had survived in poetic usage but were no longer used in actual speech. He kept rhetorical diction (that is, the " high " style taught in the treatises on rhetoric, a heritage from classical antiquity) wherever it seemed to him appropriate or effective. Otherwise he used a colloquial style, now and then somewhat varied to fit the speaker. His characters, including himself, talk in the ordinary everyday speech of fourteenth-century England, though they talk much better than such people ever do in real life. Chaucer's language is simply the language spoken in his home town, London, by cultivated people, in the fourteenth century. It abounds in clichés, set phrases, stereotyped expressions, or whatever you want to call them, but few of these are locutions found only in literature and freighted with centuries of poetic association; they are nearly all current coins of speech. Even such a figure as " ful lyk a fiers leoun," obviously literary in origin, belonged to common speech, and tags like " as to my dom " (" in my opinion "), which modern readers find quaint or charming, were in those days very common-place expressions indeed.

In his themes, again, and in the way he treated them, Chaucer was international-minded. He started out with subjects and methods of treatment fashionable in the western Europe of his day. He made no effort to revive the glories of the English literary past. Indeed, he probably knew little or nothing about these glories. He wrote for his own day. I may add that he made no effort to imitate the Latin classics either, not to mention the Greek classics, with which he was not familiar. Chaucer lived when the so-called Italian Renaissance was beginning, and he knew fourteenth-century Italy, but the Renaissance as a move-ment had little influence on him; he remained a full-fledged medieval. He seems to have written, in his youth, a good many lyrics, but few of these have come down to us, and his most important work lies in the field of narrative poetry. He told stories in verse.

Chaucer got most of his stories from books, and told them again in his own way, following his source closely sometimes and very freely indeed at other times. So far as we know he never invented a story, though we have not been able to find the exact source or sources of some of his poems. Certain tales of his, however, seem to have been drawn not from books but from oral sources. This holds particularly of the smutty stories. For instance, the miller's tale and the reeve's tale, Chaucer's two stories of university life, are exceedingly smutty and we have found no written sources for them. Chaucer may well have picked them up in visits to Oxford and Cambridge, or in conversation with Oxford and Cambridge men.

Chaucer's way of using tales already current, instead of inventing new ones, was regular in his time, and continued to be regular for a long time to come. Shakespeare, of course, did the same thing. Our modern insistence on originality would have seemed a mad idea to our forefathers. Everybody knows, they would have said, that the best stories are the old stories, the stories that have stood the test of time, the stories that are already familiar to the reading public. If your readers know the story you are telling, they will enjoy your version of it much better than they would enjoy something quite new and strange to them. For one thing, knowing what to expect, the strain on their nervous systems would be much less, and they would have much less trouble seeing the point when you were making a point. This principle is familiar in jokes. If you have never heard a joke before, you often have to use your wits and even so you may fail to get the point. This is embarrassing both to you and to the one who is telling the joke. How much better it works out if you have heard the joke before. Then you laugh at the proper time and the joker enjoys your appreciation and is impressed by your intelligence. In much the same way most people enjoy hearing again a piece of music which they have heard many times before, and very few people enjoy music which is new and strange to them. They must become familiar with it before they can like it.

Medieval stories usually followed familiar patterns, and the hearers or readers knew in advance what they were going to get. Yet novelty was not lacking. Each author had his own style, his own way of handling the familiar matter, and these individual differences gave to each composition its particular flavor. Things are not really so very different today, in spite of our emphasis on originality. We change the names and situations about a bit, but most plots fall into a few familiar types: love stories, adventure stories, detective stories, and the like; and the discerning reader can often predict the course of events in general if not in detail.

We cannot here examine all the works of Chaucer, and I will limit myself to two of them, his two great masterpieces, *Troilus and Cressida* and *The Canterbury Tales*. The first, commonly called *Troilus* for short, is a love story, told in typical medieval fashion. By that I mean that the love affair proceeds according to the rules laid down for literary love affairs in medieval times. How far lovers followed these rules in actual life I will not venture to say. The love code which we get in medieval love stories is known as the code of courtly love. Our modern conventions in love stories have descended from the medieval conventions of courtly love, although these have been watered down and otherwise modified as the centuries have rolled on.

When the story opens, Troilus, the hero, is not in love with anybody. He is rather boastful about his freedom and feels very sorry for the unfortunate men who have become victims of love. He is determined to steer clear of such entanglements. Any wise reader will know at once what to expect: the god of love will strike, and lay Troilus low. And so he does. Troilus one day goes to a temple (the scene of the tale is laid in ancient Troy). There he sees the heroine, Cressida. He falls in love at first sight. The procedure is as follows. Cressida looks at Troilus—just a fleeting glance. But in that moment the god of love, who dwells in the lady's eyes, shoots his arrow, which is Cressida's glance. The arrow hits Troilus in the eye, and then proceeds downward through his anatomy until it reaches his heart, where it lodges and becomes fixed.

What happens next? Troilus goes home and goes to bed. He is lovesick. His sickness brings with it a number of very definite symptoms, by which a good physician can diagnose his case, though without drugs to effect a cure. I will mention a few of these symptoms. First, a lovesick man has no appetite; he cannot eat, he refuses food. Again, he cannot sleep; he lies awake all night, tossing on his pillow, thinking about his lady. Thirdly, he is plunged into a profound depression; he is completely and totally miserable, and looks forward to death, which at least will put him out of his misery. This depression springs from his humility. He feels unworthy. His lady is so wonderful, and he by comparison with her is such a sorry creature, that he can give himself not the slightest hope of ever winning her love. For this reason he is plunged into despair. All these things sap his strength and he takes to his bed, too weak to go about his ordinary concerns: lovesick, in short.

And now a friend appears, to help him out—a go-between. In Chaucer's story this friend is named Pandarus. He is not only the friend of Troilus but also the uncle of Cressida, and therefore it is easy for him to bring the lovers together. But he has a hard time with Troilus, who long refuses to confide in him. Here we come to another principle of medieval love-making; the love affair must be secret. Troilus must tell nobody that he is in love, and most of all he must not reveal to anybody who it is that he is in love with. Pandarus, however, finally gets the lady's name out of him, and volunteers to help him win her. Troilus's ambitions, at first, are modest. He would like to be granted the privilege of looking at the lady, and even speaking to her, and, eventually, serving her, running errands for her, dancing attendance on her. This service is to be his sole reward. His humility is such that he cannot hope for more. But the appetite grows by what it feeds on, and the time will come to go further.

One thing, however, never occurs to Troilus, or to Pandarus, or to the lady. This is marriage. Here again we are dealing with a courtly love convention, according to which the affair must be with a married woman. As it happens, Cressida is a widow, and marriage would be possible enough, but nobody thinks of it even as a possibility; it is never mentioned. In modern love stories of the conventional, traditional kind the lovers finally marry and live happy ever afterward. Not so in medieval love stories. The most famous of them, of course, is that of Tristan and Isolde. In this story, Isolde, the heroine, is married to the hero's uncle; the love affair leads to adultery; the end is tragedy. In the story of Troilus and Cressida, too, the love is illicit, although no husband figures in the plot.

Through five long books the action of the poem proceeds. Cressida is very properly slow in granting her favors. She yields a little and then a little more, until at last she yields all and Troilus is well and happy again. The first night of love has a couple of details which may be of interest. Troilus, kneeling by the bed in which Cressida is lying, falls down in a swoon; he faints away, loses consciousness. This is a well-known symptom of medieval love. Before his fainting spell he bursts into tears, and tears are very important to a medieval lover, for otherwise no lady would believe that his love was genuine. I may remark at this point that it was good medieval practice for men as well as women to burst into tears at any and every appropriate occasion. Thus, in the confessional, when you were confessing your sins to the priest, unless you wept pretty copiously he would suspect that you were not really contrite, and might refuse absolution.

But to go back to Troilus and Cressida. After their first night of love they had many nights together, all in secret; nobody knew of their love except Pandarus, the go-between. But later the lovers were parted. Cressida's father sent for her and she had to go to him. Chaucer tells in great detail of the grief of Troilus and the vows of fidelity which the lovers made to each other. But Cressida proved faithless. Another lover paid court to her, and finally she took him. Troilus long refused to believe that she had played him false but at last the evidence convinced him. He was broken-hearted and courted death in battle.

With his death the story might be supposed to come to an end, but Chaucer gives it a conclusion startling to the modern reader, though characteristic enough of medieval ways of thought. Troilus is represented as going to heaven when he dies. From this point of vantage he looks down upon the earth and meditates upon the folly of earthly pleasures. He draws the orthodox Christian moral; while we live on earth we should prepare ourselves for heaven, not devote ourselves to the pursuit of earthly bliss, which by nature is transitory and vain. The story thus ends with a conventional Christian moral; even a story of illicit love is made to teach us lessons.

This ending illustrates a fundamental and all-pervading medieval belief about works of literary art. Such works are supposed to do us good; they are not merely for our amusement, but also for our instruction and moral elevation. And it is interesting to note that the moral of this story of illicit love is not what it would be today. Nowadays the moral would be: marry the girl, don't have illicit relations with her. But such a moral seems never to have occurred to Chaucer. He draws a much more general conclusion: devote your earthly life to preparation for the life eternal, not to temporal and transitory things.

We turn now to Chaucer's other masterpiece, *The Canterbury Tales*. The scene of this work, as its title indicates, is laid in England, and much of it deals with English life in Chaucer's day. It is the story of a pilgrimage to Canterbury, undertaken by a group of pilgrims who in visiting the shrine of St. Thomas at Canterbury were combining a pleasant holiday trip with spiritual uplift. The medieval substitute for the kind of trip we take nowadays in vacation time was a pilgrimage to the shrine of some saint. Such pilgrimages, however, had one great advantage over modern pleasure trips. Through pilgrimages one stored up for oneself treasure in heaven. A pilgrimage was a virtuous undertaking, good for the soul. And good for the body too. If you were sick, the thing to do was to seek cure by the miracle-working power of the relics of some saint or other. St. Thomas was well known for his power to cure the sick. And the cathedral at Canterbury had a full set of relics to use for curative purposes, relics which had every claim to genuineness, for Thomas was slain by the emissaries of King Henry II before the high altar at Canterbury. The priests had his body and his clothes, and his shirt in particular worked so many miracles that he was canonized very shortly after his death.

As you probably know, martyrs are usually made saints because they work miracles; the long delay in canonizing Sir Thomas More, the victim of Henry VIII, was due to the fact that no proof could be found that he had worked any miracles after his death. A good friend of mine, now dead, once told me that a certain priest, eager to accomplish the canonization of Thomas More, persuaded a sick parishioner of his to invoke the name of Thomas More in his prayers for recovery. He duly recovered, and the priest thought he had an excellent piece of evidence which would impress the authorities, and bring about the canonization. But when the parishioner was closely questioned, he confessed that to make things sure he had invoked the name of the Virgin Mary, and the priest's piece of evidence was rejected as not conclusive.

But let us get back to Chaucer. The Canterbury Tales is what is known as a frame story. The pilgrimage is a frame, in which are set many tales, each independent but all bound together by the fact that all are set in the same frame. We may begin by giving a very brief sketch of the frame story. About thirty pilgrims, of whom Chaucer was one, gathered at an inn in the town of Southwark, just across the Thames River from London. They were all bound for Canterbury, and decided to travel together, under the leadership of the inn-keeper, who agreed to go with them. To amuse themselves on the way, they were to tell stories. When the pilgrimage was over, and they got back to Southwark, a prize was to be given to the pilgrim who in the judgment of the group had told the best story. Each pilgrim was to tell four tales in all, so the total number of tales would be one hundred and twenty. But Chaucer died before he finished this gigantic work; we have actually only twenty-three tales, with the beginning of a twenty-fourth. Chaucer not only did not finish his work; he left only fragments of it, and we do not know just how he wanted the tales arranged. But though the work is only a series of fragments, we have enough, in quality and quantity alike, to make a masterpiece.

Chaucer begins with a prologue, in which the various pilgrims are described. When one reads these descriptions one is struck with the superlative quality which Chaucer gives to nearly every pilgrim. He starts with the knight, who is represented as perfect: he has waged war in Europe, Asia, and Africa, but always for the

Faith, never for selfish reasons. His son, the Squire, is as perfect
a lover as the father is a knight. You will remember that the
Squire loved so hot that he slept at night no more than a nightin-
gale—that is, he did not sleep at all, and how could any woman
have a more perfect lover than that. Nearly all the pilgrims are
perfect examples of their kind, though in some cases the kind is
bad. The pardoner, for instance, is a scoundrel, but the most
plausible and successful scoundrel that ever sold pardons, and the
monk is a perfect example of clerical worldliness. These are
obviously not realistic portraits, and should not be so taken.
Chaucer was trying to bring together in one pilgrimage a group
of remarkable individuals, each representing some calling or occu-
pation or social class in fourteenth-century England, but each
more than a type, each the quintessence of good or bad within
his type. By using extreme examples he secured more interest, a
greater dramatic quality, than would be possible with ordinary
humdrum average-type figures. This comes out not only in his
descriptions in the prologue but also in the course of events
during the pilgrimage.

After he has finished with the descriptions of the pilgrims,
Chaucer proceeds with his frame story. The host makes his
proposal, the pilgrims accept it, and the next morning they all
start out, on horseback, for Canterbury. At the first watering
place for the horses the host has them draw cut, to see who shall
tell the first tale. This falls to the knight, who then tells a love
story, not one of the strictly courtly kind, since it ends in marriage,
but a good old traditional story which had held its own in literature in spite of its unfashionable ending. The host now turns to
the monk, as the pilgrim next in rank to the knight, and asks him
to tell a tale. But the miller interrupts. He is drunk, and insists
on telling a good smutty story to reward the knight for *his* story.
The miller's tale is about an Oxford student named Nicholas, who
boards with an old carpenter and his young wife, and takes
advantage of his opportunities to seduce the wife and make a fool
of the carpenter. One of the pilgrims, the reeve, happens to be a
carpenter by trade, and takes offense. When the miller has told

his tale, the reeve proceeds to tell the story of a miller who was made a fool of by *two* Cambridge students, one of whom lay with the miller's wife, the other with the miller's daughter; in this way the reeve gives double measure for what he got. This device of having two of the pilgrims quarrel serves to make things more interesting and to give the tales an organic connection with the frame story. Chaucer uses the quarrel device more than once later on, though less successfully. After the reeve the cook starts to tell a story, but only the first fifty-eight lines of it have come down to us; Chaucer presumably never finished it. Here the first fragment ends. I will not describe the other fragments; there are nine of them in all.

We go back to the prologue. I quote the first eighteen lines, to give you an idea of how Chaucer's fourteenth-century English sounded:

> *Whan that April with his shoures sote*
> *The droghte of March hath perced to the rote*
> *And bathed every veyne in swich licour*
> *Of which vertu engendred is the flour;*
> *Whan Zephirus eek with his swete breeth*
> *Inspired hath in every holt and heeth*
> *The tendre croppes, and the yonge sonne*
> *Hath in the Ram his halfe cours yronne,*
> *And smale foules maken melodye*
> *That slepen all the night with open ye*
> *(So priketh hem nature in hir corages),*
> *Than longen folk to gon on pilgrimages*
> *And palmers for to seken straunge strondes*
> *To ferne halwes, couthe in sondry londes;*
> *And specially, from every shires ende*
> *Of Engelond, to Caunterbury they wende,*
> *The holy blisful martyr for to seke,*
> *That hem hath holpen whan that they were seke.*

The pronunciation of English has, of course, greatly changed since Chaucer's day. If you look at the words on the printed page, most of them will seem familiar enough to you, but they sound

strange. If King Alfred could have heard Chaucer speak, he
would have had trouble with a few of the words, but the pronunciation would have seemed much less strange to him than it does
to us. You will notice, too, that Chaucer uses a line of ten or
eleven syllables, the iambic pentameter; its name betrays the
fact that this particular metrical arrangement of a line is Greek
in origin. But Chaucer also uses rhyme, and by virtue of their
rhyme the lines fall into couplets. The iambic pentameter couplet
was the favorite verse form of the eighteenth century, as you
know; it is usually called the heroic couplet. Chaucer was the
first to use this couplet in English. The iambic pentameter more
often than not in Chaucer has an extra syllable at the end, after
the last foot. This extra syllable, always unstressed, is said to
give the line a " feminine " or weak ending. If the line has only
ten syllables the final syllable is stressed and the line is said to
have a masculine or strong ending. Examples:

> (ten syllables, masculine ending)
> *Inspired hath in every holt and heeth.*
> (eleven syllables, feminine ending)
> *The tendre croppes, and the yonge sonne.*

Chaucer was a careful metrist and an exact rhymer.

We turn now to the tales themselves. I have already described
three of them. The other twenty are a miscellaneous lot. The
man of law and the clerk both tell of a woman sadly put upon
but bearing her troubles in dignity and patience and at last
brought to safety and happiness. The shipman tells a story much
like that of the miller, though in this case a monk is the seducer,
a merchant is the cuckold, and the merchant's wife is made as
much a fool of as the merchant. The prioress chooses for her tale
a miracle wrought by the Virgin Mary.

Chaucer himself tells the tale of Sir Thopas, a parody on the
metrical romances still popular in Chaucer's day. The host doesn't
like the parody and stops him in the middle of it. Chaucer then
tries again; this time he tells a tale in prose, a highly edifying
and extremely dull story which nearly all modern readers skip but

which the host, if not the other pilgrims, seems to like; it is really a treatise on forgiveness, cast into dialogue form.

The monk, when called on to tell a tale, seems more than willing: he suggests telling the life of St. Edward, but first, he says, he will tell some tragedies, of which he has a stock of one hundred on hand at home. He actually starts on his stock of tragedies, but has told only seventeen of them when the knight stops him. The host chimes in, and calls on the nun's priest for a tale which is *not* a tragedy. The priest responds with one of the most delightful of Chaucer's stories: a fable about a cock, a hen, and a fox. This fable is done in the mock heroic style. The hero is of course the cock; the heroine is the hen; the villain is the fox. The lightness of touch and technical skill with which this story is told cannot be surpassed in the whole of English literature. I will quote one passage in illustration. The fox has seized our hero, the cock, in its mouth and is running away to the woods. The hens with their cackling (or, as Chaucer puts it, their lamentations) have aroused the neighborhood and the pursuit of the fox begins. It proceeds as follows:

> *This sely widwe, and eek hir doghtres two*
> *Herden thise hennes cry and maken wo,*
> *And out at dores sterten they anoon,*
> *And syen the fox toward the grove goon,*
> *And bar upon his bak the cok away;*
> *And cryden, Out! harrow and weylawey!*
> *Ha ha, the fox! and after him they ran,*
> *And eek with staves many another man:*
> *Ran Colle our dog, and Talbot and Gerland,*
> *And Malkin, with a distaf in hir hand;*
> *Ran cow and calf, and eek the verrey hogges,*
> *So were they fered for berking of the dogges*
> *And shouting of the men and wimmen eke,*
> *They ronne so, hem thoughte hir herte breke.*
> *They yelleden as feendes doon in helle;*
> *The dokes cryden as men wolde hem quelle;*
> *The gees for fere flowen over the trees;*
> *Out of the hyve cam the swarm of bees;*

> *So hidous was the noise, a! benedicite!*
> *Certes, he Jakke Straw, and his meynee,*
> *Ne made never shoutes half so shrille,*
> *Whan that they wolden any Fleming kille,*
> *As thilke day was made upon the fox.*
> *Of bras they broughten bemes, and of box,*
> *Of horn, of boon, in whiche they blewe and pouped,*
> *And therwithal they shriked and they houped;*
> *It semed as that heven sholde falle.*

You will notice here how Chaucer piles up his material, how he uses exaggeration, extremes, to gain his effect: in this case, a comic or even farcical effect. He overwhelms you with a tremendous mass of stuff, all pertinent but never before brought together in such quantity and diversity.

The physician tells the old story of Virginius and Virginia. Then comes the pardoner with a sermon as good as the pardoner himself is evil, a sermon on the sin of cupidity, the very sin of which he is constantly guilty, so that he can indeed preach with authority on this subject. The wife of Bath tells a fairy tale with an Arthurian setting—hardly what one would have expected of the wife, after her prologue, but the story ends with a husband reduced to complete submission and a wife triumphantly sovereign in the household, and that is the wife of Bath's notion of a happy marriage. I will quote the beginning and the end of this story by way of illustration. After the wife's prologue the friar has something to say about its undue length, and his words offend the wife, who pays him back by beginning her tale with a savage attack on the mendicant orders:

> *In th'olde dayes of the king Arthur,*
> *Of which that Britons speken greet honour,*
> *Al was this land fulfild of fayerye.*
> *The elf-queen, with hir joly companye,*
> *Daunced ful ofte in many a grene mede;*
> *This was the olde opinion, as I rede.*
> *I speke of many hundred yeres ago;*
> *But now can no man see none elves mo.*

For now the grete char'tee and prayeres
Of limitours and other holy freres,
That serchen every lond and every streem,
As thikke as motes in the sonne-beem,
Blessing halles, chambres, kich'nes, boures,
Citees, burghes, castles, hye toures,
Thropes, bernes, shipnes, dayeryes—
This maketh that ther been no fayeryes.
For ther as wont to walken was an elf,
Ther walketh now the limitour himself
In undermeles and in morweninges,
And seyth his matins and his holy thinges
As he goth in his limitacioun.
Wommen may go saufly up and doun,
In every bush, or under every tree;
Ther is noon other incubus but he,
And he ne wol doon hem but dishonour.

The tale proper deals with a knight who is tricked into marrying an old hag. On their wedding night she argues with her husband so persuasively that he submits himself fully to her authority:

And thus they live, unto hir lyves ende,
In parfit joye; and Jesu Crist us sende
Housbondes meke, yonge, and fresh abedde,
And grace t'overbyde hem that we wedde.
And eek I preye that Jesu shorte hir lyves
That wol nat be governed by hir wyves;
And olde and angry nigardes of dispense,
God sende hem sone verray pestilence.

Another fairy tale is that of the squire, but the setting is oriental; Chaucer left this tale unfinished.

The friar and the summoner attack each other by tales at the expense of a summoner and a friar respectively. The merchant tells a savage tale about married life, in which the husband is cuckolded. The franklin also tells of married life, but he presents another point of view, and all ends well. The second nun, like the monk, has a saint's life on hand, but she proceeds to tell it without preliminaries; it is the life of St. Cecilia. The canon's yeoman talks about the canon, his master, who was an alchemist, and tells a tale about alchemy. The manciple tells a tale of cuckoldry, and the parson ends the collection with a sermon in prose on the subject of penitence.

The great diversity of subject-matter here is obvious. The themes, however, may be grouped in various ways. Several of the tales deal with married life, and several deal with the particular theme of cuckoldry, which may or may not involve a serious discussion of marital problems. Thus, the merchant's tale deals with cuckoldry and includes serious if bitter discussion of marriage. The miller's tale likewise deals with cuckoldry, but includes no serious discussion of marriage; it is light (farcical, indeed) in its treatment of the theme. But I need not multiply illustrations.

Another grouping, which would overlap the first, may be made of tales that deal with clerics. These worthies are handled very roughly in every case; their besetting sin is adultery. In such tales Chaucer is not attacking the church, nor is he attacking abuses in the church. He is simply repeating stock stories of a cynical type, stories which he found amusing and tells again for us in his own way.

Love stories are surprisingly few. Only the knight and his son the squire tell anything that can be called a love story, though Chaucer's own tale of Sir Thopas is a parody of such a story. We get two sermons, and a prose treatise (the tale of Melibeus) which is a moral instruction if not exactly a sermon. Several of the tales may be classified as smutty stories.

Chaucer got his tales from all kinds of sources; he shows himself a widely read man. It has been thought by some that he used his stories to characterize the pilgrims who told them, but this theory makes Chaucer into a writer far more modern than he really is. In his assignments of tales to the various pilgrims Chaucer shows a due sense of propriety: the gentry tell stories befitting their social respectability, and the smutty stories are put in the mouths of the common herd. But it would be a great mistake to interpret a given story as serving primarily to characterize its teller as an individual. Indeed, some of the tales seem quite unsuitable to their tellers as described in the general prologue. Thus, the monk of the prologue is no scholar; on the contrary, he scorns literary study and devotes himself to hunting. But when he is called upon to tell a tale he becomes a very learned, bookish man. In the same way, the merchant of the general prologue is quite different from the teller of the merchant's tale. Actually the stories are told for their own sakes, and the pilgrims who tell the stories serve primarily as mouthpieces for the author.

We may conclude with a look at Chaucer's poetic art. His salient marks are narrative skill, lightness of touch, mastery of technique, and ease and naturalness of style, a style essentially unstudied or even colloquial in its characteristic effects. Nobody could tell a story better than Chaucer. He lacks sublimity, the grand manner; but he is capable of pathos, tenderness, and the like. In range he thus falls behind Shakespeare but outstrips Milton. He wrote for his own time, but his sympathetic understanding and interpretation of life has kept him green through the centuries, and he is probably more read today than ever before in all the history of English literature. Chaucer is one of the great figures in European literary culture. He stands the test of study wonderfully well. After some fifty years of close association with him, I enjoy him more than ever, and find fresh beauties with each new reading. Such richness is rare. I commend him to your attention. He is worth knowing well.

VII

The Works of Rabelais

LEO SPITZER

FRANÇOIS Rabelais was born toward the end of the fifteenth century in the fertile province of France, Touraine, the son of a jurist. He became a member of the mendicant order of the Franciscans. As such, he studied the classics, especially the Greek authors revived at that time by the Renaissance movement. He studied them, evidently, so lovingly that his Greek books were confiscated by his austere fellow monks. A papal decision let him pass over from the Franciscans to the Benedictines, and with the help of a humanistic bishop he was made a canon and allowed to devote himself to medical and scientific studies. Without permission from his superiors he later left the service of the church and became a lay brother—in the phrase of the times *per saeculum vagatus est,* he strolled through the secular world.

In 1531 we find him as a candidate for a bachelor of medicine and as a lecturer on Hippocrates and Galen at the University of Montpellier, in 1532 at Lyons as a physician and editor of medical and juridical books—and of popular almanachs. This greatest comic writer indeed began his literary career by modestly continuing a story in pseudohistorical vein about the giant Gargantua which had already had great currency with the public—the *Chronique gargantuine.* The first original work of Rabelais is the *Chronique pantagrueline,* which appeared in 1532 and gave the story, contrived by Rabelais, of a supposed son of Gargantua, Pantagruel. This book appears now in Rabelais' works as book II, book I being a new *Gargantua,* by which Rabelais replaced in

1534 the popular *Chronique gargantuine*—a tale which then must have seemed trifling to the successful writer of the *Pantagruel*.

In the same year Rabelais visits Rome as the physician of the bishop and of Cardinal Dubellay. Later he received a papal absolution for his vagabond life and was reinstated as a Benedictine. He went to Paris where he won the support of King Francis I. In a revised edition of *Gargantua* and *Pantagruel* he deletes heretical passages that had incurred the wrath of the clerical authorities of the Sorbonne—without the desired effect, however, for his third book (*Tiers Livre*) was also censured by the Sorbonne.

In 1551 Rabelais becomes a parish priest at Meudon near Paris —the lewd stories about the *curé de Meudon* are not to be taken seriously, for the simple reason that during the two years that he held this office his place was actually filled by a substitute. The publication of his fourth book (*Quart Livre*) in 1548 provoked a furore: the Sorbonne condemned it, but King Henry II, then in conflict with the pope, supported Rabelais. Rabelais seems to have died in Paris in 1553.

All serious contemporary accounts concur in presenting him, not as a debauched monk, then a commonplace in religious propaganda of all shades, but as a learned scholar and a brilliant conversationalist—as an *omnium horarum homo*, a man fit for every moment, as Cardinal Dubellay put it. He was a churchman become a humanist who fought all his life for his intellectual freedom and paid for it by perpetual insecurity like other writers of that turbid period, Marot, D'Aubigné, and the martyr Etienne Dolet. A posthumous fifth book appeared in 1564: in the form in which we have it today, it cannot be by Rabelais but it follows a plan which must go back to Rabelais. Thus the five books, written over a period of thirty years of continuous wandering and of a life lived at the perilous border between Catholicism, Calvinism, and Humanism, cannot show that unity of plan and that purity of form which we are accustomed to find in Renaissance writing. Rabelais is indeed the acme of disorderliness and improvisation at a time when Ariosto and Camoens were showing the world the possibility of modern epic poems which can vie with those of the ancients. In addition, the temperament of Rabelais was not fitted for verse, least of all for lyrical verse. He is a prose writer who uses verse only occasionally for satirical purposes.

The first book tells us about the birth and youth of the giant Gargantua, the king of Utopia (behind this pseudogeographical datum, borrowed from Thomas More, Rabelais' own home country, Touraine, seems to be hidden, as other place-names indicate). Gargantua, the Big-Throated One, son of Grandgousier (Big-Gullet) and of Gargamelle (Big-Throat)—all Rabelaisian heroes are thirsty individuals—was born in the following manner (I am quoting from the superb English translation by Urquhart): " her fundament escaped her in an afternoon, on the 3rd day of February, with having eaten at dinner too many tripes, in fact 16 quarts, two bushels, three pecks and a pipkin full."

Gargantua is first shown to us in his tremendous physical development, then as a prankster-student in Paris where he feels obliged to climb the towers of Notre Dame, to make the great bells ring and, " which whilst he was doing, it came into his mind that they would serve very well for tingling on his mare's neck." So he takes away the bells and the Sorbonne must send one of its eminent orators to ask them back. The speech of this messenger, embellished as it is by scholastic Latin and by syllogisms, is quite ineffectual—and it turns out to be superfluous in the first place since Gargantua has meanwhile quietly given back the bells. As for his intellectual development, Gargantua is first shown studying under a scholastic teacher, then, with greater success, with a humane Renaissance scholar. But the studies are interrupted by a summons from his father whose kingdom has been invaded by King Picrochole (Bitter-Gall)—a choleric and quixotic would-be conqueror who is quickly defeated by Gargantua with the help of a heavy-drinking, heavy-eating, swashbuckling monk Jean des Entommures (John of the Hashed Meat). This representative of the life of the flesh is rewarded for his exploits in war by being given the position of an abbot in a convent founded expressly for him, the Abbaye de Thélème (Abbey of the Free Will) whose motto is *Fay ce que voudras*— "Do what you like!" Handsome boys from twelve to eighteen and pretty girls from ten to fifteen will retire there to have a good time of free development and will leave the abbey in order to marry—a bold sixteenth century anticipation of the American coeducational college.

The second book centers round Gargantua's son, Pantagruel, a name again alluding to thirst (Pantagruel supposedly *pants* for drink). Gargantua is a giant king with Renaissance ideas, only more advanced than his father, thanks to the possibilities given to the young generation, which Gargantua describes in a father-to-son-letter to the student Pantagruel at Paris: ". . . the age," he says, " was not so proper and fit for learning as it is at present, neither had I plenty of such good masters as thou hast had. For that time was darksome, obscured with clouds of ignorance and savoring a little of the calamity of the Goths, who had, wherever they set footing, destroyed all good literature which in my age hath by divine goodness been restored, unto its former light and dignity, and that with such amendment and increase of knowledge, that now hardly should I be admitted unto the first form of the little grammar-school boys, I say, I, who in my youthful days was, and that justly, reputed the most learned of that age. . . . Now it is that the minds of men are qualified with all manner of discipline, and the old sciences revived, which for many ages were extinct. Now it is that the learned languages are to their pristine purity restored." Gargantua is writing here with the tone of Francis I, the Restorer of the Fine Arts in France.

Now a new protagonist enters the stage: Panurge (*Pan-urgos* means in Greek " do-everything," a man gifted for everything, especially for mockery) is a sharp-nosed roving scholar and rogue, a skeptical, witty, resourceful, boisterous, and cowardly ne'er-do-well, the Falstaff of Pantagruel. Panurge, accompanied by Pantagruel, tours the universities of France, learns how to dance and fence at Toulouse, how to love at Avignon (because, Rabelais

tells us, this is papal domain), how to play ball at Orléans, and
how really to study at Paris. There, for instance, he goes through
the catalogue of the scholastic convent library of Saint Victor,
finding for our benefit such perhaps imaginary book titles as " The
Apparition of St. Gertrude to a nun who was with child," " The
Lord's prayer of the apes," " the bibbings of the tippling bishops."
In the midst of such studies a new war breaks out, this time
against a certain race of people called the Dipsodes (the thirsty
ones). During one of the battles a companion called Epistemon
suffers the misfortune of having his head cut off—immediately
Panurge, who is " good for everything," succeeds in replacing the
head properly and, by means of an ointment, restores Epistemon
to life—whereupon Epistemon starts describing his experiences
in the place he had gone in the few moments he had been separated
from his head, the place being Hell where he saw Alexander the
Great patching shoes, Nero fiddling, and Cleopatra selling onions.

In the third book, which comes closest among Rabelais's books
to being unified, the characters of the giants recede into the
background and Panurge becomes the main protagonist. He has
been rewarded for his military services, not like before him Jean
des Entommures with a convent, but with a chateau: as was
to be expected from his Bohemian habits, all is soon in disorder
and Panurge conceives the idea of taking a wife unto himself who
should straighten things out. In order to settle this weighty
problem, whether to marry or not to marry—the value of woman
and marriage was then a burning problem for loftier Renaissance
minds than Panurge's—he seeks advice from many sources of
wisdom. He consults first his Socratic King Pantagruel, the conversation between them proceeding as follows:

. . . Nevertheless, quoth Panurge, If I understood aright, that it were
much better for me to remain a bachelor as I am, than to run headlong
upon new hair-brained undertakings of conjugal adventure, I would
rather choose not to marry.

Quoth Pantagruel, Then do not marry.

Yea, but quoth Panurge, would you have me so solitarily drag out
the whole course of my life, without the comfort of a matrimonial

consort? You know it is written *Vae soli* (Woe to the Lonely One!) . . . .

Then marry, in the name of God, quoth Pantagruel.

But if, quoth Panurge, my wife should make me a cuckold; as it is not unknown unto you, how this hath been a very plentiful year in the production of that kind of cattle. . . .

Then do not marry, quoth Pantagruel. . . .

After two pages of this rhythmical sequence *Mariez-vous donc!*— *Point donc ne vous mariez*! the hapless Panurge is still where he was. Nor is the issue settled by opening at random the pages of Homer and Virgil in search of an oracle, nor by analysis of dreams, nor by consultation of the Sibylla, nor by visits to representatives of all the professions: to a poet, a theologian, a physician, a philosopher, a judge—all presented as caricatures (for instance, the judge arrives at his verdict by throwing dice). At last it is the court jester of King Francis, Triboulet, who seems to have found the wisest solution, which consists, however, of postponing the solution and thereby assuring us of the continuation of the tale: Triboulet advises Panurge to go to China, there to consult the oracle of the Divine Bottle which is presided over by the Priestess Bacbuc (a Hebrew name meaning bottle).

The fourth book is devoted to the voyage to China undertaken by Pantagruel, Panurge, and Friar John—an Odyssey in which there is combined the theme, full of actuality in the sixteenth century, of the Northwestern passage to Asia, with timeless allegorical satire on human weaknesses. The countries or islands visited on a route that takes the party from Saint-Malo in Brittany round North America to East Asia, are all fantastic nowherelands: the Island of the Papefigues who make a fig to the Pope finds its foil in the Island of the Papimanes, the maniacs of Popery; the island of Messer Gaster, whose eyes are even bigger than his belly, turns out to be the land of the ostensibly fasting clerics.

In the fifth book, a continuation of the fourth with allegorical satire becoming even more pungent, there appear again countries inhabited by figures to whom Rabelais is hostile, lawyers and

Catholics. The Island of the Church Bells, for instance, is inhabited by strange birds under the rule of the Popinjay (and of his different wives, the Popinjesses): the ruling hierarchy includes Cleric-jays, Monk-jays, Bishop-jays and parallel feminine Cleric-jesses, Bishop-jesses, etc. Finally the seafarers arrive at the oracle of the Priestess Bacbuc, in whose underground temple they hear a voice from within a bottle pronounce the magic word that is to be the solution of Panurge's problem: *Trink*—" drink! " And Bacbuc said to Panurge, " You have soon had the word of the Goddess Bottle and the kindest, most favorable, and certain word of answer that I ever yet heard her give, since I officiated here at her most sacred oracle; rise, let us go to the chapter, in whose gloss that fine word is explained." In the chapter she shows to Panurge a silver book, supposed to contain the " gloss " to the word of the oracle: the book has the form of a breviary but is in reality a flask of Phalernian wine drawn by Bacbuc from a boiling spring in the temple. While Panurge drinks the wine, Bacbuc explains, " You must know, my beloved, that by wine we become divine. Your academies assert the same, when they make the etymology of wine from *vis*, strength, virtue and power; for it is in its power to fill the soul with all truth, learning and philosophy."

While the voyagers elaborate on the solution of the riddle, in verses inspired by Bacchic frenzy, each of them in his individual way (Panurge, for example, sees himself happily married and exercising splendidly the main function of a husband), the Priestess bids them farewell with the following speech: " Now, my friends, you may depart and may that intellectual sphere whose center is everywhere and circumference nowhere, whom we call God, keep you in his almighty protection. When you come into your world, do not fail to affirm and witness that the greatest treasures, and most admirable things, are hidden underground. . . . and your philosophers, who complain that the ancients have left them nothing to write of or invent, are very much mistaken. Those phenomena which you see in the sky; whatever the surface of the earth affords you, and the sea, and every river contains is not to be compared with what is hid within the bowels of the earth. . . . Beseech the Almighty that he out of his infinite goodness may not only make his creatures, but even Himself known to you! You will be guided by two lanterns: first God's gracious guidance, then man's assistance. Now, in God's name, depart, and may He go along with you!" (*Allez, amis, en gaieté d'esprit!*)

This whole lengthy and incoherent, formless and rambling tale, crammed as it is with ancient learning and a popular farcical spirit of Gauloiserie—what does it ultimately mean? [1] In the prologue to the first book Rabelais admonishes his prospective reader to follow the example of the dog, the most philosophical animal as Plato says in Book II of the Republic, of the dog who worries a bone until he has found a little marrow: similarly the reader will find in Rabelais' book a *substantifique mœlle*, a substance hidden behind the allegorical surface, indeed the most glorious doctrines and dreadful mysteries, religious, political, and economic. On the other hand he tells us that he has written his book, at odd moments, while eating and drinking, for the benefit of the " most illustrious drinkers and you thrice-precious syphilitics." Consequently, the allusion to the philosophical marrow cannot be taken too seriously; it is only a humanistic taunt directed against the medieval habit of allegorical explanation of literature.

Since we cannot derive any clarification of the meaning of the books from the author, let us, in the fashion of Panurge, consult the authorities, in this case the literary historians. These generally tell you that Rabelais is a propagandist of Renaissance ideas and that the *substantifique mœlle* is the doctrine of the emancipation of man's mind and senses from the coercion of the otherworldly and ascetic dogma of the Church. Thus Rabelais

[1] I have dealt with this question in a study contained in my book " Romanische Stil- und Literaturstudien," I (Marburg, 1931), and again under the title " Le prétendu réalisme de Rabelais," in *Modern Philology*, XXXVII (Chicago, 1939-40).

would be, along with the free-thinking Montaigne, one of the ancestors of eighteenth century enlightenment and deism, of Locke, Voltaire, Rousseau, and Goethe. You will find in the current monographs about Rabelais separate chapters, full of excerpts from Rabelais' work torn from their context, dealing with Rabelais' educational theories, his philosophy, religion, and politics. Accordingly, the Abbey of Thélème would represent a model of modern education as seen by Rabelais and the oracle *Trink* of the Pristess Bacbuc an exhortation to increasing intellectual thirst, in line with the intellectual thirst expressed by a Giordano Bruno. The program of Thélème might be accepted in this light were it not for the personality of the director of this program, the debauched and comic monk Jean des Entommures, and in the chapters on the oracle of Bacbuc we cannot forget the farcical allusions to drinking and fornication. The word *Trink*, taken from the lowly language of the guzzling Swiss mercenaries, carries connotations of vulgarity. And what shall we think of a Chinese priestess bearing a Hebrew name whose oracle speaks the German of the *Landsknechte*? It is precisely when Rabelais is expounding the ideas most dear to him that he indulges in the utmost of whimsicality and buffoonery. How is this to be explained? As a device to disarm the ecclesiastical authorities by pretending that his ideas are only jests? If so, his biography has shown us that he did not succeed with his strategy since his books incurred ecclesiastical condemnation and his life always skirted danger. Perhaps, then, this spirit of the farce was no secondary thing, but is a primary element of his creative mind. For we should note that also in his direct satire Rabelais is moved not only by hatred, but by an enjoyment of the fantastical shapes his satire helps him create. For example, who can read his allegorical presentation of the figure *Antiphysie* (Counter-Nature), whose children walk on their heads, with the feet upward, because the Creator has shown by the example of the trees that the roots (equivalent to man's hair) should be below, the branches (corresponding to man's legs) above—who can read this satirical allegory which caricatures medieval nature symbolism

—who can read this *myth* of Rabelais' without the feeling that he must have experienced true artistic enjoyment in visualizing human beings walking on their heads, just as much as Dante enjoyed the visual picture of the punishment of the Pope, who in his life had been guilty of simony, of reversing divine values, and now in Hell is buried head downward, while his feet, continually singed by flames, protrude from holes in the marble slab. Such scenes, apart from any didactic intention, represent the play of free imagination and appeal to the artistic sense of the reader precisely because they transcend any model in reality—a type of art, incidentally, which we moderns are perhaps better able to understand than were our ancestors, given the development of modern art away from precise models in reality. Rabelais is then deliberately seeking for what is not real, and neither in his didactic nor in his satirical tales should we look only for his serious intention. The Rabelaisian in Rabelais is his capacity for comic visualization of what has never been seen.

Let us study in detail some of those semi-serious conclusions Rabelais is fond of extracting from a fantastic context: for example, the famous eulogy of the debtors and creditors delivered by Panurge. Pantagruel has asked this improvident fellow, always out of pocket, when he would finally stop making debts. Panurge answers: on Saint Never-Never's day. To make debts is something creative—to make *something* out of *nothing* is what the Creator did. And indeed the debtor when he circulates among his creditors, who watch his movements to see whether he shows any inclination of settling up that day, moves like a god among human beings. Moreover, debts are the general principle which holds the universe together: what would the cosmos be if the stars did not borrow their light from each other (the moon from the sun), if the elements did not borrow and lend among each other (by transformation of water into air, of air into fire), if one man did not borrow and lend to his fellow man, if the body of man, that microcosm, were not based on debt and credit (the blood-circulation being nothing but such a business transaction). Consequently, Nature has created man in order that he may borrow and lend. And now comes this significant exclamation of Panurge: " *Vertugoy, je me noye, je me perds, je m'esgare on ce profond abisme du monde*—By God, I sink, I drown, I perish when I enter into the consideration of the profound abyss of this world, thus lending, thus owing. Believe me, it is a divine thing to lend; to owe, an heroic virtue."

This last paradox is proclaimed by the most unheroic and unvirtuous Panurge who a moment ago had only intended somehow to justify his personal weakness, but suddenly creates before us a vision of the well-ordered universe that functions harmoniously thanks to the sympathy and generosity of the elements. Inspired as he becomes by a pantheistic, religious and poetic frenzy, he comes to experience the Dionysiac fever of the priest in Greek mysteries: at the climax of his vision he feels his own absorption by the God he has evoked; he is swallowed up into the abysmal richness of the world which he himself had opened up before us. Out of this hypocritical ne'er-do-well and debt-maker Panurge, there has developed a seer who divines the mysteries of the universe, an *artist*, a *demiurge*, a *Panurgos* who recreates the universe and its processes—his transformation anticipates the visions of *le Neveu de Rameau*, that nephew of the famous composer whom, two centuries later, Diderot shows us as he experiences the cosmic exaltations and trances of a genius—without ever becoming one, as Diderot makes it clear. Rabelais, less disillusioned than Diderot, fails to distinguish between real and sham genius. His Panurge becomes a visionary genius before our eyes. He develops out of poor material, no better than the *Neveu de Rameau*, out of a type of Frenchman whom we know so well from French literature (Sganarelle, Mascarille, Gil Blas, Figaro) and whom we see appear with Panurge for the first time: the self-satisfied, sensuous and cynical *blagueur* who, disillusioned with the world as he is, never allows things to be what they are, but either takes important things lightly or blows up small things to sham importance, and in any case provides for himself an ideological alibi with which to live with the feeling of his personal superiority. Could it perhaps be that the curve described between

Panurge the *blagueur* and Panurgos the visionary, between the prankster and the singer of World-Harmony, is perhaps Rabelais' own artistic path—did he, the *omnium horarum homo*, find in himself a perpetual clown who was able, on the spur of the moment, to transform himself into a prophet of the mystery and harmony of life? And it is indeed very difficult with Rabelais to tell where the clown leaves off and the mystic begins. Rabelais may at any moment engender gratuitous visions out of the fullness of his imagination, with no limit set to his Homeric fabulating mind.

As we watch Panurge, the true protagonist of Rabelais' work, moving through four of the books, we will discover that his whole character is built on gratuitous mental freedom—that is mental freedom for its own sake. His is the mind that frees itself from outward reality by building up a world of fancy for its own pleasure. We see him first on his return from Turkey, covered with wounds, his clothes in rags, fainting from hunger and thirst. He does not begin his conversation, however, with references to his condition and to his need for help; instead he has the leisure to answer Pantagruel's questions with lengthy, rhetorical speeches in a dozen languages (including Hebrew and Basque), only at the end to ask for help in plain French. He allows himself the sly pleasure of showing off his linguistic superiority, in a non-sensical postponement of his real and truly urgent purpose. This is self-enjoyment of resourcefulness in the abstract, quite detached from reality.

Later we learn that Panurge never carries weapons with him—obviously he knows that the weapon of his mind cuts more sharply than a sword. His pockets are instead filled with gadgets or trinkets which may serve for tricks he performs on innocent victims: a sharp little knife for cutting purses, little horns full of fleas and lice which he borrowed from the beggars of St. Innocent to cast into the necks of the daintiest gentlewomen he could find, plus needles and thread the better to sew people together—in short the apparatus of a rogue who enjoys the gratuitous act, not of charity, but of amorality. That Panurge is indifferent to his own practical advantage is illustrated also by the scene of the consultation of Pantagruel about the marriage question, a scene in which he seems less interested in a solution than in the dialectical play of his mind with which he provokes now a yes, now a no, *just for the hell of it*, priding himself on his own mental freedom and power of analysis. In fact, Rabelais never tells us whether or not Panurge ever does marry although the problem of this marriage provides the plot for three books—as though Rabelais wished to intimate that neither this problem nor this plot are of any importance.

Panurge's relationship toward money is also quite idealistic: though he knows sixty-three ways to procure money, he knows many more ways to get rid of it. He steals coins from indulgence boxes, to spend them in order to procure an hour of sensuous love for frustrated women. His most famous prank, cruel and criminal as it is, has become proverbial in France (*les moutons de Panurge*): in order to humiliate the bourgeois pride in posses- sions of the sheep-raiser Dindenault, he decides to destroy his flock by throwing the bell-wether into the water, whereupon the whole flock follows, dragging with it its owner (who happens to have in his pocket a sum of money he owes to Panurge). Thus our sixteenth century figure represents an ancestor of those protagonists of twentieth century French novels (by André Gide, Valéry Larbaud, *et al.*) who perpetrate gratuitous crimes out of boredom in order to assert their moral autonomy. Only the *actes gratuits* of Panurge are relatively more gratuitous than those of the rich *blasés* of our day: they are performed by a social outcast.[2]

Panurge is not the only character who embodies that particular Rabelaisian quality of gratuitous reality. The stories of the giants are similarly situated on the border-line between phantasmagoria and realistic description. We hear, for example, that Pantagruel with his tongue only half extended is able to protect a whole army from rain as a hen does her chickens. And " I who relate to you

---

[2] The connection between the " acte gratuit " in Gide and in Rabelais has been established by the Swiss-American scholar Werner Vordtriede.

these so veritable stories," says Rabelais, "went along full two leagues upon his tongue, and so long marched, that at last I came into his mouth. But, oh gods and goddesses, what did I see there! [I] saw there great rocks like the mountains of Denmark— I believe that those were his teeth. I saw also fair meadows, large forests, great and strong cities, not a jot less than Lyons or Poictiers" and finally Rabelais saw a fellow who was raising cabbages in order to sell them " in the city which is here behind."

" Jesus! " said I, " is there here a new world? "

" Sure," said he, " it is never a jot new, but it is commonly reported that without this, there is an earth, whereof the inhabitants enjoy the light of a sun and moon, and that it is full of very good commodities; but yet this is more ancient than that." And another fellow found there was a bird-catcher who tended his nets to catch the pigeons which fly from that other world into Pantagruel's mouth everytime he yawns; and in his throat there are two cities called Larynx and Pharynx; at this time they are being laid waste by a plague which has killed in one week " more than 280,016 people "—a plague caused by the stinking breath of the giant after he had eaten garlic.

The literary historian will not fail to point out that Rabelais here combines two sources, the popular tale of good-hearted giants and the facetious account by the Greek satirist Lucian of a journey through the throat of a whale. But who does not sense that to these literary sources Rabelais has added that particular feeling of bewildered elation which his contemporaries must have felt when faced, no longer with the hermetically closed, boxed-in cosmology of the Middle Ages, but with the discovery of new worlds and ever widening perspective? They must have asked themselves, like Rabelais walking on the tongue of the giant, with their confidence in the existence of only one world shaken, " Which of the two worlds is the old, which the new one? And which of them is real? " Once it is granted that a new world is possible, man, proudly, if not too assuredly, may strike forward into the infinite, the unreal, the utopia, the nowhere.

The feeling of relativity newly gained in the sixteenth century, the feeling of " all coherence gone " which will inspire Pascal's theo-philosophy in the seventeenth and which will be exploited much more timidly in the eighteenth century in *Gulliver's Travels* and *Micromégas*, was not nearly as frightening to the first Renaissance thinkers as it is to our modern so-called " one world " which again tends to become a boxed-in world, the finite world of Einstein which also includes " one death," atomic death. The sixteenth century felt the infinite to be life-giving and friendly, a realm where man will be eternally able to drink at the inexhaustible springs of Nature. The generous Pantagruel, like the generous priestess Bacbuc, represents a universe that is good and cheerful and works for the good and for gaiety. The medieval giant Pantagruel who has become a Platonic philosopher-king suggests, by his name, also *pan*, the universe; and the gigantic dimensions of his body which he uses for the good represent the gigantic dimensions of the goodness of this earth. We modern readers are astonished at the carnality of such an imaginary figure and at the precise realism with which it is presented. But for Rabelais to imagine a figure is to incarnate him. His is a flesh-giving imagination in a period which resuscitated the flesh.

We have just spoken of the vistas of new worlds which Rabelais, like his contemporaries, saw with delight opened up before him. But there is still another new world which existed for the humanist Rabelais and which he felt to be as palpable as the flesh of his imaginary characters, and this is, to use the title of a famous dictionary of the sixteenth century, *The World of Words*, a world emancipated from the tutelage of pure logic and of every-day reality, a world with its own laws over which Rabelais ruled as a king. To grasp better the peculiarity of the artist of words Rabelais, let us compare him for a moment with the representative poet of the Middle Ages, Dante.

In comparison with Rabelais, Dante's style is simple, lucid, and functional: with the latter the words, the allusions, the similes, the metaphors, and the word repetitions are used exclusively in order to make an obscure thought (a vision) clear to the reader. In an age which believed in the sole importance of eternal verities transcending ordinary human understanding, the poets spent their whole effort on bringing these verities close to the understanding of the reader. If Dante wished to make us realize how the shadows in Hell crowded around him to see the traveler from the earth, he will use a simile such as: " they knitted their brows at us like an old tailor peering through the eye of his needle." Dante is not interested in the tailor who is brought in only for the sake of the visualization of a world no human eye has ever seen, a visualization which has succeeded so well that for a moment we believe ourselves truly to be in that world along with Dante. On the contrary, when Rabelais wishes to explain to us the marrow supposedly contained in his work by way of the simile of the dog with the bone, he will say: " If you have seen him, you might have remarked with what devotion and circumspectness he wards and watcheth it: with what care he keeps it; how fervently he holds it, how prudently he gobbles it, with what affection he breaks it, and with what diligence he sucks it." Here the one action of the dog is broken down into six stages to which are made to correspond six psychological attitudes and the syntax of the sentence produces an onomatopoeic effect, as though we heard the dog panting for his much-coveted marrow. Obviously Rabelais is not only interested in the philosophical implication of his simile, for the moment he sees mainly the dog, the animal vitality of the beast he has created. The simile is no longer functional, it has become autonomous.

Of course, we may surmise that Rabelais wished to imply that philosophical activity should possess the same vitality and passionate impact as the crave of an animal for food, but it is clear that he spends his whole effort on giving artistic evidence to this animal crave. In our passage, at least, the breaking down of one action into six stages corresponds to outward reality because the dog's action can be divided by slow motion into these six steps. But what should we think of the episode of the cynic philosopher Diogenes in which his traditional act of rolling his barrel is described by Rabelais with sixty-four verbs: " There I say in great vehemency of spirit did he turn it, veer it, wheel

it, frisk it, jumble it, suffle it, huddle it, tumble it, hurry it,
jolt it, jostle it, overthrow it, evert it, invert it, subvert it . . ."
and so forth and so on, with technical terms following which
are derived from all the different crafts, military arts, and the
natural sciences. This cornucopia of words truly exceeds the
intended meaning. Of course, the intended meaning is, in our
particular passage, a prologue in which Rabelais apologizes to
King Francis for not having taken part in his glorious war by
pointing to the ancient philosopher who was satisfied to roll his
barrel, while his fellow Corinthians were all engaged in military
activities. The meaning in this passage is to imply slyly by the
sixty-four verbal synonyms that Diogenes' meditation was at least
as varied, as valuable and as real as sixty-four different outward
activities of his fellow citizens taken together—that philosophical
(or in Rabelais' case, literary) activity is the true activity of
man. But while there is a motivation for such rhetorical redund-
ance it cannot be denied that Rabelais enjoys the wealth of words
for their own sake. He creates a world of his own peopled by
mysterious beings called words, evoking meaning, not subject
to it. Now if words reach autonomy they are likely to do what
organic beings are able to do: with Rabelais they possess genera-
tive capacities of their own. When he hurls at his enemies of
the Sorbonne the epithets:

Sophistes, sorbillans, sorbonagres, sorbonigenes, sorbonicoles, sorboni-
formes, soboniseques, niborcisans, sorbonisans, saniborsans—

this name-calling is surely due to his humanistic hatred against
theological obscurantism, invective being a favorite procedure
with the humanists; but humanistic hatred and humanistic style
alone cannot account for what is in reality multiplication, before
our eyes, of word-monsters. Here satire does not mimic its object,
but creates it. The words expand beyond their natural limits
to produce a climate of irreality superimposed upon reality: what
is the reality of beings called *niborcisans* or *saniborsans?* This
dizzying phenomenon of words emancipated from meaning is
unique, not only in French but in all Romance languages which

have in general preserved as a sacred heritage the ancient Roman respect for the monumental value of the word-as-it-is, which may be chiselled in inscriptions on stone. We may, for example, contrast the inscription on the gate of Hell as imagined by Dante in which the solemn integrity of the word is preserved:

> *Per me si va nella città dolente,*
> *per me si va nell' eterno dolore,*
> *per me si va tra la perduta gente,*

with Rabelais' inscription on the gate of the abbey of Thélème in which entrance is forbidden to the Hypocrites:

> *Cy n'entrez pas, hypocrites, bigotz,*
> *Vieux matagotz, marmiteux, borsoufles,*
> *Torcoulz, badaux, plus que n'estoient les Gotz*
> *Ny Ostrogotz precurseurs des magotz,*
> *Queux mitouflés, frapars, escorniflez*
> *Befflez, enflex, fagoteurs de tabus:*
> *Tirez ailleurs pour vendre vos abus!*

In this colossal onomatopoeic sequence of vilifications which I can never read aloud without a shudder of fear before the words become autonomous, the grotesque art of Rabelais is at its acme: usual French words are here assembled according to sound, rhyme and rythm; they are transmogrified by the linguistic alchemy of Rabelais to give a sensuous impression of the being of the hypocrites (by the muffled sounds *fl*)—and at the same time of the whip with which Rabelais lashes out against them (the *go* syllables in *cagots, magots,* to create a climate of grotesque nowhereness on the brink between the comic and the dreadful, between the amusement provoked by automatic repetition of sounds and the fear inspired by the unknown shapes the sounds suggest. Again we see how monsters multiply in hydra-like fashion. The late Gothic gargoyles with their manifold irrational shapes have found here an acoustic equivalent—only the medieval hate of the devil has given way to a humanistic hatred productive of linguistic deviltry, and unholy words.

In tamer passages of Rabelais we may watch the transition from a medieval to a humanistic treatment of language. In the futile speech of the messenger of the Sorbonne who asks Gargantua to give back the stolen bells, we find such odd specimens of scholastic and maccaronic Latin as:

*Omnis clocha clochabilis in clocherio clochando clochans
clochativo clochare facit clochabiliter clochantes*

—a nonsensically axiomatic sentence which means simply: " all bells ring." Here the disappearance of meaning before mere sound is intended satirically as parody of contemporary scholasticism which was satisfied with meaningless, learned-sounding verbiage. But as always with Rabelais satire does not explain his creation: we sense Rabelais' positive delight in meaningless sound. And if Rabelais is able to envisage the possibility of language without meaning, it is precisely because he has witnessed the phenomenon of the medieval scholastic language become, out of self-exhaustion, devoid of meaning.

In the human language as such, apart from such pathological exceptions, Rabelais must have recognized the paradox which haunted him in his whole artistic activity: his fiction creates *unreal reality*—so does language in general. In an episode of the fourth book, the episode of the " unfrozen words," Rabelais has created a myth which centers precisely on the intangible, but at the same time tangible, aspect of language. As they are sailing in the Arctic regions, the party of Pantagruel suddenly becomes aware of sounds in the air, without being able to discover their source. They hear voices of men, women, horses, sounds of trumpets and drums. Panurge is afraid as usual and advises them to flee, but the humanist Pantagruel, by way of explanation, is immediately ready with ancient literary parallels referring to the possibility of sounds becoming frozen. And the skipper confirms Pantagruel's suggestion: " Be not afraid, my lord, we are on the confines of the Frozen Sea, on which, about the beginning of the last winter, happened a great and bloody fight between the Arimaspians and the Nephelobates. Then the words and cries of men and women, the striking of battle-axes, the striking of armors and harnesses, the neighing of horses, and all other martial din and noise froze in the air, and now, the rigor of the winter being over, by the warmth of the weather, they melt and are heard." Panurge the skeptic asks to see some such not yet melted words, whereupon Pantagruel throws handfuls of them on the deck of the ship, here throaty insults and bloody words, there golden and green and azure words. No passage could show better how for Rabelais language has become an atmospheric element which now coagulates, now evaporates, now is a reality, now is not. And here modern linguistic science cannot but acknowledge the rightness of Rabelais' poetic view: do our linguists not speak of " petrified expressions "? It remained for the dadaistic and surrealistic poetry of our century to capitalize on the automatic and petrified in the language of our age of mechanism and social standardization. The automatic writing of Rabelais is inspired by his happiness over the possibilities given to human expressivity—that of James Joyce, on the contrary, is overhung with his pessimism about a civilization felt to be on the verge of disintegration.

Summing up our analysis of the historical significance of Rabelais, we may say that he came at that moment of the Renaissance movement when man had learnt to realize the power and potentialities given to man. And Rabelais, like his character Panurge, used this power gratuitously, " for the hell of it." His epic which includes all the tremendous knowledge of which humanism was capable is obviously, as Bacbuc's speech showed us, conceived as an epic of human cognizance, a glorification of cognizant man, but the goal ultimately arrived at is mainly the cognizance of his cognitive power without any practical results of his cognizing activities being shown to us. We only learn that man can and should drink at the springs of knowledge for the sake of drinking. Rabelais' Argonauts bring home from their voyage no golden fleece, only the enigmatic word *Trink*. Neither have they reached at the end of their expedition a higher stage of development: Pantagruel and Panurge are in the fifth book

what they were in the second, in this inferior to medieval protagonists such as Parzival or the traveler to the beyond, Dante.
While we are reminded in the case of Rabelais' heroes of
Goethe's maxim: "One does not travel in order to arrive, one
travels in order to travel," we must remember that Goethe himself
allows his protagonists (Wilhelm Meister, Faust) to reach new
stages of development. In his static conception of characters
whose categorical imperative we would think it should be to
develop, Rabelais is quite isolated: his characters seem in truth
to be only pretexts for the free play given through them to ideas:
in the story of the unfrozen words Pantagruel and Panurge have
no other function but to help a myth, emancipated from reality,
into being. Never after Rabelais will we find thought playing
with life and man so freely and so joyfully.

Similarly his vitality which exists only for the sake of vitality
accepts no limits. We should not be astonished at his failure to
arrive at formal beauty, at serene and balanced composition,
at true imitation of Greek art: had he been an Ariosto, a Camoens,
a Ronsard, he would have been limited by artistic form. But
Rabelais' art is life untamed, it lives in the moment, the law
of its being is freedom from law, improvisation, the dart and the
spurt, the drive towards the unlimited, the unreal, the colossal,
the grotesque, the macabre (his hypervividness sometimes comes
close to the cramp of death). From classical civilization he,
proceeding quantitatively, appropriated only the enormous arsenal
of facts and those innumerable possibilities of life which fascinated
his encyclopedic mind, and he mixes with the ancient elements,
without scruple or sophistication, the gross monkish satire, the
medieval slapstick farce and the spirit of fleshly French *gauloiserie*.
He represents for us that unique moment in Occidental literature
when Renaissance man, become conscious of the boundless
resources of the life of this world, experienced the rapture of
this very discovery without yet having achieved the new style
of life and art which should have been the necessary consequence
of this discovery. Outside of Italy, works of art of the Renaissance
serenity of Raphael or Ariosto are rare. Very soon after Rabelais,

the spirit of the Counter-Reformation will set in to curtail the
boundless aspirations of man; in French literature it is Malherbe
who is said by Boileau to have set a more limited task for the
Muse (*et la Muse réduisit au devoir*) —in other words, it was
Malherbe who ushered in that French neo-classical literature
which is a literature of the Counter-Reformation, of rules and
canons, of what historians of art call the baroque age. The
seventeenth century satirist Labruyère will find in Rabelais the
taste of the rabble (*le goût de la canaille*), and Rabelais' *gauloiserie* will remain only as an undercurrent in French literature,
chastened by classical taste, with Molière, La Fontaine and
Voltaire.

From the seventeenth century on what is not refined is not
worthy of literary expression in France, and Rabelais, apart from
nineteenth century Romantic lovers of the colossal and the
grotesque such as Balzac, V. Hugo, Th. Gautier, Flaubert, will
generally figure as a writer more praised by manuals of literary
history then actually read. It is the classic or baroque age that
has categorically opposed the bold rejection of the limits of the
finite world of reality that was characteristic of Rabelais. It
will insist again, as had the Middle Ages, on the distinction
between this world of appearances and the reality which is behind
it, which may be either transcendental as in Calderon (life a
dream from which the Christian should awake), or disillusioned
to the point of nihilism as in Shakespeare's well-known lines:
" Life's but a walking shadow, a poor player that struts and frets
his hour on the stage . . . it is a tale told by an idiot, full of
sound and fury, signifying nothing."

A spurious legend has it that Rabelais died with the words on
his lips: " Draw the curtain, the farce is ended." This sentence
Rabelais cannot have said: he is no baroque writer of disillusionment. For him, as you know him now, this world was a deep
ocean into whose treasure-containing waves he was ready to dis-
solve: " *je me noye, je me perds, je m'esgare on profond abisme
de ce monde*,"—a universe seen not in its clear contours and finite
limitations, but as an infinity of creative possibilities which en-
raptured that dionysiac mind.

VIII

Shakespeare's Hamlet

DON CAMERON ALLEN

WHEN DANTE STOOD at the foot of the purgatorial mount, he saw a dark shadow which he recognized as the soul of his old friend Casella, a musician of Florence. Saddened by his arduous voyage through Hell and eager for the solace of song, he spoke wistfully to the unembraceable shade: " If a new law take not from thee memory or skill in that song of love which was wont to calm my every desire, may it please thee therewith to comfort my soul, that, with its mortal form journeying here, is sore distressed." [1] So Casella began to sing a ballad of Dante's own making, and Virgil, like a generous poet, drew near to hear his protege's music; but the song was never finished, for Cato, who is the particular genius of this part of the *Purgatorio*, interrupted and reminded the poets of their elected task. This is no time for relaxation, no time to be listening to music or poetry, no time for the ephemeral pleasures and finite activities of the world. The ascending course lies steeply ahead; " Haste to the mount and strip you of the slough that lets not God be manifest to you." [2]

I know of no better parable of the non-humanistic life than this, for here in Dante's Purgatory we have a clear example of what might be called the vertical life. The proper direction of mortals is upward. Earth is thrust behind and man climbs toward God. Even the poetic fiber of the *Divina Commedia*, the plain, strong, muscular structure of the Dantean line, demonstrates in its economy, in its aloofness and want of elaboration, in its cool

[1] *Purgatorio*, II, 106-11.   [2] *Ibid.*, II, 122-23.

syllogistic mood, the withdrawal of medieval man from sensuous existence and his eagerness to obtain those permanent realities of a spiritual order that have their residence in the mansionhouse of faith.

But Dante was hardly dead before Francesco Petrarca found a soft route to the Kingdom of Heaven. The race is no longer to the swift nor the battle to the strong, for it is the lover who wins now, the lover who sees the grace and goodness of God in the blue mysteries of his lady's eyes. The staircase to Heaven can almost be built in an idle moment and it is a comfortable stairway of easy inclination. There are, of course, occasions when Petrarca talks like Dante, but the essential difference between the two men becomes apparent as we read the third book of Petrarca's *Secretum.* For two books St. Augustine has been lecturing Petrarca on his waywardness, and at this point in the dialogue he charges him with neglecting his spiritual offices in order to pursue worldly love and worldly fame. To the first accusation, Petrarca cries out: "Pray what have I done that you should desire to relieve me of the finest passions of my nature, and condemn to everlasting darkness the clearest faculties of my soul." [3] To the second condemnation he replies almost casually: "What must I do then? Abandon my unfinished works? Or would it be better to hasten them on, and, if God gives me grace put the finishing touches to them . . . for hardly could I bear the thought of leaving half completed a work so fine and rich in promise of fame?" [4] There are times in the *Canzoniere* and the *Epistolæ* when the note of regret and recantation is heard, and then Petrarca is more like Dante, but the cult of the vertical life is beginning to waver and the celestial voice of the great medieval organ is growing fainter and fainter.

It is a commonplace to observe that Dante made silent and secret love to Beatrice and transmuted her into a spiritual symbol, that Petrarca loved Laura humanly but purely and made her a means of his recognition of the love of God, but that

---

[3] *Op. cit.*, in Opera (Basel, 1554), I, 377.   [4] *Ibid.*, p. 385.

Boccaccio loved his Fiammetta as carnally as a man can love a
woman and let it go at that. This is a commonplace but a distinguished one, for it helps to indicate the transition from the other-
worldliness of the Middle Ages to the worldliness of the Renaissance. The *Decamerone* does much to betray the secret, for the
heroes and heroines of that book are people who are generally
too much in love with the world, and we know in what section
of the Hereafter Dante would have placed most of them. Then,
too, we must remember that Boccaccio, though he sometimes
trembles, never recants; he sees that there are spots in his life
and his profession, but he has a leopardlike affection for spots.
A sure witness of his worldliness is his Italian style. The lushness
of its imagery and the languid and processional march of the
sentences is most different from the austere and frugal manner
of Dante. For man is no longer in a hurry and there is plenty of
time to recline in gardens, to tell stories, and to listen to poetry
and harmony. The fair Pampinea, a queen of fabulists in the
Decamerone, gives us a hint of the new diapason when she urges
her companions to leave plague-ridden Florence for a country
villa.

There will our ears be entertained with the warbling of the birds,
and our eyes with the verdure of the hills and the valleys; with the
waving of cornfields like the sea itself; with trees of a thousand
different kinds, and a more open and agreeable prospect than these
desolate walls. The air also is pleasanter, and there is a greater plenty
of everything, attended with fewer inconveniences.[5]

We cannot imagine stern Cato listening to this invitation to
worldly relaxation, but this is 1348 and Cato is in Purgatory;
moreover, the bella donna is talking the new language of humanism, the language of a movement that avoided the vertical life
of faith and sauntered along the horizontal way of the reasonable
life, the way that was eventually to be called " progress."

It is always difficult to explain these shifts in human attitudes
because there are invariably as many explanations as there are

[5] *Op. cit.* (Ed. Scherillo, Milano, 1924), p. 21.

expositors. We are also aware that most of the so-called humanistic qualities can be found to some degree in men of the Middle Ages, but there is a difference in emphasis, a change in tone, and it is this difference and this change that count. For me this alteration can be explained in part by the new value that the Renaissance placed on reason and by the new goals that the horizontal life set for man. I do not know whether the reason was idolized because the Renaissance was infatuated by man and his world or whether the Renaissance abandoned the hard spiritual quest of the Middle Ages because it was enchanted by the independent reason. All that I know is that reason was exalted by the humanists in a way that the men of the Middle Ages— even the scholastics—would have considered unfitting, and that in the play of *Hamlet*, just as in the play of *Faustus*, we have a morality that informs us about the plight of a man who was so seduced by the lure of reason that he wandered apart from the vertical road of faith.

If we go back to the opening centuries of the Christian Era, we find that *faith* is a word used to describe the sort of knowledge that man receives through revelation and that the word *reason* designated the kind of wisdom that is acquired through the analytical and synthetical functions of the human mind. The lore of faith, the Fathers tell us, comes from the Scriptures, the tradition of the Church, and the private inspiration of a few holy men. Reason is a lesser light. It provides us with knowledge by testing the truth of things against the " ideas " or " essences " and by arriving at conclusions through " the contradictoriness of opposites." So an early Christian who regarded faith as his mainstay did not have to reject reason, but he was, nonetheless, faced with a trying set of questions. Was reason prior to faith or faith to reason? Does one come to faith through reason and has reason any force in determining the verity of revelation? Granting that a rational proof of the existence of God is possible, is revelation needed at all? Do reason and faith supply information about different and distinct fields of ignorance or is it possible to assume that in certain circumstances they are equally valid in

the same field? This last question was the most troublesome
and the thinkers of the Middle Ages were never successful in
resolving it.

The controversy about these two sources of knowledge began
early in the Christian Era with the taunts of pagan philosophers
and the doubts of early Christians who had been educated in
Greek philosophy. We can follow the debate as it runs through
the pages of Clement of Alexandria, of Origen, and of Tertullian.
We hear the fourth century Ambrose insist that faith alone has
weight in all questions concerning the mysteries of theology. We
see Augustine bend towards reason, but we know that he felt
that faith was the best criterion of judgment. We hear John
Scotus and Anselm defend reason but stamp it as inferior to
faith. The commonplaces of this discussion are like battle cries.
"Reason will tell us about the creatures and this knowledge will
lead us to God." "Reason is less than faith, but one must reason
about what one believes." "Reason will take us to the door of
Heaven, but faith lets us in." Then St. Thomas, stirred by this
trouble and by the echoes of a similar quarrel in Islam, attacked
the problem once more. Faith and reason are different in assent
and subject; they are distinct in that one is willed and the other
is not. Reason is able to supply some of the metaphysical information that men desire, but faith is far more accurate and
universal.

St. Thomas' resolution of the problem was wise, but unsuccess-
ful, and the confusion of the early humanists about the respective
boundaries and eminence of faith and reason is a testimony to this
fact. Petrarca has great difficulty in separating the two modes of
knowing; he is continually confounding saints and philosophers.
Nicolas of Cusa, mindful of the long scholastic tradition, is forced
to admit that men will never know the dividing line between
reason and faith. Ficino founders in his attempt to reconcile
philosophy and theology, an attempt that culminates in his effort
to see Socrates as a foreshadower of Christ. A further symptom
of the spreading ailment is to be found in the writings of Pico
della Mirandola, the fabulous youth who was Ficino's friend. In

celebration of the humanistic movement, Pico della Mirandola composed an oration in praise of the dignity of man that is known to every student of the Renaissance. He imagines an extra-Mosaic episode in which God appears to Adam and informs him that he has free-will and reason by means of which he may rise to celestial heights or sink to brutish depths. In this oration he speaks largely of reason and will, and not at all of faith or works. Dante, I think, would have turned pale to hear him. Yet Pico and his readers were all good Christians; they simply failed to notice that reason and its child philosophy were slowly trespassing on those areas of knowledge that had once been protected by faith and theology.

Whenever a humanist talks about reason, he hangs it about with laurel; but he often means many different things when he uses the word. In the best sense, reason was a sort of inner harp that maintained, if properly tuned, an isochronic vibration with the great universal harmony. By harkening to this inner symphony, man might charm the beasts of passion that prowled the forests of his body, and so, as Pico suggests, he might learn to live as a man and not as a brute. But reason led to other ends and it is interesting to observe that the patristic and medieval thinkers had foreseen these ends and warned man against them. In the Baconian sense, reason could reduce itself to a practical interrogation of nature, an end good in itself if properly limited, but one that led man to speculations about the universe as a mechanism or to theories about the possibility of other inhabited worlds beside the Adamic earth, theories which did much to destroy some of the most important substructures of man's belief in the watchfulness of providence and the single intent of the Creation.

From these swamps of doubt, reason drew men into utilitarian and iconoclastic studies. A new system of *real politique* replaced the hierarchical state doctrine of the Middle Ages. Physiology and heredity rather than original sin begin to be the explanation of man's moral nature; then the new ethnology, by noticing that morals and customs varied from land to land, suggested that one might question the doctrine of a universal moral law with its ancillary schemata of rewards and punishments. But the new reason went still further. The Fathers had denied the right of man to measure the nature of faith or revelation by reason, but in their attempts to make revelation plain and faith exact, the men of the Renaissance, especially after the Reformation permitted each man to read the Scriptures by the light of his own reason, eventually succeeded through their controversies over the text, the canon, the historicity, and the fidelity of many parts of the Bible in reducing that major document of revelation to the level of ordinary literature. We must not forget that all of this was going on in the top circles of intellectual society or, at any rate, it is only on this level that the disturbance occurs. An evidence of this emotional crisis is the growing pessimism, the increasing world-weariness, and the mounting burden of incertitude that one encounters as one reads through the literature of the age.

To this last group of world-weary and reason-worn creatures the character of Hamlet belongs. When I say this, I do not mean that this is the purpose of the great tragedy. The pre-text is simply a problem in revenge that is as old as the Oresteia; the theme is how a man got in his own way; but the orchestration of the play has many motifs, and the humanist's exaltation of reason, and where this exaltation leads men, is one of them. I am aware that these motifs are elusive and often contradictory, that they cannot be pinned, as so many butterflies, to a board, but I also feel that Shakespeare could not escape his ambient. Whatever a poet does he pays for with a piece of himself, and though it does not follow, as some commentators have thought, that in the character of Hamlet we have the character of Shakespeare, yet we have a piece of that character and a piece of its age. So to the consternation of some critics, I shall try to see in *Hamlet* evidences of this conflict that I have been describing. To this end I shall try to read the play like a man of the Renaissance. One may laugh at this proposal and regard me as exceptionally naive and one may properly object that I can no more read the play of *Hamlet* in this fashion than as a disbeliever in Dionysius I can read the *Bacchanals* with the eyes of a Greek. With this objection I am forced in part to agree, but I must also insist that the understanding of all literature is a matter of memory. I can no longer read *Hamlet* as I read it twenty years ago, or a year ago, or last month, but I can partially recollect how I read it and that adds to the multifariousness and pleasure of my reading. And so I shall attempt to remember how *Hamlet* might have been read in 1603, and though my recollections are vague and filled with inaccuracies, yet I hope thereby to add one more facet to that distorted and mishapen crystal that is my recollection of Shakespeare's play.

I shall begin by pointing out that Hamlet is a humanist prince of the type found frequently in France and Italy and occasionally in England. When his father was murdered, Hamlet was a student at Wittenberg, that famous Protestant university where Melanchthon introduced the new learning. With this as our clue, we understand Hamlet's versatility. He is widely read; he knows history, politics, and philosophy; he has studied classical literature and he knows his mythology. He is a critic, too, especially of the contemporary stage. He is a rhetorician and a connoisseur of acting. Like so many humanists, he is also capable of writing bad poetry. But though he is learned, he is no narrow intellectual. Ophelia tells us that he was once " the glass of fashion and the mould of form "; and though Ophelia is a good deal of a debutante, there is no reason why we should doubt her word. Following the precepts of experts like Castiglione, Hamlet has not neglected the cultivation of his body; and though he may have grown " fat and scant of breath," the falling curtain indicates that he is still an able swordsman. He has, then, all of the paradoxical versatility that we are accustomed to find in aristocratic humanists. He can be calm when he should be angry; angry when he should be calm; he can turn from poetry to murder; from cursing to tears; from love to hate; he is the serpent and the dove; the lion and the fox.

This Hamlet, whom I have been describing, existed before his father's death, and he still exists in the play before us. But the world in which he formerly seemed to live has changed, and it has changed because the shock of the elder Hamlet's death and Queen Gertrude's sudden marriage has set Hamlet on a different course of thought and this course has led him to inspect his ideals. To get to the center of Hamlet's mystery, let us contemplate the world in which he once imagined that he lived. This was the world of medieval idealism; the world from which men woke up. In his uncritical youth, Hamlet thought of kings as tall fearless men, handsome as Apollo, with their beards " a sable silvered." These kings took David as their pattern and regarded themselves as the fathers of a people, whom they ruled by the examples of the patriarchs. Widowed queens were mindful of the ecclesiastical laws and faithful to the memory of their husbands. They knew the common gloss of theologians on the life of Abraham and took tutelage in wifehood from the story of Sara. Younger brothers and uncles were versed in the dicta of the Christian political thinkers and did not aspire to an unmerited throne, for they knew that Heaven had not ordained that the younger should contend with the elder for the imperial circle. Young virgins were secret in their love and faithful to their troth; they lent themselves in no way to conspiracies against the beloved. The pages of the example books were filled with accounts of good, grey-haired councillors, who restrained erring monarchs with word and deed. Of them no usurping king could say, as King Claudius does of Polonius, " Nor have we herein barred your better wisdoms, which have freely gone with this affair along." [6] From this dream of an ideal world, Hamlet has awakened into a dream of reality. " O God I could be bounded in a nutshell and count myself a king of infinite space were it not that I have bad dreams." [7]

The transcendental background that the Middle Ages provided has collapsed for Hamlet. He can no longer look towards the realm of the ideal which is one and constant, and so he must fix his gaze on a horizontal plane that is filled with a multitude of moving figures with fluctuating values. Hence he ceases to be an idealist

[6] I. 2. 14-16. The New Cambridge text is cited throughout.
[7] II. 2. 260-62.

and a man of faith and becomes a critic and an historian. His first speech in the play is an indication of the new point of view. " Seems, Madame," he says to his mother, " I know not seems." [8] Having discovered this sharp scalpel for the dissection of humanity, Hamlet proceeds to demonstrate how men deceive themselves and others.

Polonius, who appears to the Queen as a " good, old man," [9] is a frequent butt of Hamlet's new cynicism. He gives his children copybook advice, but he cannot trust them. He suspects the virtue of his daughter but does not hesitate to sacrifice it to political designs. He sets a spy on his son. He is well aware of the market value of a lie, for " with this bait of falsehood we take this carp of truth." [10] He pretends to be pious, but he is ready to make the rites of religion subservient to practical politics. Since he has a vestigial conscience, his deeds are the worse.

> *We are oft to blame in this*
> *'Tis too much proved—that with devotions' visage*
> *And pious actions we do sugar o'er*
> *The devil himself.*[11]

Polonius, like other of the characters, is a product of the new practical reason that got men on in the world. He knows the advice of Machiavelli, for, at best, he is a Machiavellian with slight regrets.

But we must not forget Hamlet's two school-fellows, Rosencrantz and Guildenstern, friends of long standing. We know how they should regard the Prince for we have read the great literature on friendship and we have heard of Orestes and Pylades, Achilles and Patroclus, David and Jonathan. These young men are unfortunately not the sort of friends that we have encountered in books; they sell themselves to Hamlet's enemy in hopes of advancement, and so they become " my two schoolfellows whom I will trust as I will adders fanged." [12] In contrast to them is the parvenu

[8] I. 2. 76.
[9] IV. 1. 12.
[10] II. 1. 63.

[11] III. 1. 46-49.
[12] III. 4. 203.

Osric, a young man " spacious in the possession of dirt." [13] Though Osric is harmless, he is a stupid man and, consequently, a social climber. He has all the veneer of a gentleman but none of the inward qualities of a gentleman. He has gotten the fashionable court dialect by rote but there is no mind behind his talk. He is one of those whom " the drossy age dotes on "; [14] one who " complied with his dug before he sucked it." [15]

Laertes, the son of Polonius, is to the manner born and so his faults are more elaborate than Osric's. Unlike Hamlet, Laertes is still delighted by externals. Hearing of his father's death, he demands, as Hamlet does not, immediate satisfaction but his reasons are different. It is not that he loves his father with a mighty love but that the code requires him to be an avenger. Then, too, it is not his father's death that troubles him so much as the cheap and unceremonious funeral that the King has provided for the corpse of Polonius. When Hamlet begs his forgiveness, Laertes, though satisfied in himself, refrains from announcing the fact until he can consult " some elder masters of known honor . . . to keep my name ungored." [16]

All of these characters are imbued with the devisings of the practical reason. They are in love with the world; and though they may have spiritual whisperings, they stuff their ears against them because they know how such murmurings handicap a man eager for fame and fortune. King Claudius is the best example. He is not a bad king; he treats ambassadors well and he avoids war by diplomacy. He is a drunkard, but the reasons for his alcoholism are obvious. He has gained his throne by conspiracy and he has committed the sin of the Borgias. For King Claudius, wanting the valor of his elder brother and of his nephew, is a poisoner. Englishmen of this time could imagine nothing more revolting. He has poisoned his brother and he plans to poison his nephew; he lurks behind pillars to hear conversation; he employs palace spies; and, like all varlets, he has a well-filed tongue. " The

[13] V. 2. 90.
[14] V. 2. 197.

[15] V. 2. 195.
[16] V. 2. 260-61.

harlot's cheek," he says in a moment of conscience, "beautied with plastering art, is not more ugly to the thing that helps it than is my deed to my most painted word."[17] Like Polonius, Claudius is aware of the ideal; he can try to pray; he can talk foolishly about the divinity that hedges a king; he knows his evil, but he has sold himself to the world.

We see all of these things through the window of Hamlet's reason and the mirror of Shakespeare's critical judgment, but, in truth, we have yet seen nothing that the faith of the Middle Ages had not pilloried in a hundred homilies. The difference lies in the mode of viewing. The Middle Ages measured men with the revealed level of faith, but Hamlet, the humanist, measures his contemporaries with his naked reason. But it is not that he just measures others; he is constantly measuring himself. He may set a glass up for his mother, but he has long ago gazed in the glass and seen the flaws in Hamlet. Thanks to this fact, he has not only lost his idealism but he has practically lost his faith.

It is most difficult to determine the nature of Hamlet's religion. He uses the word *God* frequently; he admits that there is a divinity " that shapes our ends ";[18] he talks of " sweet religion ";[19] and he knows that Heaven punishes the evil-doer. His father's spirit has hinted at the torments of the Hereafter and it has urged Hamlet to leave his mother to Heaven. Yet Hamlet, as other humanists, has his doubts. Though a ghost has visited him from the heat of purgatorial fires, Hamlet is not sure of the immortality of his living soul; on the other hand, he is not so utterly unconvinced that he can bring himself to end his life. Nonetheless, his doubts about the reality of " that undiscovered country from whose bourn no traveller returns "[20] would be unfitting on the lips of a man of faith. Dante and other medieval thinkers did not question the existence of this place whose geography they knew so well.

But Hamlet's uneasy meditations about immortality are further italicized by his rebellion against the indignity of physical disso-

[17] III. 1. 51-53.
[18] V. 2. 10.
[19] III. 4. 47.
[20] III. 1. 79-80.

lution. It is not death that Hamlet fears, but the fact that the flesh—that delightful and worldly substance—must decay and rot and return to dust. The tragedy is filled with complaints about this unsavoury process, and the possession of dust is one of the things that makes Osric's claim to gentility so absurd. It is unseemly, too, that a fish should eat of a worm that ate of Julius Caesar, that a great lawyer should have his fine pate filled with fine dirt, that a jester should laugh no longer because his mouth has crumbled to clay. Hamlet's bitter aversion to the common end of men is given a full voice in the one comic episode in the play, a macabre bit of humor laid in a graveyard.

If Hamlet's distaste at the thought of physical decay is an emblem of his broken faith, his dying words do not reassure us. His true friend Horatio, " more antique Roman than Dane," [21] has snatched the poisoned cup that the dead Claudius had prepared for Hamlet so that with a fatal draught he may follow his Prince in death. Hamlet knocks the potent poison from his hand and cries almost with his last breath.

> *O good Horatio, what a wounded name,*
> *Things standing thus unknown, shall live behind me!*
> *If thou didst ever hold me in thy heart,*
> *Absent thee from felicity a while*
> *And in this harsh world draw they breath in pain*
> *To tell my story.*[22]

It is idle to speculate on what Hamlet means by *felicity*, but this is not a good deathbed as the Christian Renaissance understood it. For Hamlet's mind is still on this world and on the world's estimate of his life and reputation. The speech is really most bothersome because it suggests that Hamlet, his obligation to his dead father fulfilled by accident, has returned to the idealistic pattern of his youth.

Another lesson about the nature of Hamlet's intellectual difficulties may be learned from Horatio, who is an interesting character

[21] V. 2. 352. [22] V. 2. 355-60.

because, like Laertes and Fortinbras, he is a foil to Hamlet. He is, however, a foil in another way. Fortinbras and Laertes act without thinking, whereas Horatio thinks without acting. For this reason Horatio is one of the few breathing men on stage when the final curtain falls. He, unlike the other characters, is Hamlet's intellectual equal; in a sense, he is Hamlet's alter ego. He is a humanist and a thorough-going rationalist, but he has a different temperament and, in a way, is more fortunate in his birth. As a consequence of both of these accidents, he inhabits a different philosophical house from that in which Hamlet dwells. He has seen all of the menaces of the world that Hamlet has seen, but since he lacks Hamlet's cause for action and Hamlet's intense disgust, he has retreated, not into mysticism as some sensitive and disappointed men of the Renaissance did, but into stoicism. He has joined the company of the younger Montaigne, of Justus Lipsius, and of other humanists whose experience with the bright new world had sent them into the spectator's gallery.

When we first meet Horatio, he is a complete rationalist, who has no belief in the supernatural until its existence is proved to him by " the sensible and true avouch " of his own eyes. He has long ago settled on a philosophical system; a system, as Hamlet observes, that does not embrace everything. Nevertheless, he has no thirst for worldly grandeur or fame and he is completely insulated against the world of practical reason. He is the sort of man that Hamlet himself would like to be had he no cause for action.

> For thou hast been
> As one, in suffering all, that suffers nothing
> A man that fortune's buffets and rewards
> Has ta'en with equal thanks; and blest are those
> Whose blood and judgement are so well commingled
> That they are not a pipe for fortune's fingers
> To sound what stop she please. Give me that man
> That is not passion's slave, and I will wear him
> In my heart's core, aye, in my heart of hearts
> As I do thee.[23]

---

[23] III. 2. 70-79.

The stoicism that is Horatio's escape has no attractions for Hamlet; he can admire it but he cannot accept it. For Hamlet has a worldly part to play—a part that is forced on him—and he must play this part in a world he despises. That, I think, is the focal point of his tragedy as it was an impeller of many other tragedies of the early seventeenth century. The pale cast of thought may sickly o'er Hamlet's ability to act, but act he does. No protagonist who sends five men to their deaths in the course of five acts can be described as a man whose mind has totally paralysed his arm. True, he is slow to act; he admits it himself, and we are deep in the third act before he kills his first man, but it must be noticed that Hamlet loses only one chance to run a man through.

No, Hamlet's tragedy does not reside in the fact that he does not act, but that he is forced to act in a world that he disowns and against men who are not of his intellectual proportions. His tragedy is sharpened because he has a very dubious faith in the Hereafter and only a contempt for the Here. From all of this he cannot retire. He cannot follow Horatio into stoicism or Claudius into a drunkard's oblivion or Ophelia into true madness. So he knows all of the ennui, all of the disgust of men who have thought themselves out and have little to turn to except a death they hate. His thoughts on suicide, his conviction that most men are dishonest and most women strumpets, his assurance that all men are evil are symptoms of this disease.

I have of late—but wherefore I know not—lost all my mirth, forgone all custom of exercise; and indeed it goes so heavily with my disposition that this goodly frame, the earth, seems to me a sterile promontory; this most excellent canopy, the air, look you this brave o'erhanging firmament, this majestical roof fretted with golden fire, why it appears no other thing to me than a foul and pestilent congregation of vapours. What a piece of work is a man! How noble in reason! How infinite in faculty, in form and moving! How express and admirable in action! How like an angel in apprehension! How like a god! The beauty of the world! The paragon of animals! And yet to me, what is this quintessence of dust? [24]

---

[24] II. 2. 306-20.

This is the way men talk when life has gone stale. For the world, as Hamlet says, is what you think it. " There is nothing good nor bad but thinking makes it so." [25] For Hamlet the world is bad, yet he must play a role in it, and since he suspects that his acts will breed no real good, he detests his part. So he proceeds to his doom with a fortitude that is hardly Christian.

> If it be now, 'tis not to come; if it be not to come, it will be now; if it be not now, yet it will come; the readiness is all. Since no man has aught of what he leaves, what is't to leave betimes? [26]

We have come from the threshold of Purgatory to the Globe Theater on the Bankside; and in the years that this journey has cost us, we have watched men turn away from the other-worldliness of the great Italian to the this-worldliness of the clever Elizabethans. Faith, which once stood soliliquizing on the forestage of men's lives, hides now like a petty player in the tyring-room while reason, swollen with vanity and applauded by men, gesticulates and rants before the pit. Unfortunately, for the later Renaissance, the shift in the *dramatis personae* does not make for a pleasanter two hour's entertainment, for reason is a capricious and doubtful player and the parts in which he takes the stage are likely to bring bitterness. And so it is by no literary coincidence that Dante's pageant of faith has come to be called *The Divine Comedy*, whereas Shakespeare, when he embodied the eventuation of reason in human form, was forced to write on the titlepage, *The Tragedy of Hamlet*.

---

[25] II. 2. 256.   [26] V. 2. 231-35.

IX

The Comedies of Molière

HENRY CARRINGTON LANCASTER

THE GREAT pulpit orator, Bishop Bossuet, wrote about Molière:
" His comedies are full of impious and infamous expressions.
He encourages disgraceful tolerance in husbands and invites the
wives of jealous men to avenge themselves in shameful fashion."

Bossuet, of course, lacked a sense of humor. Most orators,
except Winston Churchill, do. Otherwise, they would not be
orators.

Other writers find in Molière a moralist, one who preaches the
doctrine of the golden mean, of nothing too much, of follow
nature. On this account he has been given to children to read
and has been recommended for those who are in mental trouble,
so much does he represent a sane outlook upon life.

Who is right, Bossuet or the others? I think that both are
wrong if they look upon Molière as primarily either a moralist
or an immoralist. I do not doubt, of course, that one can find
moral—occasionally immoral—instruction in Molière's characters,
that one can see in his plays the unhappiness that certain affecta-
tions, certain vices bring, but I deny that this was his principal
concern, that he wrote plays, like Bernard Shaw or Brieux, in
order to preach, or that there is no conflict in the ideas that he
sets forth.

If you read the *Précieuses ridicules*, you will conclude that a
father or guardian can choose a better husband for his daughter
or ward than she can herself, but if you read the *School for
Husbands*, or the *School for Wives*, you come to the opposite
conclusion. In the *Learned Ladies* Molière makes a servant say:

" When one makes oneself understood, one always speaks well,"
a doctrine that no poet, no professional writer can accept, though
it is quite in its place in the play. Molière can preach if his
characters are addicted to preaching, but this is not his main
concern. If you look upon him as primarily the man of the stage,
the actor-manager-dramatist, you will find remarkable unity in his
life and in his work and at the same time you can explain why he
has been considered a moralist or, if you agree with Bossuet, an
immoralist.

Molière was not born to the stage, as were some of his colleagues.
He early became an actor for love of the profession, not because
he could find no other way of making a living. And he adopted
the profession so completely that he is known to us, not by his
real name, but by the name, Molière, that he assumed when he
began to play. He was the oldest son of a successful Parisian
upholsterer named Poquelin, one who was so successful that he
was upholsterer to His Majesty, Louis XIII, when his son was
born in January, 1622. The youngster came into the world in the
heart of Paris, not far from the one official Parisian theater of
the time and not far from the Louvre, to which his father was
admitted in order that he might patch up the royal tapestries.
Nor was he far from the great French market-place or from the
quarters of plain people that surrounded it. Born into a prosperous middle-class family, he had ample opportunity to observe
Parisians of higher or lower degree than his father and himself.

He also came into contact with actors. He knew a family named
Béjart. The father, who was a sergeant-at-arms, must have had
difficulty in supporting his large family. The children relieved
him by going on the stage. Madeleine, Joseph, Geneviève, and
Louis all became actors, as did many years later the last child,
Armande, who was to marry Molière. Madeleine was probably
the first to play. We have a poem that she addressed to a leading
dramatist. She, her brother Joseph, and her sister Geneviève
joined forces with Molière as soon as he came of age and was
able to make use of the money left him by his mother. He had
already received a good education in the humanities and probably

in law. As soon as he obtained his inheritance, he invested it in creating a troupe, composed of himself, three Béjarts, and several other young people. They called themselves the Illustrious Theater, illustrious in name alone.

This was in 1643, when there were in Paris two well-established theatrical companies, those of the Hôtel de Bourgogne and the Marais, though Paris was then about the size of Newark or Indianapolis. Molière and his friends rented a hand-ball court, had a carpenter set up a stage and some boxes for spectators, and gave plays there till they were obliged to move to another court. Their affairs were in such bad shape that Molière was arrested for the debts of the troupe and was liberated only when his father paid them. After two or three years the situation became so hopeless that the troupe broke up and left Paris. Molière and the Béjarts stuck together, while their comrades went elsewhere. Molière's departure from Paris may be compared to the flight of Mahomet from Mecca. In both cases the exile led to a period of preparation outside the capital and to a victorious return.

Molière and the Béjarts attached themselves to a provincial troupe headed by a certain Dufresne and protected by a duke who lived in southern France. They wandered all over the country, playing where they could, having difficulties with small-town authorities, in danger from those who took part in the civil war of 1649–53. Molière became more and more important in the troupe until about 1650 he was made its leader. He studied his comrades, learned how to advise them, how to make them work together. He also began to write plays for the troupe to perform. During these years he learned to know more of France than Paris; he was able to study life in villages and small towns, the ways of peasants, of petty office-holders, and of rustic nobles, all of whom were to reappear in his comedies.

Under his management the troupe became the most distinguished French company outside of Paris. In 1658 he returned to the capital and was allowed to act in theaters that belonged to the government. The year following his return he delighted Paris with the *Précieuses ridicules* and after that new plays came thick and fast from his pen. He had learned that one road to success was a provision of new plays, as these could not be acted by other troupes until they were printed. And his comedies were so many and so popular that he made his theater the chief place in France for comedy. He won the patronage of the king, who gave his troupe an annual subsidy and had it play frequently at court.

But Molière had to fight his way—first against the troupe of the Hôtel de Bourgogne, next against opposition from the church, lastly against his own poor health. Not only did he fight, but he found in his opponents material for comedy. He burlesqued the acting of his rivals. He dramatized the doings of hypocrites and their dupes. He gave his cough to one of his characters and made fun of the doctors who failed to cure him. Let's look at these three classes of opponents in greater detail.

First the rival actors. In the *Précieuses ridicules* a mock-nobleman declares that he will give a play he has written to the Great Actors, that is, to those of the Hôtel de Bourgogne, for they alone know how to roll out a verse and to wait for applause. This seems to have been the first shot in the battle. The rival actors replied by having authors parody Molière's plays and printers seek to pirate them. The more successful Molière became, the more hostile were his rivals, who felt that he menaced their pre-eminence. When Molière wrote the *School for Wives*, friends of the older troupe attacked it savagely. Molière replied by his *Critique*, a playlet in which the *School for Wives* is discussed, the sensible characters approve of it, and it is condemned by a jealous poet, a prude, and an empty-headed young nobleman. Then followed a number of short comedies in which Molière is criticized in turn, and a second reply of his, the *Impromptu de Versailles*, in which Molière puts himself and his comrades on the stage and he burlesques for their benefit the acting of his rivals.

This celebrated literary quarrel, distinguished from others by the fact that the majority of the documents concerned are in dramatic form, resulted in making the *School for Wives* an extremely popular play and in advertising Molière and his troupe. He remained on unfriendly terms with the actors of the Hôtel.

After his death some of his actors went over to the rival troupe, but enough of them remained to keep the company going. Soon most of the actors of the Marais were joined to those of Molière's troupe, and finally in 1680 the troupe of the Hôtel and the company that had been Molière's were permanently united. This troupe became known as the French Comedy or the French Theater, to distinguish it from the Italian troupe that was acting at Paris. It was in this way that the Comédie Française came into being, born of Molière's troupe and that of the Hôtel de Bourgogne. Molière's share in its creation is recognized by the fact that the theater in which the company performs is often called Molière's House and by the fact that his plays have been acted there more frequently than those of any other author. And this troupe, active in Paris today, has the longest history of any company of actors that has ever existed. Obviously Molière as a manager met with no small success.

And now as to clerical opposition. A number of people were disturbed by the *School for Wives*, finding in it passages they considered indecent and accusing Molière of attempting to parody the Ten Commandments. They joined the jealous dramatists and the rival actors in attacking Molière. A group known as the Company of the Holy Sacrament got wind of the fact that Molière was writing *Tartuffe* and decided at a meeting in April, 1664, to seek to have the play suppressed. They appealed to the Queen Mother, who was a devout Spaniard, and to the Archbishop of Paris. Molière managed, however, to give three acts of his five-act comedy as part of an elaborate festival at Versailles, but further performances were forbidden for five years, though he was allowed to read his play in private homes and he once gave it in his theater with altered names. By 1669 the Queen Mother had died and her son allowed the comedy to be acted. After such a build-up, *Tartuffe* became, of course, the leading attraction of the century.

During the period in which he could not play *Tartuffe*, Molière brought out *Don Juan* and introduced into it scenes in which hypocrisy is laughed at. The play was immediately criticized by a priest and was withdrawn after four well-attended productions. Subsequently Molière thought it wise to abstain from controversy of this nature. *Tartuffe*, it is true, became his most successful play, but after *Don Juan* he wrote no play that could bring down upon him the wrath of the clergy. Instead he turned to the medical profession, substituting those who care for the body for those who concern themselves with the soul. *Don Juan* marks the transition. It is the last play to be criticized by churchmen and the first to introduce criticism of the practice of medicine.

By wearing a physician's robe Don Juan's valet has been able to prescribe for several peasants. His master thinks his prescriptions will do as well as those of the licensed practitioners, for cures wrought by the latter are usually accidental. His valet accuses him of being an unbeliever even in medicine, as he doesn't have faith in senna, or cassia, or emetics.

This was only a beginning. Soon Molière had written a farce called *Love as a Doctor,* or *The Four Doctors*, in which we see four physicians of whom one insists upon bleeding, another on the use of antimony, while the others, though willing to take milder measures, are great sticklers for form. They visit the girl who is supposed to be ill. One of the physicians, upon recognizing a servant girl he had seen at a house where the coachman was ill, gives this proof of his reverence for authority: He asks about the health of the coachman for whom he has prescribed. Lysette, the maid, answers: " He is dead."

Dr. Tomès: Dead!
Lysette: Yes.
Dr. Tomès: That can't be.
Lysette: I don't know whether it can be, but I know that it is.
Dr. Tomès: He can't be dead I tell you.
Lysette: And I tell you that he is dead . . . and buried.
Dr. T.: You are mistaken. Hippocrates says that these sorts of illnesses end only on the fourteenth or the twenty-first day, and it is only six days since he fell ill.
Lysette: Hippocrates may say what he pleases, but the coachman is dead.

Then comes the consultation held by the four doctors, who seat themselves and cough:

Dr. Dès Fonandrès: Paris is very large; you have to take long trips when business is active.

Dr. Tomès: My mule is excellent for such trips. You wouldn't believe how far she can go in a day.

Dr. Dès Fonandrès: I have a horse that can't be tired out.

Dr. Tomès: Do you know where I've been today? I went to the Arsenal, then to the Faubourg Saint-Germain, then to the Marais, then to the Saint-Honoré Gate, then to the Faubourg Saint-Jacques, then to the Richelieu Gate, then to the Place Royale.

Dr. Dès Fonandrès: My horse did all that today and more, and besides I visited a patient outside of town.

Dr. Tomès: By the way, which side are you taking in the quarrel between Dr. Theophrastus and Dr. Artemius?

Dr. Dès Fonandrès: I'm for Artemius.

Dr. Tomès: So am I. It is true that his opinion killed the patient, but Theophrastus ought not to have had a different opinion from that of a colleague older than himself. Don't you agree with me?

Dr. Dès Fonandrès: Certainly. We must always respect formalities, whatever may happen.

Dr. Tomès: A dead man is only a dead man. No conclusion is to be drawn from his death. But the neglect of a formality injures the whole medical profession.

The next play in which Molière ridiculed the profession was *The Doctor in Spite of Himself*. Here we see no physician, but a wood-chopper named Sganarelle who had once been the valet of a physician and had picked up scraps of Latin and of medical talk. He is forced to put on a doctor's robe, but he soon enjoys it, for he finds that, thanks to the robe, to his bad Latin, and to his nerve, he gets along quite nicely in the profession. He is called in to diagnose the case of Lucinde, a girl who has suddenly become dumb. Here is the scene of diagnosis:

Sganarelle: Well, what's the matter? What pains do you feel?
Lucinde: Ha, hi, hom, han.
Sganarelle: What's that?

Lucinde: Han, hi, hom, han, hai, hi, hin.

Sganarelle: What?

Lucinde: Han, hi, hom.

Sganarelle: Han, hi, hon, han, ha. I don't understand. What the devil of a language is this?

Géronte (the girl's father): That's her illness, sir. She has become mute without our ever discovering the cause. That's why her marriage has been delayed.

Sganarelle: Why?

Géronte: The man she is to marry wants to wait for her to be cured.

Sganarelle: And who is this fool who doesn't want his wife to be dumb? Would to God that mine were. I'd take good care not to cure her.

Géronte: We beg you to do what you can for my daughter.

Sganarelle: Don't worry. Tell me, does this illness oppress her much?

Géronte: Yes, sir.

Sganarelle: So much the better. Does she feel great pains?

Géronte: Very great.

Sganarelle (to Lucinde): Give me your arm. (He feels her pulse.) There's a pulse that indicates that your daughter is mute.

Géronte: Yes, sir, that's her trouble. You found it out right away. . . . But what is the cause of the trouble?

Sganarelle: It is that she has lost the power of speech.

Géronte: Very good, but what made her lose her power of speech?

Sganarelle: All our best authorities will say that it is caused by an impediment in the action of her tongue.

Géronte: But what is your opinion about this impediment in the action of her tongue?

Sganarelle: Aristotle says about that . . . some very fine things.

Géronte: I believe it.

Sganarelle: He was a great man.

Géronte: Yes, indeed.

Sganarelle: To return to our argument, I think that this impediment in the action of her tongue is caused by certain humors that we learned men call peccant humors, peccant, that is, peccant humors, inasmuch as the vapors formed by the outpouring of the influences that arise in the region of illnesses, coming, so to speak, to . . . . Do you understand Latin?

Géronte: Not at all.

Sganarelle: You don't understand Latin?

Géronte: No.

Sganarelle: Cabricias arci thuram, catalamus, singulariter, nominativo, haec Musa, la Muse, Bonus, Bona, Bonum, Deus Sanctus, Est ne oratio latinas? Etiam, oui, quare, pourquoi, quia substantivo, et adjectivum, concordat in generi, numerum, et casus.

Géronte: Oh, why haven't I studied?

And the diagnosis continues, including the remark that the heart is on the right, the liver on the left, which brings a protest from Géronte, who had always supposed the heart to be on the left, the liver on the right, but Sganarelle gets out of the difficulty by answering:

Yes, it used to be that way, but we doctors have changed all that and we now practise medicine by new methods.

Géronte: That's what I did not know and I beg your pardon for my ignorance.

After emphasizing the real physician and the fake physician, Molière decided to concentrate upon the patient, upon the man who is hipped about himself, who thinks he is ill, but isn't.

Molière, of course, had never studied modern psychiatry. He did not know that, if a man thinks he is ill, he *is* ill, that a so-called imaginary invalid is a person mentally ill. However, in drawing his *Malade imaginaire,* he depicted a person who talks about his ailments and worships his physicians in a way that may be familiar to many of us. He is so much convinced of his doctor's infallibility, that, when he is told to walk up and down, he asks if he should walk up and then down, or down and then up. He also asks him how many grains of salt he must put on his egg.

He plans to marry his daughter to a young physician in order to have one always at hand, but his plan fails, his daughter marries another man, and, on the advice of his family, the imaginary invalid decides to become a doctor himself. This decision prepares the way for a grand ballet in which druggists, surgeons, and physicians march in and take their places around the hall. The presiding physician than calls upon his colleagues to put questions in Gallic Latin which, if properly answered, will permit the admission of the Imaginary Invalid into their profession. The first doctor asks why opium puts one to sleep: *"Domandabo causam et rationem quare Opium facit dormire?"* The Invalid replies that there is in opium a dormitive virtue that dulls one's senses. Whereupon the chorus applauds.

Similar questions and answers follow. The Invalid swears to obey all the laws of the faculty, and the president confers upon him the right to prescribe, to purge, to bleed, to pierce, to slash, to cut, and to kill with impunity throughout all the earth.

Thereupon the surgeons and druggists dance around the Invalid, wishing long life to the new doctor who has spoken so well, a thousand years in which he may eat and drink and bleed and kill:

> *Vivat, vivat, vivat, vivat, cent fois vivat,*
> *Novus doctor qui tam bene parlat!*
> *Mille, mille annis, et manget, et bibat,*
> *Et seignet, et tuat!*

But the doctors were avenged. At the fourth performance of this gay comedy-ballet Molière, who was playing the imaginary invalid, was taken seriously ill, managed to stagger through his role and to get home, where, a few hours later, he died.

As he was only fifty-one, he might have given us many more delightful comedies, but, when he was on his death-bed, he had at least the satisfaction of knowing that he had accomplished much as actor, manager, and author of comedies.

As television had not been invented in his day, we cannot judge his acting except by the statements of his contemporaries. Even his enemies admitted that he was a great actor when they claimed that it was the acting of the *School for Wives* rather than its verses that made it succeed. The daughter of one of his comrades, herself at one time a member of his troupe, wrote of him as follows:

He was neither too fat nor too thin; he was tall rather than short; he carried himself well, showed a fine leg. He had a large nose, a large mouth, thick lips, a swarthy complexion, black and heavy eyebrows, which he moved in such a way as to render his face extremely comical. He realized that nature had refused him the gifts required by a tragic actor and limited himself to comic roles, excelling both in farce and in high comedy, in such roles as those of Arnolphe, Orgon, and Harpagon. It is in them that he seduced the spectators to such an extent that they could no longer distinguish the actor from the character he represented.

I have referred to his success as a manager. As a dramatist he had certain limitations. He did not attempt tragedy. He avoided the sentimental type of play that was to develop in the eighteenth century and is not unknown today. He wrote one tragi-comedy, but, as it failed, he tried that kind of play no further and merely incorporated some of its lines in later plays. His genius led him to comedy of various kinds, from comedy of character and comedy of manners to comedy-ballet, farce, and comedy that emphasizes music and spectacle. In these he is the supreme master, with all respect to Aristophanes and Shakespeare.

He broke away from the tradition that comedy should have in its cast only persons of the middle and lower classes. *The Misanthrope* is essentially a comedy of high society, where entertainment, love affairs, duels, lawsuits, gossip, and dabbling in literature occupy men's minds rather than the business of making a living. Alceste, the Misanthrope, is an admirable member of society, but one who renders himself comic by his inability to make social compromises. The Truth always is his guide.

" What! " exclaims his friend Philinte, " would you go and tell old Emily that at her age it is unbecoming to pretend to be pretty, and that the powder she uses shocks everybody? "

" Certainly," answers Alceste.

" And would you tell Dorilas that everyone at court is bored by his constant talk about his own valor and the distinction of his family? "

" Certainly," repeats Alceste.

And this lover of truth, however disagreeable it may be, of sincerity, of the accurate expression of one's feelings, is in love with a charming flirt, Célimène, a young widow to whom the truth has no meaning, and who is sought after by most of the men in the play.

Her admirers urge her to discuss her absent acquaintances. When she does so, she gives us a much larger picture of the society of the day than we could get from seeing only the characters in the play. There is Damon who says nothing at great length; Timante, who takes on mysterious airs, claims to have important secrets to tell, and ends by confiding in you something of no interest or importance; Géralde, who is constantly talking about horses and dogs and mentions no men and women except dukes, princes, and princesses; Cléon, who gets credit for his excellent table, but unfortunately serves there, not only delicious food, but himself.

Célimène's best scene is, perhaps, with the prude, Arsinoé, who is jealous of Célimène's youth, beauty, and attraction for men. She comes to tell Célimène of the trouble she has taken in her behalf. According to her, she had been the day before at the home of some excellent people where the conversation happened to fall upon Célimène. They said that the crowd of men who came to see her and the fact that she was much discussed caused her to be censured. Arsinoé, of course, came to her defense and said that her intentions were good, but she had to admit that Célimène did live in a way that was most unfortunate. There was nothing, of course, really immoral, but a woman should avoid the shadow of a suspicion. You understand that I'm telling you all this purely for your good.

Célimène smilingly thanks her for her kindness. " Far from taking it badly," she says, " I'm going to show how much I appreciate it by telling you something in return. The other day I was at the house of some admirable people who happened to talk about you. They said that you were forever discussing honor and good behavior, always appearing shocked at any suggestion of indecency, continually criticizing others, but that you beat your servants and fail to pay them, make vain attempts to appear beautiful, and would be glad to be the heroine of a love-affair. I defended you, but all were against me and pointed out that you would do well to look after your own conduct before showing so much interest in that of others.

The Misanthrope is a comedy of character, but it is not the first. Molière had already written the *School for Wives*, in which there is a dominant character, a person with whom we might sympathize were he not warped by one characteristic that renders him ridiculous. Molière might have called his play the *School for Husbands*, but he had already given this title to another play. The principal role, one that takes up a third of the text and one that he played himself, is that of Arnolphe, whose character is altered by his attitude towards women. He is now forty-two, about Molière's age at the time, but he has never married. His reason is that he fears his wife will not be faithful, but he thinks the trouble is with women's education. He has himself hit upon a plan that will, he is sure, solve his matrimonial problem.

Some eleven years before, he had secured possession of a girl who was only four years old and had put her in the care of two ignorant and stupid peasants in order that she should know nothing about the relations between the sexes until he could himself reveal them to her. When the play begins, he has just come home after an absence of some weeks. When he sees the girl, whom he calls Agnes, he is delighted by the childishness of her conversation and expresses his joy in a monologue filled with satisfaction over his educational experiment. Immediately afterwards the trouble begins. He has hardly finished his monologue when young Horace, son of an old friend, comes to greet him, to borrow money from him, and to tell him that he has fallen in love with a girl named Agnes whom he has seen on a balcony near by and that he will use the money Arnolphe has loaned him in an effort to win her. When he has gone, Arnolphe has a second monologue differing in tone from the first. He expresses his agitation over the confidential information he has just received and decides upon an investigation.

In the interview with Agnes that follows he tries to be tactful and says that he has been told by gossips that a young man has come to see her, but that he couldn't believe it and was willing to bet . . . .

Agnes: Don't bet, you'll lose.
Arnolphe: What! Is it true that a young man . . . .
Agnes: Sure thing. He has hardly budged from our house.

Then she explains how it all happened.

I was on the balcony working in the fresh air when I saw passing by a handsome young man, who, catching my glance, bowed humbly; so I, not willing to be surpassed in politeness, made a bow to him. Then he bowed again and so did I. We kept this up till it grew dark. Next day an old woman came to tell me how deeply I had wounded the young man and how I could cure him only by letting him visit me. Of course I couldn't let him suffer, would you have done so?

Arnolphe hears of the visit, of kisses, of a ribbon the young man took. He is relieved to find that matters have gone no farther, but he thinks it advisable to marry Agnes himself as soon as possible. To prepare her for matrimony he reads her his Maxims of Marriage, which point out that a woman should seek to please her husband only, that she should receive no one unless her husband authorizes the visit, should accept no present, should never write letters, should avoid social gatherings, cards, picnics, etc. He sends her out with the programme in her hands and expresses in a new monologue the hope that, if he acts quickly, his plans may still succeed. But he gradually discovers that his method results in complete failure. He fails as a lover and as an educator. Young love triumphs over all his experience, over all the precautions that he takes. The plot is rendered comic by the fact that the two young innocents are constantly revealing to Arnolphe the progress of their love-affair. Whenever there is danger of our feeling sorry for Arnolphe, there are comic expressions or comic situations that keep us from becoming sentimental. And the monologues continue to emphasize the state of Arnolphe's emotions.

Another high comedy is *Tartuffe* in which the central character,

Orgon, is so completely unable to tell the difference between a hypocrite and a really devout person that he lets himself be deceived by a dead-beat, who brings discord into his family, interferes with his daughter's marriage plans, and seeks to seduce his wife.

You may ask why *Tartuffe* was attacked by church organizations, though Molière made it plain that he is holding up to scorn hypocrites and their dupes, not really pious people and those who trust them. It was probably because there were in the Company of the Holy Sacrament and similar societies not only hypocrites who did not like to see themselves unmasked, but sincere people who, while they might not object to the play as a whole, were shocked by certain passages, such as those in which Tartuffe to make love uses the language of prayer and the arguments of the casuists whom Pascal had attacked in the *Provincial Letters*. Says Tartuffe to Elmire:

> The love that attaches us to beauty that is eternal does not stifle in us love for what is temporal. Our senses may readily be charmed by Heaven's perfect creations. The delights of Heaven are reflected in others, but they show in you their rarest marvels . . . . I have not been able to look upon you, perfect creature, without admiring in you the Author of nature and without feeling my heart fill with love when I contemplate the most beautiful portrait in which the Creator has painted Himself. At first I feared that this secret ardor was a clever trap set by the evil one, and, thinking that you were an obstacle to my salvation, I resolved to avoid you, but at last I came to understand that my feeling may not be guilty and that I can reconcile it with good conduct. That is why I allowed it to take possession of my heart. . . . And now in you is my hope, my welfare, my tranquility. Upon you depends my suffering or my beatitude.

Another comedy is *l'Avare* in which the central character is a wealthy business man, who is rendered highly amusing by his avarice. In the *Learned Ladies*, instead of having one central character, we have three women, a mother, her daughter, and her sister-in-law, who together represent the neglect of domestic duties for what they consider higher matters.

One of Molière's most interesting and most celebrated productions is the *Bourgeois Gentilhomme*. He apparently conceived it as a comedy of character in which the chief person, Monsieur Jourdain, was to be a merchant who would render himself ridiculous by his efforts to ape the nobility. While he was at work on this play, a Turkish mission visited Paris, was shown the splendors of the French court, but expressed no surprise or admiration. The court wished Molière to avenge it by burlesquing Turkish customs, and, for this purpose, put at his disposal a Frenchman who had traveled in North Africa, Syria, and Turkey. This man conferred with Molière and with Lulli, the opera composer, who was to write the music for the play. Molière arranged his plot in such a way that Jourdain would be deceived into thinking that he would be made a Turkish nobleman by a special ceremony, and it was in this ceremony that the knowledge the traveled Frenchman had of manners and of costumes could be employed. The ceremony and the ballets give the work the tone of an extravaganza, but much of it is nevertheless comedy of a high order.

Jourdain wishes to have an education, not for the sake of culture or the development of his powers, but in order that he may act the nobleman. He would practise writing in order to write courtly love-letters. He would learn to fence because noblemen fight duels. Whenever he learns something new, he loves to go and brag to his wife and his servant about his acquisition. Here are some samples of his conversation:

The professor of philosophy asks him what he wants to learn. Jourdain replies; " All I can. I am angry with my parents because they did not make me study all branches of knowledge when I was young."

The Professor of Philosophy: " That is a reasonable feeling. *Nam sine doctrina vita est quasi mortis imago.* You understand Latin of course." Jourdain: " Yes, but act as if I didn't. Explain what it means."

Then the professor tells how to make the vowels that Jourdain has been making ever since he learned to talk. Jourdain confides in him that he wishes to write a love letter he can drop at the feet of a certain noblewoman.

Professor: Do you want to write in verse?

Jourdain: No, no verses.

Professor: You want only prose?

Jourdain: No, I want neither prose, nor verse.

Professor: But it must be one or the other.

Jourdain: Why?

Professor: Because, sir, there are only these two ways of expressing oneself.

Jourdain: There is nothing but prose and verse?

Professor: No, sir. All that isn't prose is verse and all that isn't verse is prose.

Jourdain: And when one speaks, what is that?

Professor: Prose.

Jourdain: What! When I say, " Nicole, bring me my slippers and my night cap, it's prose?

Professor: Yes, sir.

Jourdain: In faith, I've been speaking prose for over forty years without ever knowing that I was doing it; and I am very much obliged to you for having told me that.

So much, indeed, that he hastens to show off his newly acquired learning. After talking to his wife of other matters, he says:

Do you know what you are saying?

Mme Jourdain: Yes, I know that what I am saying is well said and that you ought to live differently from the way you do.

Jourdain: I'm not talking about that. I'm asking you what are the words you are saying.

Mme Jourdain: They are words that are very wise and that's more than your conduct is.

Jourdain: I'm not talking about that, I tell you. I ask you what I am speaking with you, what I am saying at this time, what is it?

Mme Jourdain: Nonsense.

Jourdain: Oh, no; it's not that. What we are both saying, the language that we are speaking.

Mme Jourdain: Well.

Jourdain: What is it called?

Mme Jourdain: Its called whatever one wishes to call it.

Jourdain: It's prose, ignorant woman.

Mme Jourdain: Prose?

Jourdain: Yes, prose. All that is prose is not verse; and all that is not verse is not prose. That's what comes from studying!

Jourdain feels that to complete his role as a nobleman he must have a noblewoman as his mistress. He accordingly arranges to entertain a certain Dorimène, who is brought to his house by Dorante, an impecunious nobleman who for some time has been borrowing money from Jourdain. Dorante arranges to have an elegant meal brought in, for which, of course, Jourdain pays, the nobleman pretends to the young woman that he is giving her the dinner and has merely borrowed Jourdain's house for the occasion. The three sit down after Jourdain has paid Dorimène elaborate compliments. Six cooks who have prepared the feast dance a ballet, then bring in the table covered with food. But in the middle of the dinner Mme Jourdain arrives and breaks up the party. Dorimène, shocked to find that she has been deceived, leaves in haste. Jourdain scolds his wife, who replies that all women will be on her side. Left alone, poor Jourdain laments: "She came in at a most unfortunate moment. I was in humor to say some very pretty things and I never before felt that I had so much wit."

Just think of all the clever things you were about to say when you were interrupted and give your sympathy to Monsieur Jourdain.

Molière is full of expressions like this that can easily be applied to our own experience. Take, for instance, the famous phrase in the *Fourberies de Scapin*, "What the devil was he going to do in that galley?" "*Que diable allait-il faire dans cette galère?*" A young man needs money. His valet tries to extract some for him from his miserly father. He pretends that the son was invited by a Turk on board his boat, was given delicious fruit, and, while they were eating, the galley put out to sea and the Turk now insists on the payment of 500 francs if the father does not want his son taken to Algiers. The father laments, tries to find a way out and every now and then repeats "What the devil was he going to do in this galley?" Of course, that is not the question. The important thing is to get the money and ransom the young man, but the miser is very human when he keeps asking the question.

The next time you lose your pocket-book, or break your glasses, or a plate you value, see if you do not ask yourself why you did something or went somewhere, though, if your question were answered, it would not find your pocket-book for you, or mend your glasses or your plate.

There is this permanent quality in Molière's work. There is also a picture of life in seventeenth-century France, drawn boldly and with comic effect. The king is, of course, referred to in flattering terms. Nothing else would have been possible in a play acted in Paris, but Molière had other reasons. He needed the king's protection and he probably had a high opinion of Louis XIV, who, up to the time of Molière's death, seemed to be an excellent young ruler. He had not yet revoked the Edict of Nantes, involved his country in lengthy wars, or ruined its financial structure.

Molière's nobles may be persons with whom we sympathize, or they may be held up to ridicule. When Molière first returned to Paris, he put on the stage, not a real marquis, but a valet disguised as one. A few years later he dramatized real marquises in all their finery and futility. Soon the young marquis became a conventional comic figure, especially amusing as he could be easily compared with the living marquises who were sitting as spectators on the stage.

Another type of aristocrat that Molière cartooned was the country nobleman, the fellow left high and dry by the tide that carried the capable and cultivated nobles to Versailles. M. and Mme de Sotenville, for instance, who appear in *George Dandin*. They make me think of a half-starved turkey-gobbler and his hen. They are still able to strut and to gobble about the achievements of their ancestors in the crusades, but they are forced to marry their daughter to a peasant, whose financial assistance they accept, but whom they keep at his social distance despite the fact that he has become their son-in-law.

The bourgeois constitute the largest class in Molière's comedies. One may, like Jourdain, be seeking to leave it, or he may, like Mme Jourdain, prefer to stay in it and to have a bourgeois son-in-law. He may be a miser like Harpagon, or a spendthrift like his son. Or he may be an excellent member of society.

And there are representatives of the workers, the clever valets and the peasants. Here again the character may be held up to ridicule, as is Gorge Dandin, or he may be presented sympathetically as are the peasants in *Don Juan*.

Molière had a great gift for entering into his characters and making them live. He often distinguishes them from one another by their speech. He employed material supplied by the Romans, the Italians, the Spaniards, by French dramatists and novelists, and by the life about him. Such material he made his own and presented in such a way as to produce highly comic scenes, sometimes at the expense of the plot. As someone said of Shakespeare, he is full of quotations. Here are some of them:

May propitious Heaven give us children of whom we are the fathers.
One dies only once and it's for such a long time.
Nice people know everything without studying.
Outside of Paris there is no salvation for gentlefolk.
Bolts and bars don't make the virtue of women and girls.
I should like to know if the great rule of all rules is not to please and if a play that has reached this goal has not followed a good route.
To esteem everybody is to esteem nobody.
It is true, my reason warns me every day, but reason is not what regulates love.
Age will bring anything, but at twenty it's no time to be a prude.
He who would drown his dog accuses him of being mad.
I live on good soup, not on fine talk.
In the good old days women thought only of their households. Their books were a thimble, thread and needles with which they prepared their daughters' trousseaux, but now they are far from such habits, they want to write and become authors . . . . And in this vain pursuit of knowledge, they know nothing about my dinner.

A learned fool is more of a fool than an ignorant fool.

When a shoemaker makes shoes, he can't spoil a piece of leather without having to pay for it, but a doctor can spoil a man without its costing him anything. It's always the fault of the man who dies. And among the dead there is the greatest discretion in the world, no one of them has ever been heard to complain of the doctor who killed him.

Molière impressed himself so deeply upon his countrymen that, twenty years after his death, an author of comedies declared that it was useless to try to excel in his profession. " If I imitate Molière, I am accused of plagiarism; if I write differently from him, my critics say, ' Ah! that is not Molière! ' "

Let me close with a tribute from Austin Dobson: [1]

> *True Comedy circum praecordia ludit—*
> *It warms the heart's cockles. 'Twas thus that he viewed it,*
> *That simple old Critic, who smote on his knee,*
> *And named it no more than he knew it to be.*
> *" True Comedy! "—Ah! there is this thing about it,*
> *If it makes the House merry, you never need doubt it:*
> *It lashes the vicious; it laughs at the fool;*
> *And it brings all the prigs and pretenders to school.*
> *To the poor it is kind; to the plain it is gentle;*
> *It is neither too tragic, nor too sentimental;*
> *Its thrust, like a rapier's, though cutting, is clean,*
> *And it pricks Affectation all over the scene.*
> *Its rules are the rules* ARISTOTLE *has taught us;*
> *Its ways have not altered since* TERENCE *and* PLAUTUS;
> *Its mission is neither to praise nor to blame;*
> *Its weapon is Ridicule, Folly its game.*
>
> *" True Comedy! "—such as our* POQUELIN *made it!*
> *" True Comedy! "—such as our* COQUELIN *played it!*
> *It clears out the cobwebs; it freshens the air;*
> *And it treads in the steps of its Master,* MOLIÈRE!

---

[1] " La bonne comédie," *Collected Poems* (London, 1913), 598-99.

X

Goethe's Faust

ERNST FEISE

GOETHE's *Faust* was begun in 1772 by the young poet, then twenty-three years old, in the exuberant spirit of his generation which rebelled against the rationalism of its elders; it was continued toward the close of the century by a mature and experienced master and statesman, imbued with the conviction of his philosophical and ethical obligation even in his poetry; it was completed in 1832 by a sage who viewed life with serenity but humility, as a symbolic struggle between the creative and destructive forces in man.

Historically speaking, the genesis of this work *Faust* reaches from the time of Frederick II of Prussia and Louis XV, over the period of the great upheaval in France and the conquests of Napoleon, to the July Revolution of 1830 and the first conceptions of a world economy and of modern imperialism.

Biographically speaking, we see the fiery youth improvising poetic rhapsodies among his comrades of the Storm and Stress movement at the beginning of his literary career, while at its close the somewhat unapproachable Weimar Excellency is discussing problems of scientific method and world politics with distinguished guests from Europe and America. A few months before his death, Goethe lays away the sealed manuscript of the Second Part of *Faust* as a bequest to a coming generation.

NOTE: The *Faust* quotations are taken, separately or combined, from the renderings of George M. Priest (A. Knopf, N. Y.), Van der Smissen (Dutton & Co., N. Y.), and John Shacross (Scholartis, London).

Today it stands before us like one of those monumental European edifices at which centuries have built, the nucleus a Gothic cathedral, surrounded by Renaissance galleries, flanked by classical columns, and crowded in by warehouses and banks. Its action spans three thousand years, its earliest events take place after the Trojan War, when the Greek Helena returns from Troy to Sparta, and it ends with a project of modern imperial colonization and the wresting of land from the destructive wrath of the ocean for the peaceful pursuits of a democratic population. But in spite of all its apparent disparity there is a unity of idea, a unity of experience (those of its author), and a unity of action, centered in the figure of its hero, who is the representative of a great soul-myth of old, such as Prometheus, the Wandering Jew, and Don Giovanni—the myth of Dr. Faustus.

Johann Faust, around whom this myth crystallized, was an actual historic person who lived between 1480 and 1540, a Renaissance man like Paracelsus, full of the self-confidence of man's newly acquired power and sure of his ability to fathom and master life's riddles and problems with the tools of science. He was a scholar thirsting for supernatural knowledge, and, since the natural means of attaining it are denied him, ready to turn to magic, ready to conjure up spirits which, he believed, controlled the elements of our cosmos. His Christian brethren crossed themselves when meeting him. Catholics called him a vain quack and boaster; Protestants saw in him an unwelcome fellow-rebel. For what they called God he called nature; where they sought revelation, he sought power forbidden to man. His pantheistic enthusiasm was condemned by the stern logic of the scholastics; his magic practices ridiculed by the cool research of the humanists. Popular belief, unable to grasp the nascent vision of a new conception of life, reduces his figure to that of a trickster magician and fantastic traveller, who signs away his soul to the devil, indulges in carnal pleasures, attains the love of a satanic strumpet heroine, called Helen of Troy, with whom he begets a son and is taken to Hell by the deceitful tempter. This is the picture of him that we get from the compilation of legends which an enterprising publisher,

Spiess, printed in 1587 as a thriller for credulous readers. This folkbook survived in various versions until Goethe's childhood; and Goethe must surely have witnessed the puppet play *Faust*, which was at that time performed at city and country fairs.

The only worthy dramatic attempt to treat this great myth, Marlowe's *Faustus*, came to Goethe's attention in 1818, too late to add anything of importance to his own dramatic conception. But even Marlowe, dramatist of the superman, and obviously sympathetic toward a figure like Faustus, was unable to overcome the traditional view that Faust is a great sinner and must atone for his godless and overweening pride.

An entirely new conception of man's task on earth and his relation to God was necessary to do justice to the dramatic potentialities latent in the figure of Faustus—and it was left to the young Frankfurt dramatist to recognize them.

Goethe had just attained national fame through his tragedy *Goetz von Berlichingen*, which was based on the autobiography of a valiant rebel knight of the sixteenth century. He was now wavering between plans for dramas on Caesar, Mahomet, Prometheus, and Faust. Why was it that only Faust impressed himself so vividly upon the poet's mind that he over-shadowed all the other heroes? Was it only that a Caesar or a Mahomet demanded an extensive historical study? Or was it rather that Goethe could identify himself more closely with the great magician and his despair at the limitations of man's knowledge? Goethe's adventures in alchemy and natural science, no doubt, had already taught him how arduous the path of knowledge was. But the decisive stimulus must have been his actual acquaintance with a man who seemed to him the embodiment of a Faustian soul. This was Johann Gottlieb Herder, the critic and philosopher whose intellectual crisis Goethe witnessed with his own eyes in Strassburg when only twenty-one years old. Here was a man, endowed with the richest gifts of the mind, a volcano of encyclopedic plans, striking out in all directions of human knowledge, yet disgusted with book-learning, having left a most desirable position as a teacher and preacher in his Baltic home, cursing his own bookish bent and thirsting for a vigorous active life, dreaming of reforms for the education of his people, indeed, for a whole reorganization of his Russian fatherland, nay, for a reorientation of humanity itself.

In Herder's personality there was stuff for a drama, and his writings revealed an entirely new conception of poetry and of life. What value, Herder asked, had poems conceived by reason instead of being poured out by a pulsing heart? What effect could be felt from characters of drama who were hemmed in by petty conventions and who turned criminal because they were unable to realize their personalities in a narrow bourgeois sphere? What were all these versified moralities in comparison to the giants of Homer and Shakespeare? Where were the transports of a Pindar, where the great lyric outbursts of pristine sweeping emotion in the face of the great wonders of life? Abstraction had dried up the sources of spontaneous feeling, the well-springs of all poetry and of life itself. The oneness of body and soul, the harmony of nature and spirit had been destroyed in the materialistic conception of man as a mere animal or by the idea that reason was the only faculty worthy of man. Soulless ran the machine of the universe. What prayers could reach the ear of a God who was the winder of this machine?

Goethe's Faust was the protest against such a soulless, bloodless, joyless, lifeless conception of the world. This is the mood of the opening monologue, in which Faust turns away from his academic life to invoke the spirit of the universe with the aid of his book of magic. As in Marlowe's play, he scorns the knowledge of the four academic faculties which he has been teaching.

> FAUST: *No dog but such a life would spurn!*
> *Therefore to magic arts I turn,*
> *If haply, spirits aiding me*
> *By act and utterance I may see*
> *The heart of many a mystery:*
> *That I no more need tax my brain*
> *To prate of things beyond my ken:*
> *But learn what 'tis that at life's core*
> *Sustains the world for evermore,*

Behold the very seeds of life,
Nor waste my days in wordy strife.

. . . .

Ah! woe is me! still must I dwell
In this accurst, this musty cell,
Where even the blessed light of day
Thro' dim panes sends a feeble ray!
Heaped round with books in mouldering piles,
Which worms consume and dust defiles:
Its lofty walls from vault to floor
With smoke-stained paper smothered o'er!

. . . .

Out! Out! into the open land:
And this dark book of secrecy,
By Nostradamus very hand,
Is it not guide enough for thee?
Then shalt thou learn how move the stars,
And Nature teaching thee to seek,
Thy soul shall burst its prison-bars,
As spirits onto spirits speak!

   (He regards the sign of the Macrocosm, [i. e. the spirit
       of the universe])

How all things weave one whole together,
And live and work in one another!
How heavenly beings sink and rise,
Exchanging golden chalices!
On fragrant wings diffusing bliss,
Piercing the earth or soaring to the skies,
Blending all life in mystic harmonies!
A wondrous spectacle!—but nothing more:
Where, endless Nature, shall I reach thy core?
Where reach those breasts, of life the fountain-head,
Those breasts, which nourish Heaven and Earth,
For which the heart yearns in its dearth?
They flow apace—and must I pine unfed?

Because this spirit of the universe may be approached only
through contemplation while Faust yearns for active participa-

tion, he turns hopefully to a spirit more akin to human nature, the Earth Spirit, who appears to him in a terrifying flame:

FAUST: *Thou wraith of flame, thou canst not make me fear!*
'Tis I, 'tis Faust! thy fellow and thy peer!

SPIRIT: *In the floods of life, in action's storm*
Up and down I wave,
I sway and soar,
Birth and the grave
A sea without shore,
A varied weaving,
A radiant living,
Thus at time's humming loom 'tis my hand that prepares
The robe, ever living, the deity wears.

FAUST: *Swift spirit who from end to end*
Circlest the world, how like I feel to thee!

SPIRIT: *Thou'rt like the spirit thou doest comprehend,*
Not me! (disappears)

FAUST: *(collapsing) Not thee?*
Whom then?
I, Image of the Godhead!
Not like even to thee?

This monologue and the exorcising scene are the core of the Faust action in Goethe's first fragmentary version of the play, the so-called *Urfaust*, written in the early seventies. But into this action Goethe wove a secondary plot, not originally connected with the Faust legend, which also was suggested to him by an actual experience, the execution of a girl of twenty-five. Susanna Margareta Brandt was a servant girl at an inn in Frankfurt. Abandoned by her lover, she did away with her illegitimate child; for this crime she was imprisoned in St. Catherine's Tower, a block from the Goethe home, and executed on January 24, 1772. Several members of Goethe's family were connected with her trial, and we still possess the legal documents copied by his father's scribe. One sentence in these depositions re-echoes in the only prose scene of the drama, left exactly as it was in the *Urfaust*, " *Sie ist die erste nicht* " (" she is not the first one "), probably the nucleus of the Gretchen drama, in which Faust curses Mephisto, the devil, for these cynical words:

MEPHISTO: She is not the first.

FAUST: Not the first! Misery! misery! too great for any human
             soul to conceive that more than one created being could
             sink into this agony, that not the first, writhing in mortal
             torture, atoned for the guilt of all the rest in the eyes
             of the Eternal. It pierces me to the marrow, the misery
             of this single being; you grin indifferently at the fate of
             thousands.

We still sense in this scene how the young poet was shaken through and through by the tragedy, and we find the trace of this emotion even in his *Shakespeare Oration* which was composed about this time: " No one reaches the goal toward which he set out so longingly . . . he finally falls into a pit dug for him God knows by whom and is deemed as nothing." The essence of Shakespeare's tragic principle seems for Goethe to lie in the clash between the will of the individual, that is, " the presumed freedom of our will with the necessary course of the whole." Shakespeare is seen perhaps through Spinoza's eyes in the following words: " What we call evil is only the other side of the good, which belongs inexorably to its existence as the tropics must burn and Lapland freeze so that there may be a temperate zone."

So " deemed as nothing," this giant of the mind, Faust as well as the humble, plantlike, touchingly natural girl—" freedom of will," " necessary course of the whole "—is our drama not on the way? " Evil the other side of the good "—does not Mephisto, the devil, emerge, the sensual, the carnal side of Faust the thinker, the urge to procreation in the innocent, pure mind of Gretchen? The pit is dug by their own natures. The first part of the tragedy now takes shape in ballad-like, song-like dramatic sketches such as " Gretchen at the spinning wheel," flashes of an action, written from 1772-75, only fragments of a drama, even after the addition

of a few scenes during the late eighties, until, at the end of the
century, the work is resumed.

We leave the *Urfaust* and now turn to the first part of the
drama as we know it today and which we owe to Schiller's
constant and spurring enthusiasm. The naturalistic and rhapsodic
improvisation of the young Goethe changes to a well-planned
production, carried out according to a preconceived idea. Scenes
have to be filled in and a radically new solution sought. Faust
and Gretchen must be saved. The titan drama of the *Urfaust*
is changed to a mystery play of Faustus Everyman.

The play proper begins with The Prelude in Heaven, where
the devil, Mephisto, appears among the retinue of the Lord of
Hosts. He, the representative of darkness, the nihilist, the destroyer, finds nothing worthy of praise in all of God's creation and
proposes a wager that he can lead Faust, whom the Lord expressly
recognizes as his servant, to damnation. The Lord replies:

> *You shall have leave as you prefer*
> *So long as earth remains his mortal dwelling;*
> *For man must strive and striving he must err.*
> *Let it be so: to you is given the power*
> *That may seduce this soul from his true source,*
> *And drag him down with you in fatal hour,*
> *If you can wholly bend him to your force.*
> *But stand ashamed when called on to confess:*
> *A good man in his dark bewildered course*
> *Will not forget the way of righteousness.*

But Mephisto in his megalomania hopes to fool even the Lord,
who, of course, can hardly make a wager since he is all-knowing.
The Lord clearly expresses the fact that the devil is only his
instrument for stimulating man's eternal striving, lest

> *Man's efforts sink below his proper level,*
> *And, since he seeks for unconditioned ease,*
> *I send this fellow who must goad and tease*
> *And toil to serve creation, though a devil.*

Although in all of the early versions of the Faust legend the

pivotal interest hinges on Faust's eternal damnation—and Faust's
very pact is at once regretted by himself on account of this—we
are in Goethe's version principally concerned with Faust's earthly
life, namely with the question: Will Mephisto be able to lead
this man so far astray that he become bogged down in coarse
debauchery, instead of continuing his striving in spite of all errors,
of pursuing his path through the world, which is the task imposed
upon him by his creator and which ultimately may lead him to
his creator?

What changes, now, are necessary in the *Urfaust*, to harmonize
its fragments with this new interpretation? That first monologue
in which Faust turns from the academic world may stand as it
is, as well as Faust's disillusionment over his vision of the two
spirits—that of the world and that of the earth. But to go back to
the grubbing life of a scholar after these glimpses into the infinite
is also impossible to Faust. His laboratory disgusts him:

> *You instruments, you mock me to my face*
> *With wheel and spindle, cylinder and cog,*
> *For nature keeps her veil inviolate,*
> *Mysterious still in open light of day,*
> *And where the spirit cannot penetrate*
> *Your screws and irons will never make a way.*

There seems one last resort to penetrate the mysteries of
creation: means by which he may break the confines of human
individuation and seek the infinite by dissolving into the cosmic
all. It is not what we generally would call suicide. A vial of
poison beckons from the shelf:

> *Now is the time by deeds to demonstrate*
> *To face the dark abyss without a care*
> *Where Fancy dooms itself to tortures of its own,*
> *And strive undaunted to the thoroughfare*
> *About whose narrow mouth the flames of Hell are blown.*
> *This to resolve with courage unalloyed*
> *And at whatever risk to mingle with the void.*

But as he is about to drink the potion, the Easter message of the

passion play chanted in the near-by church stays his hands.
Memories of long-lost childhood faith are reawakened:

> The song of innocence, the joy of spring
> And thoughts of youth this solemn hour have brought me.
> In my last step a childlike wavering.—
> Begin once more, oh sweet celestial strain.
> Tears dim my eyes: earth's child I am again.

But only for hours of respite is he drawn from the brink, to
be thrown anew into deeper gloom and despair.

What is life worth to a man like Faust? In his haunting search
for the infinite, for life's creative sources, he finds no answer. All
of life's joys, he knows, are transitory, while he wishes them to be
infinite; and if they were infinite, he would nevertheless tire of
them because of his infinite striving which drives him from one
experience to the next. It is illusion—what we now call " the
will to believe "—which spurs man from disappointment to disappointment, and this illusion he curses in whatever form it may
appear, as self-esteem, as honor, fame and dream, as worldly goods
and as love,

> Accurst be Hope and Faith's devotion
> And Patience curst above them all.

But without illusion can life still be endured?

At this moment Mephisto must enter the play, he " who must
goad and tease and toil, to serve creation though a devil,"
Mephisto, the disillusioned, the nihilist, but himself a victim of
illusion, hoping to win Faust's soul by offering him his services
and by dragging him down into the depths of the only kind of
pleasures he can imagine, the material and carnal. And now
follows a most peculiar pact between the two servants of the
Lord, Faust the god-seeker and Mephisto the destroyer, a pact
radically different from that of the old conceptions in the early
Faust legends and in Marlowe. Mephisto proposes to serve him
on earth if Faust will serve him in a hereafter. Faust, however,
is not interested in any question of the beyond; on the other hand

he also scorns the paltry gifts Mephisto is able to offer on earth.
He knows that any fulfilment of his striving is forever denied
to him, but also knows that he can never cease to strive. Life is
his task and his despair:

> *That yonder irks me not at all,*
> *First let this world in ruins fall,*
> *The other may then have its day.*
> *'Tis from this earth that all my joys are born,*
> *This sun it is that lights me when I mourn:*
> *From them if I can once be torn,*
> *Then come what will or may,*
> *I am not anxious, I to hear*
> *If in the future we shall hate and love:*
> *Or whether in that other sphere*
> *Exists an " under " and " above."*
> *What can you give, poor devil, then?*
> *Could beings such as you surmise*
> *What yearnings move the souls of men?*

So all Faust can offer instead of a serious pact is a contemptuous
I dare:

> *If ever slothful limbs I stretch at ease*
> *On downy couch, be that the end!*
> *If thou with flattery so canst ply me,*
> *That pleasing to myself I be,*
> *Or with indulgence satisfy me,*
> *Then be that day the last for me,*
> *This bet I offer. . . .*

In other words, in this paradoxical affirmation of an unconscious
will-to-life, Faust has nothing to gain from his bet: if he should
lose and be contented, his life is over; if he should win, his misery
will continue. His only gain would be the confirmation that he
is right, that the devil is not only stupid in that he is never able
to grasp man's *real* nature, but that he is also powerless. This
is tantamount to saying that evil and hence the devil is non-
existent, that nothing can divert Faust from following the course

of eternal striving. So sure is he of his everlasting dissatisfaction that he can top his assertion with these hyperbolic words:

> *When to the moment I shall say:*
> *Linger a while, thou art so fair!*
> *Bind me in fetters fast that day,*
> *Then e'en perdition I will dare.*

Mephisto accepts the pact, although Faust's first demand seems quite ridiculous to him; namely that he, Faust, expects with the help of magic to gain at least the sum total of all human experience.

> *I'll sound the heights and depths that man could know,*
> *Their very souls shall be with mine entwined,*
> *I'll load my bosom with their weal and woe,*
> *And share with them the shipwreck of mankind.*

Thus the stakes are laid down. The game may commence. Mephisto loses the first round; for at a vulgar academic drinking bout, Faust remains a disgusted spectator. The devil suspects that the aged professor needs a rejuvenation and leads him to the witch's kitchen to decrease his age by thirty years through a magic potion.

> *A dose like that within your guts, my boy,*
> *And every other wench is Helen of Troy,*

Mephisto ventures to prophesy as Faust lingers at the sight of a naked beauty in the magic mirror of the witch. It is to prepare him for the temptation of sex, the most fundamental experience man shares with all forms of life. But man differs from all other creatures in this: while they mature toward and end in the process of procreation, his experience and growth are twofold: physical and spiritual. The former is sexus, the urge to satisfy his desire to procreation, which, however, partakes, *qua natura*, of the sanctity of life. The other is Eros, the great god of creation, in whose flame man's soul is purged and lifted into a loftier sphere of being. But the cunning of nature makes use of the animal side of man to lure him into this fire in which his alloy is tested.

Mephisto, the nihilist, knows only of sex; in Faust's soul, earthly and divine nature are at war with each other.

With the skill of the master, Goethe now fuses the *Urfaust* tragedy of the Frankfurt servant girl with his new conception of the drama. Faust, the restless breaker of all bounds, whose mind has plumbed all depths of thought and set out to storm through the world of human experience, is arrested in his course by the love of a simple, plantlike, genuine, and (in her own compass of life) perfect being. Seldom has a poet used less artifice in conveying to us the touchingly virgin nature of an unfolding love as in that scene in the Garden of Gretchen's neighbor, where she begins:

MARGARET: *Yes, out of sight is out of mind, they say!*
To you politeness comes so easily:
But then, you've many friends, and they
Are all far cleverer than me!

FAUST: *Believe me, love, what men call clever*
Is mostly empty show—

MARGARET: *How may that be?*

FAUST: *Alas! that innocence and candor never*
Should know themselves and their own worth!
That meekness and humility,
The richest dower of bounteous Mother Earth—

MARGARET: *If you but for a moment, think of me,*
Through many a weary hour I'll think of you!

FAUST: *Then you are much alone?*

MARGARET: *Yes, though our household's but a little one,*
The work is still to do;
We have no maid: and I must keep all nice,
Must sew and knit and cook and toil the livelong day:
My mother is in every way
So careful and precise.
Not that she needs to pare things down:
We're not as pinched as many are:
My father left us well provided for,

A cottage and a garden by the town:
But now my days are still as anything!
My brother 's soldiering,
My little sister 's dead.
While yet she lived she gave me trouble enough,
But still I never wished to throw the burden off,
So dear she was to me!

FAUST: *An angel if like you!*

MARGARET: *My father died before she came:*
My mother was at death's door too:
Yet she got well: but never was the same,
Nor could she hope to feed the little one;
And thus I came to nurse it quite alone
On milk and water till it seemed my own:
Upon my lap, my arm it lay:
Sprawled, laughed and grew from day to day.

FAUST: *Life's purest joy, believe me, has been yours!*

MARGARET: *Yes, but I also had my anxious hours!*
By night its little cradle lay
Close to my bed: it scarce could move, but I
Awoke straightway.
First I would give it food, then let it lie
Beside me: then to check its crying fit,
I'd rise, and walk about and dandle it;
Then dawn would see me at the washing-trough,
Or busy with the fires or setting off
To market: so it went from rise to set!
No easy life nor always cheerful, Sir,
Yet sleep and food taste all the pleasanter.

.   .   .   .

FAUST: *Have you forgiven me*
My wanton act, my rash intrusion,
When I delayed you at the minster door?

MARGARET: *In truth Sir, I was all confusion.*
For no such thing had happed to me before.
No person e'er spoke ill of me:
Was it, I asked myself, that he could see

In my behavior aught unmannerly,
Unmaiden-like? He seemed to take for granted
So light a wench would give him all he wanted.
Yet in my heart a feeling grew
That seemed to plead your cause with me.
I was right angry, I confess,
That I could not be angrier with you.

Faust recognizes that her existence *is* and deserves purest human happiness in the fulfilment of her destiny as a loving woman, that he " the monster without goal and rest, who like a cataract from rock to rock roars foaming to the abyss " can only crush her in his plunge. Eros bids him flee, sexus Mephisto drives him on and triumphs. Her mother, her brother are destroyed. Gretchen herself, abandoned, kills her new-born child in a fit of insanity and is thrown into prison. But she submits to human justice rather than to be torn from prison by Faust and his hellish companion—and for this attains Heaven's forgiveness. Faust's better soul emerges, when through the memory of her pure love he rushes from the carnal debauchery of the witches' Sabbath into which Mephisto has plunged him. Under the burden of his guilt he curses the day on which he was born.

We come to the Second Part of *Faust*, which is by no means a book with seven seals, as people often seem to think. It is in many ways even easier to understand than the first part, in which a tense and swift dramatic action is condensed.

Faust is now about thirty years old. Thus seven decades of his life, with new aspirations and failures, are still to be dealt with, for he dies a centenarian; hence it is clear that Goethe's technique of presentation must undergo a radical change, especially since the action is to encompass the whole world as a stage. No longer can the dramatist be principally concerned with realistic happenings, but instead he presents us with a typifying, general, symbolic picture of human life, sometimes abbreviated in lyric scenes, sometimes expanded into grand and pageant-like *revues* of aspects of society, of history, of human institutions. We see the *content* of experience rather than the *experiencer*; Faust acted upon rather than acting; and we often ask ourselves, is it Faust or is it humanity as a whole which is presented here as the protagonist, whose life and evolution we view in these broad panoramas on the stage?

The very first scene of the second part gives us a clear example of such a symbolic device, a lyrical and operatic picture, in which Ariel and kind spirits of nature sing of their endeavors to revive the horror-stricken hero, in appeasing the furious conflict of his heart, healing the wounds of his remorse, and bathing him in waters of forgetfulness, so that at the rising of a new sun he can face life with a vigorous resolution, which he voices in a beautiful monologue.

No longer will he attempt to view the absolute, the transcendental (symbolized by the sun), but strive to recognize the divine in its reflection, in ever-changing life itself:

> *Behind me therefore let the sun be blazing.*
> *The cataract in gorges deeply riven*
> *I view with growing rapture and amazing.*
> *To plunge on plunge in thousand streams 'tis given,*
> *And yet a thousand, downward to the valleys,*
> *While foam and mist high in the air are driven.*
> *Yet how superbly o'er this tumult sallies*
> *The many-colored rainbow's changeful being;*
> *Now lost in air, now clearly drawn, it dallies,*
> *Shedding a fragrant coolness e'er when fleeing.*
> *The* rainbow *mirrors human aims and action.*
> *Think and more clearly will you comprehend it:*
> *We* have *life in light's colorful refraction.*

Faust now enters the great world of politics. At the court of the Empire, where feudalism is declining and the state in full decay, he fills the treasury by inventing paper money. The resulting ease and luxury engender the wish for extraordinary entertainment, and he is requested by the emperor to exorcise the spirit of the most beautiful woman, Helen of Troy. Magic alone can span millenia, but magic of a special sort, the magic of man's mind. Mephisto can only advise in this matter; Faust's genius alone can execute the awesome task of descending to the arch-mothers, custodians of all forms of creation, there to seek that famous image of womanly beauty and to spirit her before the spectators at the court. But when she appears here, she is but a shadow, a form of past life, which, however, through her physical perfection so kindles the passion of Faust, that he wishes to possess her; a vain attempt in which he almost loses his life through his own sorcery; for ideals cannot be possessed by force.

(Just as we here envisage only the idea of Goethe's work, and could really experience it, make it our own [to introduce an approximate comparison] only by giving ourselves over to an actual performance of it, so Faust has to submerge himself in Greek antiquity, re-live the ages which produced the ideal that has remained the symbol of highest beauty in the soul of humanity to our day, and without which—whether we are conscious of it or not—we should be lacking a vital part of our cultural heritage, should be reduced to a more primitive stage of our human development.)

Faust's attempt to take physical possession of Helen's shade causes an explosion that nearly cost him his life. Mephisto then takes him back to his old study. Chance has it that here Faust's former famulus believes that success has finally crowned his long labors to produce a human being chemically in a test tube. It may only be due to Mephisto's magic help that Homunculus (i. e. the little man) is born, a mere spirit without a body, able to exist only in the glass vial. The introduction of Homunculus is a magnificent dramatic device; for Homunculus, mere spirit, and therefore gifted with superhuman knowledge, in his striving to obtain a body, to really become, constitutes a contrast to Faust, who would like to possess Homunculus' unlimited vision untrammeled by time and space. But Homunculus is also a parallel to Helena's evolution from spirit to human embodiment. Moreover he furthers the dramatic action in that he, as pure spirit, can see what Faust is dreaming, can perceive the picture of Helena for whom he is longing.

Homunculus now directs Faust and Mephisto to hurry to the

plain of Pharsalus, Greece, where at this moment the Classical *Walpurgisnacht* is being celebrated. On this night all the spirits of Greek mythology, ranging from the most hideous and animal-like forms upward to high physical beauty, griffins, sphinxes, nymphs, sirens, centaurs, and gods of earth and water, assemble on that battlefield of antiquity; for it is the anniversary of the battle between Caesar and Pompey, by which the fate of the Roman Republic was sealed forty-eight years before the birth of Christ. Here in Thessaly, Faust re-experiences the gradual evolution of the Greek ideal of beauty and is now adequately prepared for his meeting with Helen, who is just returning from Troy to her home in Sparta.

An ingenious telescoping of history sets in, somewhat puzzling even in this atmosphere of magic. We ourselves re-live it by descending into mankind's phylogenetic soul, into mankind's *becoming* as remembered growth and development of humanity through the centuries. This is the stuff of which man's soul is made.

Just as Faust has seen mythological figures, which really evolved in time, juxtaposed in space on the plains of Pharsalus, so Helena, the symbol of highest feminine beauty, descends into her memories of gradual *becoming* in the minds of men. Once in prehistoric times a mere object of man's lust and a chattel to be conquered and possessed by him, she now, for the first time in her existence, attains a personality. In Faust, the medieval conqueror of the Greek Peloponnesos and the representative of a knightly court-ship, engendered by the Christian reverence for Mary, the Queen of the Heavens, she meets a suitor who treats her as an equal and asks for the favor of her hand, a favor she alone shall grant.

Their union means the blending of North and South, of modern romantic and ancient classical culture. Its symbol is their son Euphorion ("the one filled with the joy of living"). Euphorion combines in himself the principle of beauty symbolized by his mother with that of eternal striving represented by his father. Hence his deeper significance must be the yearning for a life in

absolute beauty, an ideal which is incompatible with the exigencies
of earthly existence.

Static beauty and dynamic striving are irreconcilable. A
dramatic device like Homunculus, Euphorion symbolizes Faust's
restless onward bent. He rises into the air, a second Ikaros, loses
the firm earth from under his feet and plunges into the void,
drawing his mother with him into the night of Orcus. All that is
left to Faust is the memory of the experience of beauty, which,
however, has increased the stature of his soul and the compass
of his striving to heroic measure.

Mephisto now views the world with him from a high mountain
range and offers him—tempter like Satan of old—the joys of an
Oriental despot, but Faust scornfully replies:

> *Indulgence does debase.*
> *The deed is everything, the glory naught.*

With Mephisto's help he defeats the enemies of his emperor
and receives from him in fief a strip of land along the sea where
he sets out to " limit the bounds of that watery deep, and force
it far away within itself to keep." Here we find him measuring
his strength with that of the element, lord of vast fleets, incurring
new guilt " since war and trade and piracy are just triune and
can't be parted," as Mephisto says, and who should know better
than he, the devil?

Faust's spirit is undaunted as ever, but he is beginning to tire
of magic and wishes he could face his task like any other human
being:

> *Not yet have I won through to liberty.*
> *Could I but magic from my pathway banish*
> *And all its spells unlearn and bid them vanish!*
> *Nature! Stood I before thee as a man alone*
> *It were worth while to be a man, I own.*
> *Such was I ere in darkness I did grope*
> *And wildly cursed myself, the world, and hope.*

Now his hour of greatest trial has come. Four gray spirits
approach his manor, Want, Debt, Distress and Care; while three

of them have no power over the rich and mighty, the fourth, Care, is not so easily deterred and enters through the keyhole. Faust, who has heard the uncanny whispering of these spirits, asks:

Is some one here?

CARE: *The answer must be: Aye!*

FAUST: *Who art thou then?*

CARE: *Here once for all am I.*

FAUST: *Go, get thee hence!*

CARE: *I am where I should be.*
        Hast never care and worry known?

FAUST: *I have but hurried through the world, I own.*
        Every desire as by the hair I seized,
        Relinquished what no longer pleased,
        I've but desired and then achieved each hour,
        Then wished again, and so with mighty power
        Stormed through my life; grandly at first indeed,
        But now, grown wary-wise with measured speed.
        This globe is well within my ken;
        The view beyond is barred to mortal men.
        A fool who yonder turns his blinking eyes
        And deems his like are found above the skies!
        Let him stand fast and look around him here!
        Not to the strong is mute this earthly sphere.
        What need of roaming through eternity?
        Can he not grasp what he doth know and see?
        So let him walk throughout his earthly day,
        Though spirits haunt him, going his own way,
        Let him find pain and bliss as on he stride,
        He! every moment still unsatisfied.

CARE: *Whoso in my toils is caught*
        Finds the world is good for naught;
        Gloom forever round him lies,
        Suns for him nor set nor rise;
        Though his sense be sound and whole
        Darkness dwelleth in his soul;

Of his store of blessedness
Naught he truly can possess;
Good and bad luck turn to whim,
Wealth but hunger means to him;
Be it bliss or be it sorrow,
He defers it til the morrow,
Looking to the future ever
And his goal attaining never.

FAUST: *Unblessèd sprites! Thus ye befool and craze*
Mankind a thousand times with fond illusion,
Emmeshing us in toils of wild confusion.
From demons I can ne'er break free, I know,
But though the strong spiritual bond one may not sever,
Thy might, o Care, great and insidious though
It be, I will acknowledge never! never!

CARE: *Then learn it now; I leave behind*
My curse to be on thee attending.
Throughout their lives are mortals blind;
So, Faustus, be thou too at thy life's ending!
                    (She breathes on him)

FAUST: *(blinded) Night presses round me, deep and deeper still.*
And yet within me beams a radiant light;
What I have planned, I'll hasten to fulfill;
Only the master's word has weight and might.
Up from your couches, vassals, man by man!
Triumphantly show forth what boldly I began.

. . . .

A swamp along the mountain-chain
Which poisons all I have retrieved,
This noisome pool too will I drain;
Then were this last the greatest I've achieved.
For many millions thus I space provide
Where, though not safe, active and free they may abide.
Within, the land shall be a paradise,
Although the flood outside may rage and rise;
Yet, as it gnaws to pierce the sheltering wall,
To stop the gap they hasten one and all.

> *Ay! from this maxim I will never swerve,*
> *The last conclusion still of wisdom true:*
> *He only life and freedom doth deserve*
> *Who day by day must conquer them anew.*
> *And so, by danger girt, shall childhood here,*
> *Manhood and age pass many a strenuous year.*
> *Such busy throngs I fain would see,*
> *On free soil standing with a people free.*
> *Then to the moment might I say:*
> *" Linger a while, thou art so fair! "*
> *For so the traces of my earthly day,*
> *Though aeons roll, can perish ne'er.*
> *In the presentiment of such high bliss*
> *I now enjoy the highest moment, this!*
> > *(Faust falls back, dead)*

MEPHISTO: *Him can not pleasures sate, no bliss suffice:*
> *Fast shifting shapes forever him entice.*
> *The poorest moment, emptiest and last*
> *The poor wretch wished to hold it fast.*
> *Who me so stoutly did withstand,*
> *Time conquers him—Here lies the old man in the sand.*
> ·
> *So it is past. What therefore can one glean?*
> *It is the same as had it never been*
> *And yet whirls on as if 'twere not destroyed.*
> *I'd choose instead the everlasting void.*

And here we must ask who has won the wager? It has been argued that Faust does not say the fatal words to the moment: " linger a while, thou art so fair," but only foresees the time when he *might* say so. Yet there can be no doubt that he has revoked his curse upon life and has given assent to life as it is. On the other hand, the devil may sneer at him for prolonging this moment, the poorest and emptiest of all (for in his blindness Faust mistook the sound of spade and pick which were digging his grave for that of the work on his reclamation project), yet Mephisto cannot claim to have " seduced his soul from his true

source " nor " dragged him down with him in fatal hour and
wholly bent him to his force."

Neither Faust nor Mephistopheles foresaw the course of events.
The Lord alone was right in His predictions; and He may now
send His angels, who carry Faust's immortal parts upwards
through the vast heavenly realms. In their journey upwards
these immortal remains become purified through further striving
and transformation until " una poenitentium, formerly called
Gretchen," may lead him to higher spheres. Here all-pervading
celestial love, " the ever womanly," bestows on him the grace
of the Highest, which alone hallows all who have fallen short of
the glory of God. The Chorus Mysticus concludes:

> *Things that are transient*
> *As symbolic appear;*
> *All imperfection*
> *Is perfected here;*
> *That which no tongue can tell,*
> *Here it is done;*
> *The ever womanly*
> *Leadeth us on.*

XI

Crime and Punishment

N. BRYLLION FAGIN

NINETEENTH-CENTURY Russia contributed to the literary world three novelists of magnificent stature: Turgenev, Dostoyevsky, and Tolstoy. Of these three Dostoyevsky is the most original. Turgenev and Tolstoy, great as they are—each in his own way—fit into the main stream of European literature; Dostoyevsky does not. He is more complex as a personality and more distinctive as an artist. He is by all odds less even, less disciplined, less polished, and more difficult to understand, to account for, and to evaluate. He is a phenomenon in both Russian and world literature: erratic, contradictory, yet searingly memorable.

Fyodor Mikhailovich Dostoyevsky was born in Moscow in 1821, the son of an army surgeon who was a dipsomaniac, a violent, tyrannous and suspicious husband, and a cruel father. He was so despotic a master that his own peasants killed him by smothering him with cushions. Fyodor's elder brother, Mikhail, died of an unspeakable disease; his younger brother, Nikolai, inherited his father's dipsomania; his sister Barbara accumulated a great deal of wealth but was murdered for her miserliness. There can be no question that in *The Brothers Karamazov* Dostoyevsky recalled his own family: old Fyodor Karamazov is certainly reminiscent of what we know of the author's father, and Ivan is a portrait of the author himself.

Dostoyevsky's childhood was harsh and unhappy. Yet he managed to secure a good education. He attended private schools, learned French, studied philosophy, and entered a school of engineering. Upon graduation in 1843, he received a commission in the army. But he found army life boring. He preferred the more carefree though uncertain life of literary Bohemia. His natural instability manifested itself early; he was childishly extravagant, a passionate gambler, incalculably moody, shy and arrogant by turns, and either excessively gay or excessively sad. His health was equally uncertain. He suffered from epilepsy and insomnia; yet he was a prodigious worker, often writing all night.

He began his literary labors by translating Balzac's *Eugénie Grandet*, but after meeting Turgenev, who was three years older, he decided to attempt a novel of his own. Although he was steeped in Romanticism—having devoured the works of Schiller and Byron—he began as a Realist. *Poor Folk*, his first novel, was published in Nekrasov's *Petersburg Almanac* in 1846, when he was twenty-five years old. The story is told that when Nekrasov, who—although of the same age as Dostoyevsky—was already a well-known poet, first received the manuscript he and his friend the novelist Grigorovitch sat up most of the night to finish reading it and, at 4 A. M., rushed to Dostoyevsky's home to kiss him. Even before its publication the book was hailed by the great critic Belinsky who, on the strength of it, solemnly announced to the public the birth of a great Russian writer. *Poor Folk* struck the key of Dostoyevsky's characteristic melody; it indicated the milieu in which he was to labor so tirelessly and superlatively all his life. He was to become, unlike Turgenev, not the novelist of landed gentry and quiet country life, but a transcriber of city streets, of dark brooding rooms, of anguish and despair, of the secrets and terrors of life. Twenty years later, in 1866, he was to achieve his deepest expression of the fetid life of the city in *Crime and Punishment*.

But first it is necessary to return for a little while to Dostoyevsky's own life. Biography, which is often a digression in literary criticism, is, in the case of a writer like Dostoyevsky, highly relevant and illuminating. There is so much of the man himself in his work, of his own experiences, travails, humiliations, and spiritual defeats and victories, that to ignore his biography would be to lose a valuable source of understanding.

In those early years, for instance, at the beginning of his
literary career, he felt impelled to join a group of young revolu-
lutionists known in Russian history as the Petrashevsky Circle.
Dostoyevsky himself was not a revolutionist, but his compassion
for the poor and the downtrodden attracted him to the meetings
of this group of intellectuals who seemed to be inspired by a love
of the Russian masses to seek a program for their redemption.
One early morning in April, 1849, Dostoyevsky was arrested and
taken to the Fortress of Peter and Paul where he was kept for
eight months. He was then tried and condemned to death and,
together with twenty other men, was led to a windswept square
to be shot. A platoon of soldiers with loaded rifles was already
deployed for the execution when a messenger arrived with a
commutation of the sentence. The whole proceeding, it seems, had
been intended by the Emperor as a forceful lesson to the young
revolutionaries. But, in the meantime, one of the men went mad
and another developed tuberculosis.

Dostoyevsky never forgot the lesson. Many years later, in
his novel *The Idiot*, he described vividly the terrors of a man
waiting for execution. He had turned his terrible ordeal into an
asset for his art. Perhaps another asset should be mentioned:
during the eight months of his imprisonment in the Fortress
he kept himself from going insane by reading the Bible and
Shakespeare.

His sentence was commuted to four years penal servitude in
the mines of Siberia, to be followed by four years of service in
the army as a common soldier. The horrors of his Siberian experiences are depicted in his *Memoirs from the House of Death*. It
was in Siberia that his epileptic fits became frequent tortures, and
to them was added the wracking pain of rheumatism.

It was also in Siberia, after his release from the mines, that he
married his first wife, the widow Issayeva, only to discover that
she had a lover and had no intention of relinquishing him after
her marriage. Upon discharge from the army, where he had risen
to the rank of a non-commissioned officer, he returned to Petersburg, alone, and threw himself into literary activity. He published

short stories, a minor novel, his *Memoirs from the House of Death*, and, together with his brother Mikhail, edited a magazine, *The Times*.

Then he fell in love again, this time with a girl named Apollinaria Suslova. She was an " eternal student," a revolutionary who sang the " Marseillaise," and believed in free love. She made all the overtures and begged Dostoyevsky to follow her to Paris. He agreed, but by the time he reached her two weeks had elapsed and she was now in love with a Frenchman. Dostoyevsky went to London, alone. Some years later she wrote to him that she was free again, her lover having proved unfaithful, and begged him to come to her. Should he refuse she threatened to commit suicide. He went to her and took her with him to Germany. She no doubt taught him many things about the emotion of love-hate. We have an authentic description of that emotion in Dostoyevsky's story " The Gambler." " Mlle Suslova," says the noted historian of Russian literature, D. S. Mirsky, " was a proud and . . . ' infernal ' woman, with unknown depths of cruelty and of evil. She seems to have been to Dostoyevsky an important revelation of the dark side of things."

His wife died in 1865, but not before she called him to Moscow and told him the details of her life with her lover and subjected him to other humiliations, not the least of which was her contemptuous reference to him as a " convict," a " miserable convict." The next year his brother Mikhail died, leaving to Dostoyevsky the payment of his debts and the support of his illegitimate children.

It was during that same year of 1866 that *Crime and Punishment* appeared, first serially in a magazine, and then in book form. Its success should have alleviated his financial burdens, but Dostoyevsky, being impractical in business matters, had sold the copyright of all his works for a pitifully small sum to an unscrupulous publisher. He was equally impractical in his dealings with his relatives, many of whom sponged upon him all his life.

The year after the publication of *Crime and Punishment* he married Anna Grigorievna Snitkin, a young girl whom he had engaged as stenographer-secretary. They went to live in Germany in order to escape his creditors, but he found the roulette table in Baden-Baden, and later in Geneva, beyond his power to resist and his poverty was greater than ever before. Sometimes when he won he bought for his young wife everything he saw, but the very next day he sold everything, pawned his watch and his wife's earrings, borrowed small sums—all he could get—from Turgenev and other friends and acquaintances, and lost it all.

Yet his married life was a happy one. Anna Grigorievna, twenty-six years younger than her husband, was a sensible, practical woman. She loved and understood him, watched over him, knew his weaknesses and helped him fight them, and worshipped his genius. By 1871 they were able to return to Russia, where Dostoyevsky resumed his place among the creative spirits of his generation. He died twenty years later, at the age of sixty, and was followed to his grave by an estimated populace of 40,000.

It is futile to inquire which is his greatest novel: *Crime and Punishment, The Idiot, The Brothers Karamazov,* or (in the opinion of at least one first-rate critic) *The Possessed.* All are the work of an artist of profound sensibility, of a fictive talent for which there is no other word than genius. *Crime and Punishment* will serve admirably to focus our attention upon those characteristics which are responsible for the power and overwhelming impression of a Dostoyevsky novel.

It is not wise to assume that the American reading public generally is familiar with *Crime and Punishment,* or, for that matter, with any of Dostoyevsky's novels. The pressure to read contemporary fiction—the numerous " masterpieces " hailed by book review supplements every Sunday—is formidable. The Dostoyevskys can wait. Which in truth they can. *Crime and Punishment* is as fresh today, as " timely," and as illuminating of man's life on earth, as when it first appeared under the title of *Rodion Raskolnikov* in the St. Petersburg literary journal *Russky Viestnik* in 1866.

It is difficult to indicate the mere story of this great novel, the plot, the sequence of incidents in the lives of a group of characters. A good novel can no more be abstracted or paraphrased than a good poem or a good play. A synopsis of *Hamlet* or *King Lear* discloses only the bare skeleton on which Shakespeare's tragedy is built. The wealth of detail and character perception and the pulse of life which the pages of *Crime and Punishment* contain can only be apprehended by a reading of the work itself. Yet an attempt to convey some idea of the story must be made.

A young law student, Rodion Raskolnikov, harassed by poverty, conceives the idea of committing a murder. He has been obliged to withdraw from the university, he is half starved, and he has pawned everything valuable he possessed, including the keepsakes given him by his mother and sister, who are living somewhere in the provinces, living meanly but hopeful that some day Rodion will graduate, make a name for himself, and redeem the family's fortunes. The mother has a small government pension and the sister is employed as a governess in the home of an upper middle-class family named Svidrigailov. The person Rodion has decided to murder is an old woman, a pawnbroker who has received his pledges and given him trifling sums for them. She is, he rationalizes, " a silly, flint-hearted, evil-minded, sulky old woman, necessary to no one." He plans the murder carefully and executes his plan, but he finds himself under the necessity of killing the woman's half-sister Lizaveta, an inoffensive younger woman whom he had no intention of killing. His deed fills him with horror and loathing and he is unable to profit from it. He grabs a few trinkets and a purse with money and makes his escape. He buries his loot under a stone in somebody's yard, then buries himself in his lodgings and is sick of a fever.

Just before the murder he made friends with an alcoholic named Marmeladov, a discharged government clerk—" titular counselor " is Marmeladov's own flattering description of himself—who laid bare to him his mind, his heart, and his life history. He had married, for the second time, an intelligent, well-educated, handsome woman, with three young children. But his weakness for drink lost him his position and the family was reduced to rags and starvation. His wife, Katerina Ivanovna, had contracted tuberculosis and had turned into a scolding, bitter woman. And finally his own young daughter by a previous marriage, Sonia, had taken to the streets to support the family. Dostoyevsky himself must be permitted to tell when and how it happened the first time, or rather Dostoyevsky's Marmeladov must be permitted to tell it:

. . . Katerina Ivanovna [was] walking up and down and wringing her hands, her cheeks flushed red, as they always are in that disease: "Here you live with us," she says, "you eat and drink and are kept warm and you do nothing to help." . . . I heard my Sonia speaking (she is a gentle creature with a soft little voice . . . fair hair and such a pale, thin little face). She said: "Katerina Ivanovna, am I really to do a thing like that?" . . . "And why not?" said Katerina Ivanovna with a jeer, "you are something mighty precious to be so careful of!" But don't blame her, . . . honoured sir, don't blame her! She was not herself when she spoke, but driven to distraction by her illness and the crying of the hungry children; and it was said more to wound her than anything else. . . . At six o'clock I saw Sonia get up, put on her kerchief and her cape, and go out of the room and about nine o'clock she came back. She walked straight up to Katerina Ivanovna and she laid thirty roubles on the table before her in silence. She did not utter a word, she did not even look at her, she simply picked up our big green . . . shawl . . . , put it over her head and face and lay down on the bed with her face to the wall; only her little shoulders and her body kept shuddering . . . . And then I saw, young man, I saw Katerina Ivanovna, in the same silence go up to Sonia's little bed; she was on her knees all the evening kissing Sonia's feet, and would not get up, and then they both fell asleep in each other's arms . . . . together, together . . . yes . . . and I . . . lay drunk.[1]

In the phantasmagoric days that follow the murder, Raskolnikov runs into Marmeladov again, is present at his death after Marmeladov had been run over in the street, and helps to arrange his funeral. Sonia looks upon him as an angel of mercy and,

[1] The Modern Library edition. Translation by Constance Garnett.

though she grows to love him, dares to worship him only silently and from afar. When Raskolnikov's mother and sister Dounia arrive, brought to Petersburg by Dounia's wealthy suitor Luzhin, he introduces Sonia to them and makes her sit down in their presence, as though she were a pure, respectable, and respected woman. In the end it is to Sonia that he unburdens himself of his guilt and she does not fail him: she responds with pity and terror and helps him to purge himself. " Go at once," she tells him, " this very minute, stand at the crossroads, bow down, first kiss the earth which you have defiled and then bow down to all the world and say to all men aloud, ' I am a murderer! ' Then God will send you life again."

And this is what he actually does, in time. He also goes to the police station and gives himself up to Porfiry Petrovitch, the investigator who has suspected Raskolnikov's guilt all along but being unable to prove it has bided his time and contributed to Raskolnikov's deterioration by occasional psychological probings. Porfiry Petrovitch is, incidentally, the first criminal investigator in literature to employ the methods of modern psychology in the solution of crime. M. Dupin, the French detective in Edgar Allan Poe's short stories of ratiocination, anticipated Porfiry, but Poe's character is purely mental, cold and bloodless, like a calculating machine; Dostoyevsky's investigator is a vivid personality —like all of Dostoyevsky's characters—and is fully as memorable as a person as he is as an investigator. Incidentally, also, Dostoyevsky was aware of Poe's work and was generous in praise of him. " He . . . places," he once wrote, " his hero in a most extraordinary outward or psychological situation, and, then, describes the inner state of that person with marvellous acumen and amazing realism."

But to proceed with the story. Raskolnikov is sentenced to eight years in Siberia and Sonia follows him. For some time he is sullen and apathetic, heartily disliked by the other convicts, thieves and murderers from whom he recoils in horror. He is cold to Sonia, who hovers in the distance, and accepts her love and ministrations without gratitude or even interest. She in the meantime has become a welcome visitor to the prison yard. The prisoners all take their hats off to her and call her " Little mother, Sofya Semyonovna." And then a day comes when. . . . But again it seems best to let Dostoyevsky tell it in his own inimitable way:

They were alone. . . . The guard had turned away for the time.

How it happened he did not know. But all at once something seemed to seize him and fling him at her feet. He wept and threw his arms round her knees. For the first instant she was terribly frightened and she turned pale. She jumped up and looked at him trembling. But at the same moment she understood, and a light of infinite happiness came into her eyes. She knew and had no doubt that he loved her beyond everything and that at last the moment had come. . . .

They wanted to speak, but could not; tears stood in their eyes. They were both pale and thin; but those sick pale faces were bright with the dawn of a new future, of a full resurrection into a new life.

On this note of resurrection the novel ends. Like Dickens, Dostoyevsky thought it necessary to wind up the story of every character in the book. Dounia marries Razumikhin, Raskolnikov's fellow-student and best friend, and she helps her husband establish a prosperous publishing house. Svidrigailov, the strange, dandified, lustful man in whose house she had worked and who had persecuted her with his love, commits suicide. Katerina Ivanova dies and her children are taken care of. But enough of mere plot. I am afraid that this retelling of the bare bones of the story can only prove misleading and unfair to a superb story-teller and great artist.

For what Dostoyevsky has created is a whole world, at once imaginative and real. Into it he poured all of himself, his almost supernatural understanding of his fellowmen, of their broodings and dreams, their sins and cruelties, their saintlinesses and generosities. His novel has the lurid melodrama of life itself, and its deepest tragedy; it is raw and bitter; but it is also tender and invigorating. It is intensely Russian, with the authentic reek and smell of the streets, the taverns, the dank lodging-houses, police-stations, and prisons of St. Petersburg; but it is also universal, full of the faces, voices, and idioms which we recognize in all the cities and alleys of the world.

Except on a superficial level, this is not a murder story at all. It can, of course, be read on this superficial level, and it holds up beautifully as a tale of crime, although the murder is committed early in the book by the man through whose point of view the story is told, and therefore the usual suspense as to who is the murderer is completely lacking. Nor is there much suspense in guessing how soon and in what manner Raskolnikov will be detected. For the process of his cracking up begins immediately and he gives himself away long before Porfiry Petrovitch confronts him with the accusation. The suspense lies deeper and is of a higher order. It is imbedded in two other levels, the psychological and the moral. These are related in cause and effect, in supplying motivation for the crime and the disintegration and redemption of personality.

Psychologically, Raskolnikov is an introspective, intellectually confused and emotionally unstable person. He is not clear either about the purpose of his crime nor about the dark forces that impel him to it. At one time he thinks that it was his need of money, his poverty, his inability to proceed with his education, and the deprivations of his family that impel him to kill the useless old woman. But, much later, when he confesses to Sonia, he realizes that it was desire for power, power which is " only vouchsafed to the man who dares to stoop to pick it up." " I wanted to become a Napoleon," he says, " that's why I killed her." Perhaps it was not even power, in the conventional sense of sway over other people. All he wanted, he admits a little later, was " to have the daring. . . ." " That," he summarizes, " was the whole cause of it."

Morally, or perhaps I should say spiritually, Raskolnikov embodies the duality of man who is torn between evil and good, arrogance of intellect and kindliness of nature, lawlessness and religion. In one sense, Dostoyevsky, although an intellectual himself, was anti-intellectual. He saw the pitfalls of rationalization, of overweening pride which outrages the dignity of simple

nature, of mind excluding the promptings and acceptances of
the heart. The student, the dry casuist, shouted down his own
intuitive perception of the dignity and sanctity of human life;
he overlooked both the categorical imperative and the sixth
commandment. It is only after his suffering had begun, his long
ordeal of expiation, of the education of his heart, that he understood the value of life.

"Where is it," thought Raskolnikov. "Where is it I've read
that some one condemned to death says or thinks, an hour before
his death, that if he had to live on some high rock, on such a narrow
ledge that he'd only room to stand, and the ocean, everlasting
darkness, everlasting solitude, everlasting tempest around him,
if he had to remain standing on a square yard of space all his
life, a thousand years, eternity, it were better to live so than to
die at once! Only to live, to live and live! Life, whatever it may
be! . . . How true it is! Good God, how true!" Yet even with this
new understanding of the value of life his pride of intellect is
not conquered. A few hundred pages later it flares up to exclaim,
"I've only killed a louse, Sonia, a useless, loathsome, harmful
creature." But Sonia, with her simplicity of heart, corrects him:
"A human being."

One of our own writers, Nathaniel Hawthorne, once wrote a
short story called "Ethan Brand." In it, a New England lime-
burner returns from a journey of eighteen years which had taken
him throughout the world on a strange search. He had been
searching for the Unpardonable Sin and had come back defeated
because he had found it. It was not out there in the great world,
in alien lands, in far away places, but in his own heart. The
Unpardonable Sin—"the only crime for which Heaven could
afford no mercy"—was, in Hawthorne's words, "the sin of an
intellect that triumphed over the sense of brotherhood with man
and reverence for God." By his arrogance of pride Ethan Brand
had severed the cords that bound him to the human family and
had violated the pattern of relationship which God had established. He made an outcast of himself and condemned himself
"to bleak and terrible loneliness." His heart which should have

been part of the beating heart of humanity " had withered, had
contracted, had hardened, had perished." Now he has nothing
to live for and nothing to live with and he jumps into the fiery
lime kiln. The next morning his successor arrives to clean the
furnace and finds Ethan Brand's heart, the only part of him which
the heat could not burn; it had become marble.

Raskolnikov, too, can be said to have committed the Unpardonable Sin. His mind, his intellect, planned and reasoned, made
distinctions between useful and non-useful individuals, with himself of course belonging to the first category, because, forsooth,
he was an " extraordinary " being; he had a right to live, even
at the cost of depriving another human being, an " ordinary "
person, of her life. There was no recoil from the idea of shedding
a fellow-mortal's blood; no sympathy for another's terror and
pain. The heart was dead. For just as Emerson envisaged an
Oversoul animating everything in the universe with divinity, we
may envisage an Overheart which imparts its rhythm to all living
humanity. By cutting itself off from this common heart of
humanity, by withdrawing from the communal pulse beat, an
individual heart shrivels and dies. It was only later when his
ordeal of suffering had begun that Raskolnikov realized that along
with his killing of the old woman and her sister he had killed a
principle, that in murdering them he had murdered himself, his
own humanity.

If Raskolnikov does not end like Ethan Brand it is because
Dostoyevsky reserves him for a better fate. Having no strain
of Puritan Calvinism within him, Dostoyevsky believed in the
redemptive powers of compassion and love. Sonia, the pure little
Magdalene, is Raskolnikov's way to redemption. Her compassion
and her love know no bounds and seek no compensation; she is
completely unselfish and without the slightest impulse to cast
stones. Long before the moment of glory in the Siberian prison
yard when he comes to accept her gift of love and thereby is made
whole again, reunited to life, he acquires compassion and feels the
cleansing emotion of humility before suffering and degradation
borne with meek nobility. One can never forget the moment when

Raskolnikov, knowing her story from her drunken father, how she had gone out on the streets and submitted her body to shame and humiliation to appease the hunger of Katerina Ivanovna's crying children—one can never forget the moment when Raskolnikov drops before her to the ground and kisses her feet. When she protests in anguish and perplexity, he exclaims, " I did not bow down to you, I bowed down to all the suffering of humanity." It comes like a flash of revelation; it is an impulse to adoration and a profession of utter self-abnegation. Few scenes in the whole body of fiction can equal the electrifying effect of that moment.

Raskolnikov is finally redeemed when he learns, like Sonia, simply to feel. It is then that—Dostoyevsky tells us—" Life had stepped into the place of theory." And it is then that Raskolnikov picks up the New Testament she had given him and turns to the story of the raising of Lazarus from the dead.

The man who is not redeemed, who is permitted to end in suicide, is Svidrigailov, whose only sin was that of lechery. Before he dies he reviews his life in his mind. " It's queer and funny," he says, " I never had a great hatred for any one, I never particularly desired to revenge myself even. . . . I never liked quarrelling either, and never lost my temper—that's a bad sign too." Yes, that is a bad sign. He deserves no redemption because he has not been great enough to sin greatly. Like Ibsen's Peer Gynt he has earned neither Heaven nor Hell, only the Button Moulder with his ladle to collect his remains for recasting. Redemption can only come through intense participation in life, involving great temptation, the capacity for great sin and great suffering, and the Svidrigailovs, skating on the surface of life, are too negligible to qualify for that. Their relation to humanity is only peripheral and they are contemptible rather than pitiful. They are dismissible.

But only from Dostoyevsky's book of life. To the novel, as a work of art, they are indispensable. Svidrigailov is one of the finest creations. And so is Luzhin, that self-absorbed, self-valuating, calculating peacock. Both of these negligible people, who generally play such important roles in life, are done in the round, like all of Dostoyevsky's characters. They are carefully observed and delineated. Every man, woman, and child that enters the picture of his action is captured fully and completely, not because they are needed but because for Dostoyevsky all people are infinitely interesting, infinitely important, and deserve to be portrayed, nay, must be portrayed with justice.

His description of the Svidrigailovs and the Luzhins raises the interesting question of Dostoyevsky's hardness toward them. He who was the most compassionate of writers has no glint of compassion toward them, only cold contempt. One is tempted to find in this phenomenon support for André Gide's theory that Dostoyevsky is suffering from humiliation rather than blessed with humility. This of course overlooks for the moment the perpetual duality of Dostoyevsky, the perpetual conflict within him between the memories of the indignities he may have suffered at the hands of the Luzhins and his impulse toward Christian forgiveness. This conflict is always there and supplies much of the tension that any novel of his has. It is psychological tension, which redeems much of the physical melodrama with which his novels are also full.

We must not ignore the weaknesses and the contradictions of Dostoyevsky. But what matters, in the final reckoning, is the wealth of his visions. Fyodor Dostoyevsky is one great novelist who has been able to strike off fiery lyrics out of the agonized chaos of existence. The riddle of life—with which all genuine literature, and Russian literature especially, is saturated—has through his pen become transmuted and ennobled. He has gone down to the darkest places, into the obscurest nooks of mind and matter, of impulse and urge, of vice and sublimity, and out of it all he has woven a passionate symphony, hard and irregular, rising to heights of intense terror and tenderness. Dostoyevsky is often crude, melodramatic, lurid, but never cold, and always the supreme psychologist, the prober of the obscure, the impassioned analyst of revolting forces that " normal " people are pleased to call " pathological." It is not surprising that Nietzsche should have paid him the supreme tribute of saying: " Dostoyevsky was the only psychologist from whom I had anything to learn: he belongs to the happiest windfalls of my life."

Dostoyevsky is not pleasant reading. His novels have little polish. They are morbid and harrowing. There is blood in them, and tears, and a hurricane of emotions. He writes of extreme suffering which brutalizes, but which also makes men gentle, keen, forgiving. The sympathy for the oppressed and disinherited of the earth that Dostoyevsky felt did not spring from mere good nature. He was spawned in the dirt, he lived with his " Poor People " and " The Possessed," and he came up from the " Underground " and " The House of Death." And he knew as no one else that the spirit of man is nowhere as virile as in the misery and the dirt, seeking its God, helplessly stretching itself toward the light. Among the sick and tortured, the harlots and the murderers and the drunkards he found truth, love, and brotherhood. Their suffering lifted them above the pretensions and the simulations, the pettinesses and snobberies of the balanced and happy. They debauch and they drink, but they know their unworthiness. They are humble before their God and their conscience. And in this humbleness lies their redemption. Dostoyevsky's pen was clumsy and grim and nude—like life itself— like the soul of his sublime " Idiot "!

XII

The Works of Balzac

HENRY CARRINGTON LANCASTER

W HEN Balzac is mentioned, one thinks of a long shelf of books, containing nearly a hundred novels and tales; or of Rodin's statue, square, squat, and powerful; or of the labors of scholars and collectors, such as Lovenjoul, the Belgian nobleman who spent much of his life collecting Balzac documents, and Mr. Royce in this country, who has assembled a vast amount of printed material concerned with Balzac; or the work of scholars like Marcel Bouteron in France, or my old friend Preston Dargan and the students he gathered about him at the University of Chicago. For Balzac, after attracting journalists, critics, and lecturers, has become a fruitful field for Ph. D. dissertations, not only in Chicago, but in Paris—dissertations devoted to his life, to the development of his art, to his reappearing characters, to his political and social ideas, etc.

The public may well ask what manner of man he was and why he roused so much interest that we celebrate his centennial here in America.

Honoré Balzac was born at Tours on May 20, 1799. His father came from southern France and belonged to a family of no special distinction except that his youngest brother, implicated in a murder, was guillotined. Balzac's father was a civil servant. His mother was the daughter of a cloth merchant who had become an agent of the quartermaster's department in the armies of the Republic and of the Empire.

Honoré was sent to various schools, where he failed to distinguish himself, then studied law and attended lectures at the

Sorbonne. One gathers that he spent much of his time in extensive reading. Like his mother, he was attracted by the mysticism of Swedenborg. He was also influenced by Mesmer. As he was filled with the ambition to write, his family allowed him to try his luck for a year in a garret, no. 9, rue Lesdiguières, near the Arsenal Library. He has described his life there at the beginning of one of his stories:

Love of knowledge placed me in a mansard, where I worked at night and passed the day in a neighboring library. I lived frugally, accepting all the conditions of a monastic life. One passion alone took me from my studies . . . I went to observe the manners and customs of the quarter. Since I was as badly dressed as the workmen, they admitted me freely to their groups. . . . When, between eleven o'clock and midnight, I would meet a workman and his wife returning from the theater, I would follow them and listen to their talk. First they would discuss the play, then their own affairs, while the mother dragged one of her children by the hand without listening to her complaints or requests. The husband and wife would keep counting the money they were going to receive the next day and planning how they would spend it. Then would come discussions of household affairs, protests over the high cost of potatoes, the length of the winter, the baker's bill, etc. As I listened to them, I made their lives my own, I felt their rags on my back, I walked with my feet in their leaky shoes. Their emotions became mine.

Balzac claims that during this year his chief diversion was entering in this fashion into the lives of others.

He must have gathered experience that was to be of great value to him later on, but he did not at first give much evidence of it. He composed a play called *Cromwell* that was shown to an old and rather successful dramatist, who advised Balzac not to devote his life to literature. When his year was up, he joined his family in their suburb of Paris and then returned with them into the city. There he made a number of acquaintances that proved useful to him both socially and professionally. He composed a number of novels and tales, some of them in collaboration. In 1826–28 he tried his hand at printing and brought out editions of Molière and La Fontaine, but he was soon obliged to give up the business. When he did so, he owed nearly 60,000 francs. His profit lay in knowledge that he had gained in regard to printing, knowledge that he was subsequently to use in his novel, *Lost Illusions*. Perhaps one reason for his failure was the fact that he continued to write. In compensation he brought out the very next year his historical novel, the *Chouans*, which gave him a definite and important position in the world of letters.

The work he produced before the *Chouans* is now little read, but it shows a number of tendencies that were to be subsequently developed. He had read all sorts of novels: introspective novels, sentimental novels, gruesome novels, gay novels. All left their traces in his early work. He had read such different French writers as Chateaubriand and Paul de Koch. He had shuddered over Ann Radcliffe's accounts of ghosts and evil men. He had dipped into Miss Edgeworth's *Tales of Fashionable Life*. He owed something to Cooper. We find him later on comparing the secret signals used by the police of Paris—shops, cabs, a person standing at a window—to those employed by Indians in Cooper's novels—a tree-trunk, a beaver's dam, a rock, a buffalo hide, a motionless canoe. He owed more to Sir Walter Scott, who taught him the art of preparation and gave him an interest in historical novels.

Les Chouans is historical, but it deals with very recent history, more recent for Balzac's readers than was the period dealt with in *Gone with the Wind* for our own times. Balzac probably knew men who had taken part in the rebellion of the royalist Chouans against the Republican armies, and he was well aware of the fact that to have been with the Chouans was a title to favor at the court of the restored Bourbon monarchs. This kind of history easily led to studies of contemporary life.

There were other influences. In the eighteen-twenties much interest was taken in street scenes and the description of popular types, both Parisian and provincial. Balzac himself collaborated in a dictionary of street signs, which attracted him to the physical surroundings in which he would locate the events of his tales. He had sought incidents in contemporary life to serve as examples in his *Physiology of Marriage*, another book he completed in 1829. Such interests led him to publish in 1830 his *Scenes from Private Life*, a collection of tales in two volumes that are distinctly realistic. At the same time he did not neglect another aspect of his genius, the mystical, early influenced by Swedenborg and Mesmer.

This is best illustrated by the *Wild Ass's Skin*, the *Peau de chagrin*. A young man, bent on suicide, wanders near the Seine while waiting until the darkness of night would conceal his plunge into the river. He happens to enter the shop of an aged antiquary, who presents him with the magic skin on which is written in Arabic—not, as Balzac asserts, in Sanskrit: " If you possess me, you will possess all, but your life will be mine. God wished it so. Desire and your desires will be fulfilled. But regulate your wishes by your life. It is therein. At each wish I shall decrease like your days. Do you want me? Take. God will answer your prayer. So be it! " He accepts the skin and soon discovers that it grants him whatever he wishes, but with the penalty that each time he expresses a desire, the skin contracts. We follow his career among the joys the skin at first produces, then among the efforts he makes to lead a desireless life in order to prevent the skin's fatal contracting, and finally witness his death in the fulfillment of a last desire. The obvious moral is that we wear out our lives through our desires and our exercise of power.

By the end of 1832, Balzac had developed his art to such an extent that he was able in the next three years to bring out three masterpieces: *Eugénie Grandet, The Search for the Absolute,* and *Old Man Goriot*. In these we have well developed stories, memorable characters, and the careful description of their surroundings, which are related to the main characters and help to account for their peculiarities. In each of the three novels there is a central character, warped, like many of Molière's, by a vice, but a vice that is by no means comic in its effects. If Balzac had died in 1835, he would have attained greatness by these three novels, but he still had much to add to his reputation.

Before mentioning other novels let me refer to the women in his life. He found little congeniality in his mother, about whom he wrote to a friend, " we have been badly treated by our mothers, a misfortune that develops one's sensitivity." On the other hand he was devoted to his two sisters, one of whom tells us a good deal about him.

He attracted a number of women, chiefly at first women older than himself. What did he have to offer them? He was short— only about five feet, four inches—and thick set, a bull neck described by Gautier as round, smooth, and white as a column, thick lips, a small mustache, a nose square at the end with wide nostrils, a fine forehead, thick black hair, and magnificent brown eyes with glints of gold. The wife of a general wrote about him: " There was in his gestures, in his way of speaking, of carrying himself, so much confidence, kindness, naïveté, and frankness that it was impossible to know him without becoming fond of him. His good humor was so exuberant that it was contagious."

In the day he neglected his clothes, but in the evening he often dressed with great care. A Danish poet tells of meeting him in a salon, elegantly dressed, displaying white teeth between red lips and attracting attention by his high forehead and his genial manner. Some time later, while crossing the court of the Louvre, he met a man who resembled Balzac, but whose clothes were worn out, whose boots were not shined, and whose trousers were covered with mud. " He smiled at me," writes the Dane; " at first I did not stop, but the resemblance was so striking that I turned and ran after him. ' You are really Monsieur de Balzac? ' He laughed and shook my hand."

He knew intimately Mme de Berny, a neighbor of his mother's, one who could tell him tales of the court as it existed before the Revolution. Another friend was the Duchess of Abrantès, widow of one of Napoleon's generals. She could entertain him with the gossip of the court of the Empire. Other friends were an Italian countess and the marquise de Castries. From these women he learned much about aristocracy. It is often said that, while Balzac was thoroughly at home in describing the bourgeois, he was not so successful with the nobility. Brunetière came to his defense by remarking that Balzac's ideas of aristocrats did not correspond to the conceptions of certain university professors. This was unkind, but there was probably much truth in the remark. Certainly Balzac was in a better position to judge the nobility of the first half of the nineteenth century than are critics, professorial or otherwise, of the twentieth. It may well be that the rank of these ladies had much to do with their attraction for him. He found in them, as in the workmen of his apprentice days, material to be studied. But his chief adventure in aristocracy was with quite a different person.

Evalina Hanska belonged to a noble, ancient, and prominent Polish family. She was married to a count who was twenty years older than herself and who owned fifty thousand acres of land and over three thousand serfs. She lived with her husband in a vast establishment near Kief, where, profoundly bored, she sought distraction, as others have done before and since, by reading French novels. One day her book-dealer in Odessa sent her Balzac's *Chouans*, which made a deep impression. Then came the *Physiology of Marriage* and the *Scenes from Private Life*. She wrote to him early in 1832. He answered by putting a notice in a French newspaper asking for her address. A correspondence was begun. Balzac's imagination soon had him in love with this far-away princess. " I'm like a prisoner who, from the depths of his dungeon, hears at a distance the delicious voice of a woman. . . . Without ever having seen you, I already love you too much." They met in Switzerland under the ineffective chaperonage of her ailing husband. This rival died in 1842. The following year Balzac set out for Russia, but he found the widow busy with legal affairs, objecting to his debts, and not disposed to marry him. Other visits followed, but she did not yield until a few months before his death. Balzac claimed to be in love with her, but her portraits show little charm. Her large fortune, her aristocratic birth, and the romantic background of their acquaintance may account for an emotion he mistook for love.

In the meanwhile he had continued to bring out novels and tales. These include *César Birotteau*, the story of an honest seller of perfumery and cosmetics, his financial disaster, and his rehabilitation; *Lost Illusions*, in which Balzac could use his knowledge of the printing business, of provincial society, and of life in Paris among journalists and would-be authors. A sequel to it is *Splendor and Misery of Courtesans*, which presents not only courtesans and their lovers, but thieves and murderers, police, and secret service men. Here we meet again the ex-convict, Vautrin, who had figured prominently in *Le Père Goriot* and now reappears disguised as a Spanish priest. He outwits the police and the secret service men so successfully that there is nothing to do with him except to make him one of their number. His situation reminds me of an anecdote told me recently by Dr. Abraham Flexner. It seems that he was once at a hotel in the Great Smokies. A friend called his attention to a man in his shirt sleeves sitting on the steps of the porch. " That fellow," said his friend, " has killed three men." " You don't seem nervous about sitting so near him," commented Flexner. " Oh, no," was the answer," we're perfectly safe. He's been elected sheriff." The voters in East Tennessee must have been reading Balzac.

Unlike many novelists, Balzac showed no decline in his powers. Among his leading works are two novels written at the end of his life and published together as *Poor Relations*. One, *Le Cousin Pons*, tells the story of a persecuted collector of antiques; the other, *La Cousine Bette*, gives a memorable account of a sour and vengeful old maid.

Balzac was not satisfied to limit himself to novels about certain individuals. He wanted to go farther, to describe all of French society of his time and in this way to interpret man in general as a social animal. Early in his career he had thought of writing a historical series, somewhat as Scott had written the Waverly Novels about Scotland, or as Cooper had written about American Indians. Then he had brought out in 1830 *Scenes from Private Life* and in 1831 *Philosophical Novels and Tales*. In 1834 he got out an edition of his works called *Social Studies*, divided into three parts: *Studies of Manners, Philosophical Studies*, and *Analytical Studies*. The first of these, *Studies of Manners*, was

subdivided into six groups: scenes from Private Life, scenes from
Provincial Life, from Parisian Life, from Political Life, from
Military Life, and from Country Life. He classified in this way
books he had already published, as well as those appearing for
the first time and those he intended to write, some of which were
never written. He had thought, for instance, of writing a novel
about Napoleon's invasion of Russia in which he would take the
Russian point of view rather than the French, but he never got
around to it. His idea was eventually carried out by Tolstoy in
War and Peace.

Balzac had not in 1834 selected his famous general title, *The
Human Comedy*. Just why or when he chose this title is uncertain.

Dante, as you know, had called his great poem *Commedia*
because it began in disaster (Hell) and ended in joy (Heaven).
Boccaccio had added the adjective *Divina*. Balzac was well
acquainted with the poem and had referred in 1829 to one's
arriving at the last infernal circle of the divine comedy of marriage.

Professor Baldensperger discovered that an Englishman who
had been introduced to Balzac, Henry Reeve, wrote in 1835 that
a good title for the novelist's works would be, parodying Dante,
a *Diabolical Comedy*, but it is not sure that he passed this idea
on to Balzac. Others have thought that a friend, returning from
Italy, suggested the title, or that the idea came from the work of
a Pole. It is, however, quite possible that his own interest in
Dante led him to the title without its having been suggested by
others.

As for the date, Professor Jackson called attention to Balzac's
use of the term in a letter of 1838, but the text of this letter may
well be corrupt. All we are sure of is that he called his collected
novels the *Comédie Humaine* as early as June 1, 1841. It is an
admirable title, stressing the vastness of the undertaking, its
dramatic quality, its realism, and its unity,[1] and giving a grim

---

[1] Proust (*la Prisonnière*, I, 219-20) refers to the unity the title gives to the
work, an unconscious and therefore vital unity, one not governed by logic
that would have excluded variety and chilled the composition.

satirical suggestion that recalls the famous epitaph: " Life's a jest and all things show it, I thought so once and now I know it."

It was, however, far from Balzac's intention to make a jest of his own work. He is said to have declared: " What Napoleon failed to do with the sword, I will do with my pen." It was in this spirit that he went about picturing French society.

It was a varied and intriguing society he had the good fortune to depict. Life in France had been an exciting experience for over thirty years when he began to write. Men and women of fifty could remember the days of the Bourbons before the Revolution, a time that was as dear to many aristocrats as the time known as " Before the War " was to my mother's generation in Virginia. On the other hand, many of the bourgeois and peasants had welcomed the Revolution with its slogan of liberty, equality, and fraternity. They still cherished many of its reforms without excusing the excesses of the Terror. And Balzac's own contemporaries had grown up under Napoleon's rule, when French armies had stretched from Madrid to Moscow, somewhat as those of Hitler were to do in our time, but without the aid of motor vehicles, radios, or telegraphy. After Napoleon's downfall came the Restoration and the liberal régime of Louis Philippe, a period of financial prosperity, of literary rather than political greatness, one that gave an author ample opportunity for observation and reflection.

There were in France aristocrats who, like some exiled White Russians we have met, wanted everything to be again just what it had been a half-century before. Some of them, relegated to the provinces, felt that the restored Bourbon government was neglecting them, gathered round themselves a rather forlorn society of impecunious conservatives, but at times, in order to keep the pot boiling, were obliged to marry their sons to wealthy girls of the middle class. Other nobles attracted the favor of the kings and acquired considerable influence, political as well as social. They had to compete with the power of wealthy bourgeois, some of whom were profiting by the Industrial Revolution to build up great fortunes. Below them were professional men, office holders, merchants, workmen, farmers, peasants, servants, members of the underworld, Parisians, provincials, and foreigners.

All these Balzac sets before us, shows their relations with one another, makes them live and love, earn a fortune or lose one, build up families or destroy them. His theoretical devotion to royalty did not blind him to the serious defects of the nobility: snobbishness, indifference to the rights of others, ignorance of practical affairs, unwillingness to work. One story devoted largely to them is called the *Cabinet of Antiques*. His bourgeois are an impressive group: brokers, politicians, men who had made fortunes out of buying the property of nobles during the Revolution, judges just and unjust, lawyers, doctors, civil servants, etc. Balzac was probably the first novelist to introduce into literature the man we call a traveling salesman. He is also one of the first to exploit the boarding house and its mistress. One who has read *Old Man Goriot* can never forget the Widow Vauquer, by birth de Conflans. She resembles, as Balzac puts it, all women who have had misfortunes. She never explains how she lost her fortune or how she lost her husband. The previous existence of both must be taken for granted. When we first meet her, it is early morning and she is preceded by her cat, who jumps on the sideboard to sniff at the milk kept, with small regard for sanitation, in jars covered with plates. The widow enters, dragging her feet in her slippers, wearing a dressing cap from which escapes a lock of false hair. Her face, says Balzac, is as fresh as the first frost of autumn. The wrinkles around her eyes vary her expressions, from the mechanical smile of the professional dancer to the severe frown of the insistent creditor. In short her personality explains the boarding house, as the boarding house accounts for her personality.

Balzac describes his characters' physique, their clothing, their gestures, the rooms in which they live, the small town or the quarter of Paris in which their house is situated. He tells how they make their living, often how much they earn in a year, how much they have to pay for food, rent, laundry, etc. Most writers who preceded him paid little attention to the question of money.

There are, of course, exceptions, but none went into such detail as did Balzac. So much is this the case that when Hauser, who was professor of economic history at the Sorbonne, was asked by a friend what an income of 12,000 francs a year might mean around 1830, he answered, " Don't ask economists; read Balzac." For Balzac tells you what kind of life a family leads and often how much such an existence costs. We learn, for instance, that Mme d'Espard, an extravagant woman high up in Parisian society, spends 60,000 francs a year. At the other end of the economic ladder Raphaël can live for a year on 365 francs. " Lets count," he says, " 3 sous for bread, two for milk, 3 for pork, 3 for the rent of my room, 3 for oil in my lamp, 2 for laundry, 2 for coal. That makes 18 sous. Two sous are left for unexpected expenses."

Balzac saw in his emphasis upon finances a method of adding to the impression of reality he was trying to produce. He also realized, as few had done so intensely before him, how much drama lies in the fact that we have to make our livings, in the changes of our lot occasioned by the loss or gain of a fortune, in the element of uncertainty, the lure of wealth, the crimes that may be committed in its pursuit.

He wrote so much that there was danger that the reader might lose sight of the unity he wished to give to his work. In order to avoid this effect and to bind his stories together he invented the extensive use of reappearing characters. A few have been found in his work as early as 1832. The use of them increases until in *Splendor and Misery of Courtesans*, completed in 1847, he introduces no less than 155 such characters. Sometimes a comparatively unimportant character becomes in a later novel a leading character, as is the case with Rastignac, who first appears in the *Peau de Chagrin* and becomes a chief character in *le Père Goriot*. Or an important person like David Séchard of *Lost Illusions* may play a very minor part later on, as David does in *Splendor and Misery of Courtesans*. The method makes us think we know a larger, and consequently a more significant, group of persons than those whose fortunes are described in a single novel.

They make us realize that Balzac is writing not just the story of
Grandet or Goriot, but the *Comédie Humaine*. They appeal, too,
to our vanity, just as we are pleased at a reception to find many
people we know, especially if we know more about some of them
than does the general public. For instance, in *Les Employés*
Mme de Nucingen appears at a tea. To the casual reader she is
merely a name, but one who has read much of Balzac knows that
she is one of Goriot's ungrateful daughters, married to a wealthy
Alsatian who murders French when he talks, that she has her box
at the Opera, to which she invites de Marsay, Rastignac, etc.

Although the use of reappearing characters often makes it
unnecessary for him to describe a good many of the persons he
mentions, he is so fond of such descriptions that at times they
run away with the story. *Les Employés*, for instance, becomes a
portrait gallery of civil servants rather than the presentation of
an action. Similarly he may discourse too much on certain
subjects, such as the printing business in *Lost Illusions*. As an
ex-printer himself and one who had extensive contacts with
publishers, he gives us much information of interest, but he does
it at such length that the story is unnecessarily interrupted. It
may be said in his defense that he was often desperately in need
of money and that his manner of work at times prevented him
from writing as he might have done under different conditions.

There was much, however, that was excellent in his method.
He took many notes. He always kept in his pocket a notebook
and a pencil. He did not hesitate to write down an idea that
someone else had expressed, a new word, a suggestion for characterization or description, the color of a curtain, the shape of a
mouth, a gesture, proper names. His sister declared that he
thought life could be given to imaginary characters, not by
invented names, but by names that were really in use. One day
he came home with two names he had just discovered: Matifat
and Cardot. "What delightful names," he said, "I found Matifat
in Pearl Street. I can already see my Matifat. He'll belong to
the lesser bourgeoisie with a palish cat's face. As for Cardot, he'll
be a little fellow, dry as a pebble, sprightly and gay."

But it would be a mistake to think that he was all observation. He owed as much to his imagination and to his memory, to what he had learned as a law student, to his struggles in journalism and in establishing himself as a novelist, and to his reading and his conversations.

After dinner he would go to bed about eight o'clock and have himself waked at midnight. Then he would put on his white dressing-gown, seat himself at his table, and begin to write with his pen made from the feather of a crow. His light came from a lamp or from candles. Near him was his coffee, kept warm on a porcelain heater. He would drink cup after cup without sugar. He was completely lost to all other influences, plunged deep into the sea of his imagination. He would stop writing about seven A. M., take a bath, and stretch out on his sofa. Between eight and nine the printer would bring him proof and get new copy or corrected proof. Then Balzac would go back to writing, stopping at noon for boiled eggs and more coffee. And his writing would continue until his evening meal, when friends might come in to dine and talk. He would keep up this régime for a month or two, then return to society and to renewed observation of our species.

He would sketch out a story, then go back and put corrections between the lines or in the margins, scratching out passages, sometimes shifting the position of paragraphs or even of chapters. He might at the last moment take out a description in order to use it in another story, or unexpectedly insert one in a space he had left blank. His text was deciphered with great difficulty by the printers, who prepared from his manuscript galleys that were submitted to Balzac. He treated his proof about as he had done his original sketch, adding words, phrases, paragraphs, criss-crossing his corrections until it was almost impossible to make out his meaning. The poor printers then prepared page proof, which Balzac proceeded to alter as freely as he had changed the text of his galleys.

Champfleury gives a vivid description of Balzac's method:

The printer's shop is prepared. It is stamping like a racer, ready to go. M. de Balzac sends two hundred sheets penciled in five feverish nights: a sketch, a chaos, an apocalypse, a Sanskrit poem. The shop grows pale, but it transforms the monster into signs that are more or less legible and are taken to the author. He sends back the first proofs glued on enormous sheets like posters. From each sign or word that is printed runs a pen stroke that darts and winds like a rocket and finally bursts into a rain of phrases, epithets, and nouns, underlined, crossing one another, scratched out, on top of one another. Just imagine 400 or 500 arabesques of this kind crossing one another, climbing and slipping from one margin to the other. . . . The proofs are sent back seven times in succession. At last one begins to recognize some symptoms of excellent French.

His business affairs were almost as much muddled as his proof corrections. Finding himself in debt after his printing venture, he sought to extricate himself by his writing, often signing contracts and collecting money on books before he composed them. At times he would emerge from the red, but he would spend his money extravagantly and soon find himself again in debt. He made a great deal of money, but he left debts for his wife to pay when he died.

If he had had a fortune, he would probably have written less and would have made less of the role played by money in modern life. On the other hand, the pressure of his creditors, his feverish activity at a time when most men are asleep, and his confused manner of indicating his corrections led to compositions that impress us by their range and power rather than by the perfection of their detail.

Balzac has a habit of expressing his views on things in general. Such remarks have recently been collected by Professor Atkinson into five small volumes. Many of them are platitudes, or seem to have been inspired by his aristocratic and conservative acquaintances. He refers, indeed, to himself as the disciple of M. de Bonald, the spokesman of the privileged classes. However, some of his observations give evidence of mature reflexion. I will cite one example.

In *Les Employés* he describes a talented official who has given much thought to reforming public services in the interests of economy. He would have felt at home as a member of the Hoover Commission. Among other reforms he proposed the reduction of the number of cabinet officers, to be started by uniting the ministry of the navy and the ministry of war. For him the navy appeared to be a branch of war services like the artillery, the cavalry, the infantry, and the service of supply. Was it not nonsense to give different administrations to admirals and generals, when they had the same aims: to defend the country, to attack the enemy, and to protect national possessions?

Balzac wrote this in 1837. In his novel the reform is not accepted by the government. It is opposed by too many political interests. Too many persons would lose their jobs. And it has taken us over 100 years to adopt the suggestion made by one of Balzac's characters.

He wrote a number of historical tales and in his *Contes drolatiques* sought to reproduce the style and language of French authors of the sixteenth century. He also wrote a few imaginative tales that have little contact with reality. But his chief work lies in the *Human Comedy*. Here he sought, not only to present French society of his day, but to express his ideas about man, to classify him as the naturalists were classifying animals. He admitted that a man can leave the class into which he is born, but he thought that in the main man is the product of his environment and can be classified accordingly. This is one of the reasons why he was careful to describe the environment along with the man.

Balzac believed that certain ideas pursued with passion will produce monomaniacs, may destroy them and wreck their families. This belief inspired some of his most memorable characters. Grandet, for instance, thinks only of making money and is unable to enjoy the millions he has made. He forces his wife and daughter to lead a most penurious existence, is largely responsible for his wife's death, prevents his daughter from marrying the cousin whom she loves, and dies in the situation described as follows:

When the priest came to give him the last sacraments, his eyes, which for several hours had appeared lifeless, brightened upon seeing the silver cross, the silver candlesticks, and the silver basin of holy water. . . . When the priest brought near his lips the gilt crucifix in order that he might kiss the image of Christ, he made a frightful gesture to seize it. . . . He called his daughter whom he could not see, though she was kneeling beside him, and said "Take good care of everything. You will have to give me an account of it over there."

Then there is old Goriot, who has sacrificed everything to his daughters, one of whom he married to a nobleman, the other to a wealthy banker. He used to go and stand for hours on the side of the street in order to catch a glimpse of them as they drove past in their handsome carriages. Only one of them came to his death bed and she arrived too late for him to recognize her. They sent empty carriages to his burial.

Then there is Claës of the *Search for the Absolute*. He is a descendant of a wealthy Flemish family established in northern France. He gradually spends everything he can get hold of on his experiments, carried on in his home by himself and his valet. He nearly ruins his family, but he is never convinced that the secret of the composition of matter cannot be discovered. In fact his last words are "Eureka," as if he had really made the discovery that was reserved for the twentieth century.

I may mention two others who illustrate Balzac's idea that a thought, carried far enough, will destroy the thinker and his product. One of these, Gambara, is intent upon creating a new form of music, but succeeds in making what appears to others to be merely discords; the other, the old man of the *Unknown Masterpiece* devotes years of his life to a painting which he shows with pride to two younger artists.

"Well, there it is," said to them the old man, whose hair was in disorder, whose face was enflamed by supernatural exaltation, whose eyes sparkled, and who panted like a youth drunk with love. "Ah! Ah!" he cried, "you did not expect such perfection. You expected a picture and you find yourselves before a woman. This canvas has so much depth. The air is painted so genuinely that you cannot distinguish it from the air that surrounds you. Where's the art? Gone! Vanished! There is the real form of a girl. Have I not caught the color well, and the line that seems to end the body? . . . See how the contours stand out from the background. Does it not seem to you that you could run your hands along that back? . . . Her flesh is palpitating. She is about to get up. Wait."

"Do you see anything?" one of the visitors asked the other.

"No. Do you?"

"Nothing."

They examined the painting, putting themselves on the right, on the left, in front, stooping down and rising in turn.

One of them said: "I see there only colors confusedly piled up and held in by a multitude of strange lines that form a wall of paint."

"We may be mistaken," said the other. Upon drawing near the painting, they noticed in a corner of the canvas the end of a naked foot that stuck out from this chaos of colors, tones, vague shades, a kind of formless mist; but a delicious foot, a living foot! They remained struck with admiration before this fragment that had escaped from slow and progressive destruction. This foot appeared like the torso of a marble Venus discovered in the débris of a burned city.

Balzac, of course, had not had our advantages in music and art. He had not heard twentieth-century symphonies, nor had he seen post-Cubist paintings. He did not realize that the musician and the painter he created were giving what was to be for the next century the last word in art. For him, with his nineteenth-century outlook, the genius of these men had carried them far beyond reason and art itself, into a riot of discords and of formless shapes.

Balzac's monomaniacs have attracted wide attention, but they are in a distinct minority among the hundreds of persons he introduces into his novels. He does not make the mistake of some of his realistic descendants, who give us such a gloomy view of life that they show us no characters with whom we can sympathize. One may certainly feel affection for Eugénie Grandet or for Dr. Bianchon, who was so real to Balzac that he wanted to send for him when he was dying, or for many others down to the humble water-carrier who, when his dog died, wanted to have a mass said for his soul. His dog, he said, was a real Christian who for twelve years had gone to church with him without ever barking, listening to the organ without opening his mouth, and squatting beside his master with an air that made him think he was praying with him.

The desire to give reality to persons and situations leads Balzac to seek customary gestures or phrases for his characters, as well as to describe their complexions, voices, manner of walking, etc. He also made use of documents that he would reproduce in full, as, for instance, when he gave the text in *César Birotteau* of the famous advertisement of hair-tonic, one that would do credit to a contemporary radio announcer.

He varied greatly his methods of constructing his novels. He sometimes begins with a rather dramatic scene, but more usually he prefers long descriptive passages that prepare us for the entrance of the characters. A third method, well adapted to a symbolic novel, is shown in the *Peau de Chagrin*, which begins with the hero's entering a gambling house, where an employé immediately demands his hat. This hat becomes a symbol, setting the tone for the novel. "Know this well," Balzac writes, " you have scarcely taken a step towards the green table before you've reached a point where your hat no longer belongs to you any more than you belong to yourself; you have become a stake in the game, you, your fortune, your hat, your cane, and your cloak." And so the hero soon becomes a stake in the game played by his desires and the dimensions of the fateful skin.

The story once begun, Balzac mingles action, ideas, descriptions, characterizations, sometimes overemphasizing one kind of writing at the expense of the others. But the general effect is most impressive. One is amazed that in less than thirty years of composition he created such an extraordinary number of characters and scenes.

He did not himself have a Peau de Chagrin that would fulfill any desire for the asking. His love-affairs were not durable. He never succeeded in getting himself out of debt for long. He failed in his political aspirations. He was defeated by a person of small repute when he sought election to the French Academy. Yet he must have found much happiness as he worked away by candle-light while the city lay quiet around him, the city whose life in the twenties and thirties of the century he has recorded as no one else has done. And he created by his imagination an enormous family, more real to him than most persons he had met in the flesh. Perhaps he had a Peau de Chagrin, but one that was limited in its power to literary creation. It granted his prayer that he might give life to innumerable characters, but it kept contracting with each new creation until, when he had passed the mark of nearly a hundred novels and tales, it reminded him that, though he was only fifty, life was no longer his.

XIII

Fielding's Tom Jones

KEMP MALONE

FICTION has always been cultivated in every stage of human society. But in the early periods of English literature, fictitious stories were not written down (and so preserved to us) unless they had been told in verse. Prose tales were not looked upon as artistic enough to be worth the trouble of writing down. It was not until the tenth century that a prose tale was committed to writing in English, and this tale, the story of Apollonius of Tyre, was based on a classical romance, as its name reveals. This beginning might have led to great things in prose, but it did not. The Norman Conquest brought England under the cultural as well as political domination of the French and, from a literary point of view, the French were a backward people; they still had no prose at all, and very little verse, and under their rule prose fiction, instead of making further strides, was given up. Such fiction as we have from the period after the Norman Conquest was written in verse; in other words, under the French cultural domination we got a relapse into a more primitive state of things, and this not only in literature but also in other aspects of the English people's cultural life. As Sir James Murray puts it,

Learning and literature, science and art, had attained to fair proportions in England, . . . when their progress was arrested by the Norman Conquest. . . . In literary culture the Normans were about as far behind the people whom they conquered as the Romans were when they made themselves masters of Greece, and it was not until some two generations after the Conquest that learning and literature regained in England somewhat of the position which they had occupied two centuries earlier.

When prose fiction started up again in medieval England, we find it chiefly in two forms: the so-called exemplum and the romance of chivalry. An exemplum is an illustration, anecdote, or short story, told, not for its own sake, but to point a moral. The priests used such exempla in their sermons; the exempla served to liven up a sermon and to drive home, by example, a moral lesson. Thus, a bawdy story might be a perfectly good exemplum if in it the wicked were punished and the good rewarded. In this way lots of vivid, interesting stories got written down, as parts of sermons. And great collections of exempla were made, first for the convenience of the priests, but afterwards for the reading public at large—a public not so very large in those days, it is true, since few people, except the clergy, knew how to read and write. Alongside these exempla were found a kindred type, the so-called fabliau (the name is French). The fabliau differs from the exemplum in that no moral lesson can readily be drawn from it, though it may well teach lessons of another kind. In plain English, the fabliau is usually a more or less racy story, told frankly because it is funny, and with no pretence that one's morals are improved by listening to it.

Quite different from the exemplum and the fabliau was the romance of chivalry. You are all familiar with stories about King Arthur and his knights. These stories were first told in verse, but in the later Middle Ages it became fashionable to tell them in prose. The best known romance of this kind, in English, is Malory's famous work, the *Morte d'Arthur*. It was written in the fifteenth century. There were many other romances, dealing with other heroes of history or story, such as Charlemagne and Alexander the Great. The romances were usually long drawn out, full of heroic adventures, like the exploits of knights in rescuing maidens in distress, killing three-headed giants, or dragons, fighting duels with other knights, making expeditions to fairyland,

and coming upon marvels and wonders galore. The modern romance, as distinguished from the novel, grew out of these medieval romances of chivalry. It is the novel, though, which we are to talk about here.

The word novel means " something new " and as a technical literary term it was first applied to new collections of stories of the exemplum and fabliau type—in other words, novel used to be the name for more or less realistic short stories, with or without a moral. The best known collection of such novels is the *Decameron* of the fourteenth-century Italian writer Boccaccio. Later (though not until the seventeenth century) the term *novel* was extended to long, complex stories of a somewhat similar character. It is important to keep in mind that the modern novel grew out of the medieval exemplum and fabliau, not the medieval romance. Wherever you find it funny, smutty, dealing with everyday life in a reasonably realistic way, there you may know it is true to its medieval heritage. But it is just as true to this heritage when it makes things come out right—the villain exposed and put to shame, the hero triumphant at last and rewarded with the hand of the heroine. Here the novel and the romance have something in common: both must be edifying as well as interesting. They must encourage the reader to *be* good and to *do* good by showing him how wicked vice is and how the vicious always lose out in the end. To our forefathers literature was a means to an end, and this end was moral uplift. As Fielding himself puts it, in the dedication of his *Tom Jones,*

To recommend goodness and innocence hath been my sincere endeavor in this history. This honest purpose . . . is likeliest to be attained in books of this kind, for an example is a kind of picture, in which Virtue becomes as it were an object of sight. . . . Besides displaying that beauty of Virtue which may attract the admiration of mankind, I have attempted to engage a stronger motive to human action in her favor, by convincing men that their true interest directs them to a pursuit of her. . . . Lastly, I have endeavored strongly to inculcate, that virtue and innocence can scarce ever be injured but by indiscretion; and that it is this alone which often betrays them into the snares that deceit and villainy spread for them. . . . For these purposes I have employed all the wit and humor of which I am master in the following history: wherein I have endeavored to laugh mankind out of their favorite follies and vices.

Fielding thus bears express witness to a high moral purpose in his *Tom Jones*. His attitude is typical of his age, not peculiar to himself. Perhaps in your own reading of this novel you have been chiefly struck with its bawdy scenes and the like. If so, you have missed the point. You ought to be better men and women, not worse, for having read *Tom Jones*.

When I say that the modern novel grew out of the medieval exemplum I do not mean that there were no intermediate stages and no other influences at play. On the contrary, the novel is a highly complex literary form, and its history is correspondingly involved. Much prose fiction was written in the later Middle Ages, in Tudor times, and in the seventeenth century, but the particular kind of long story which we call a novel did not come to literary maturity until the eighteenth century. The first great English novelists were Defoe, Richardson, and Fielding. The novel was born when men began to write long stories (and especially fictional biographies) in somewhat the manner which Boccaccio and others had made familiar in short stories. The two chief types of early novel are the novel of manners and the novel of adventure. The novelist of manners makes use of his story to bring out in some detail the customs and tastes of the time. The novelist of adventure makes his story more exciting, filling it with incidents told chiefly for their own sake. Such a novelist differs from a writer of romances in that his hero is rarely if ever a perfect gentleman; he has vices as well as virtues, and may even be a low character, whence the term picaresque, that is to say, roguish, applied to novels of adventure in which a rogue (that is, a thief, highwayman or the like) is the hero. But it was quite possible for a novelist to combine in one story both manners and adventures enough. Fielding does this in *Tom Jones*, a novel of manners indeed, but also one of adventures.

Tom Jones is not a biographical novel in the strict sense of the word. It begins, indeed, with the birth of the hero, but ends, not with his death but with his marriage, the idea being that, since the hero and his wife lived happy ever after, their married life offered little of interest to a novelist and was best dismissed in a paragraph or so. This kind of novel smacks of the romance in its ending. In other ways, too, it reminds us of a romance, or even of a fairy story. The heroine, Sophia Western, is a young woman without a flaw of any kind; such perfect beauty of person and character is not to be expected of flesh and blood, and will not be found anywhere on this earth of ours. Fielding has given us an ideal of perfect womanhood, not a real woman, begotten by Squire Western in eighteenth-century Somersetshire. The story of the hero's birth, too, belongs to romance; in particular, the conduct of his mother, Bridget Allworthy, cannot be explained in realistic terms, and must be interpreted as an author's trick or device, whereby he contrives to eat his cake and have it too: he makes his hero at one and the same time a true foundling and a true nephew of Squire Allworthy.

Most of the characters in the novel, indeed, are to be taken as types, humors, or even caricatures, not as products of psychological study and realistic technique. Thus, Allworthy is the ideal country gentleman, and Western, his foil, is a Whig caricature of a Tory squire. Nevertheless, Fielding, like Chaucer, gives us a multitude of beautifully realistic details, which as it were take the place of realistic characterization and enable us to think of the characters as individuals rather than as types, or at any rate to give to them particular associations in our minds.

And from the beginning we are made at home. The author takes us into his confidence at once, and chats with us throughout with so delightful an air of informality and intimacy that we live the story along with him, and feel ourselves his companions everywhere and all the time. The triangular relationship of author, story, and reader is here open and above board; we are constantly reading, not only the story but also the author's opinions about it, and about many other things, and we end up as members of the family. But I will leave off general comments, for the moment, and take up a few individual passages, passages which bring out certain features of our story worth dwelling on for a bit.

First of all, however, let us take a look at the names of the characters in the novel. Some of these names seem to have no special meaning, but others are clearly meant to serve as characterizing epithets. Allworthy describes the squire of that name well enough; throughout the story he is represented as a worthy man in every respect. The two learned men who live with him, Thwackum and Square, have names that reflect their characters. Thwackum the tutor believed in thwacking (that is, beating) his unfortunate pupils, and he put his theories into practice with a vengeance when it came to our hero, who learned his lessons to the accompaniment of constant beatings. Square the philosopher also lived up to his name in his precepts at any rate, though his practice of virtue left something to be desired. He talked constantly of the rule of right, the immutable pattern of justice and proper behavior, and he measured Tom just as constantly by this square, this rule, and regularly found him wanting. Mr. Supple, the curate, was supple indeed in dealing with that formidable parishioner of his, Squire Western, and he needed all the suppleness he could muster for the task. Western himself has a name that fits him geographically: he lived in Somersetshire, in the western part of England. The squires of the west were Tories almost to a man, and Fielding in his caricature of Squire Western was hitting at the Tory squires in general. I will comment on two more names. Sophia Western's maidservant goes by the name Honor, and one must suspect that Fielding called her that in a spirit of sarcasm or irony, as her conduct was anything but honorable. Arabella Hunt, who proposed marriage to our hero, was on the hunt for a man; certainly she made no bones about pursuing Tom. The practice of giving to characters in a story names of this kind goes back to the Middle Ages, where it is the regular thing in the morality plays, for instance.

Now for the passages. I begin with one about architecture and landscape.

The Gothic style of building could produce nothing nobler than Mr. Allworthy's house. There was an air of grandeur in it that struck you with awe, and rivaled the beauties of the best Grecian architecture; and it was as commodious within as venerable without.

It stood on the southeast side of a hill, but nearer the bottom than the top of it, so as to be sheltered from the northeast by a grove of old oaks, which rose above it in a gradual ascent of near half a mile, and yet high enough to enjoy a most charming prospect of the valley beneath.

In the midst of the grove was a fine lawn, sloping down towards the house; near the summit of which rose a plentiful spring, gushing out of a rock covered with firs, and forming a constant cascade of about thirty foot, not carried down a regular flight of steps, but tumbling in a natural fall over the broken and mossy stones, till it came to the bottom of the rock; then running off in a pebbly channel, that with many lesser falls winded along, till it fell into a lake at the foot of the hill, about a quarter of a mile below the house on the south side, and which was seen from every room in the front. Out of this lake, which filled the center of a beautiful plain, embellished with groups of beeches and elms, and fed with sheep, issued a river, that for several miles was seen to meander through an amazing variety of meadows and woods, till it emptied itself into the sea; with a large arm of which, and an island beyond it, the prospect was closed.

On the right of this valley opened another of less extent, adorned with several villages, and terminated by one of the towers of an old ruined abbey, grown over with ivy, and part of the front, which remained still entire.

The left-hand scene presented the view of a very fine park, composed of very unequal ground, and agreeably varied with all the diversity that hills, lawns, wood, and water, laid out with admirable taste, but owing less to art than to nature, could give. Beyond this, the country gradually rose into a ridge of wild mountains, the tops of which were above the clouds.

Here the important words and phrases are *Gothic, variety, ruined, ivy, unequal, owing less to art than to nature, wild mountains.* The description reflects a taste, in architecture and in landscape, characteristic of the eighteenth century, a period usually thought of as neoclassical.

Next we take up a passage that illustrates a mock-heroic treatment of the hen-pecked husband motif, one of the standby's of jokers in all ages. Here this motif is reinforced by another favorite: the beaten schoolmaster motif. In the good old days the schoolmaster spent much of his time beating knowledge into the skins of his pupils with the help of a stick, and there was nothing that these pupils enjoyed more, the rest of their lives, than seeing a schoolmaster—any schoolmaster—get a beating. But let me read the passage. Here the schoolmaster is compared to a mouse, his wife to a cat, in mock-heroic style.

As fair Grimalkin, who, though the youngest of the feline family, degenerates not in ferocity from the elder branches of her house, and though inferior in strength, is equal in fierceness to the noble tiger himself, when a little mouse, whom it hath long tormented in sport, escapes from her clutches, for a while frets, scolds, growls, swears; but if the trunk, or box, behind which the mouse lay hid, be again removed, she flies like lightning on her prey, and, with envenomed wrath, bites, scratches, mumbles, and tears the little animal.

Not with less fury did Mrs Partridge fly on the poor pedagogue. Her tongue, teeth, and hands fell all upon him at once. His wig was in an instant torn from his head, his shirt from his back, and from his face descended five streams of blood, denoting the number of claws with which nature had unhappily armed the enemy.

Mr Partridge acted some time on the defensive only; . . . but as he found that his antagonist abated nothing of her rage, he thought he might, at least, endeavor to disarm her, or rather to confine her arms; in doing which, her cap fell off in the struggle, and her hair being too short to reach her shoulders, erected itself on her head; her stays likewise . . . burst open; and her breasts, which were much more redundant than her hair, hung down below her middle; her face was likewise marked with the blood of her husband; her teeth gnashed with rage; and fire, such as sparkles from a smith's forge, darted from her eyes. So that, altogether, this Amazonian heroine might have been an object of terror to a much bolder man than Mr Partridge.

My next illustration is a passage devoted to satire on doctors.

These gentry from time immemorial have been subject to witticisms. Fielding pokes fun at the medical faculty in connection with the death of Captain Blifil, who had a stroke and died before the doctors could get there.

Death, that inexorable judge, had passed sentence on him, and refused to grant him a reprieve, though two doctors who arrived, and were fee'd at one and the same instant, were his counsel.

These two doctors, whom, to avoid any malicious applications, we shall distinguish by the names of Dr Y and Dr Z, having felt his pulse; to wit, Dr Y his right arm and Dr Z his left; both agreed that he was absolutely dead; but as to the distemper, or cause of his death, they differed; Dr Y holding that he died of an apoplexy, and Dr Z of an epilepsy.

Hence arose a dispute between the learned men, in which each delivered the reasons of their several opinions. These were of such equal force, that they served both to confirm either doctor in his own sentiments, and made not the least impression on his adversary.

To say the truth, every physician almost hath his favorite disease, to which he ascribes all the victories obtained over human nature. The gout, the rheumatism, the stone, the gravel, and the consumption, all have their several patrons in the faculty; and none more than the nervous fever, or the fever on the spirits. And here we may account for those disagreements in opinion, concerning the cause of a patient's death, which sometimes occur, between the most learned of the college; and which have greatly surprised that part of the world who have been ignorant of the fact we have above asserted.

The reader may perhaps be surprised, that, instead of endeavoring to revive the patient, the learned gentlemen should fall immediately into a dispute on the occasion of his death: but in reality all such experiments had been made before their arrival: for the captain was put into a warm bed, had his veins scarified, his forehead chafed, and all sorts of strong drops applied to his lips and nostrils.

The physicians therefore, finding themselves anticipated in everything they ordered, were at a loss how to apply that portion of time which it is usual and decent to remain for their fee, and were therefore necessitated to find some subject or other for discourse; and what could more naturally present itself than that before mentioned?

Our doctors were about to take their leave, when Mr Allworthy, having given over the captain, and acquiesced in the divine will, began to inquire after his sister, whom he desired them to visit before their departure.

This lady was now recovered of her fit, and, to use the common phrase, was as well as could be expected for one in her condition. The doctors, therefore, all previous ceremonies being complied with, as this was a new patient, attended, according to desire, and laid hold on each of her hands, as they had before done on those of the corpse.

The case of the lady was in the other extreme from that of her husband: for as he was past all the assistance of physic, so in reality she required none.

There is nothing more unjust than the vulgar opinion, by which physicians are misrepresented as friends to death. On the contrary, I believe, if the number of those who recover by physic could be opposed to that of the martyrs to it, the former would rather exceed the latter. Nay, some are so cautious on this head, that, to avoid a possibility of killing the patient, they abstain from all methods of curing, and prescribe nothing but what can neither do good nor harm. I have heard some of these, with great gravity, deliver it as a maxim, that "Nature should be left to do her own work, while the physician stands by as it were to clap her on the back, and encourage her when she doth well."

So little then did our doctors delight in death, that they discharged the corpse after a single fee; but they were not so disgusted with their living patient; concerning whose case they immediately agreed, and fell to prescribing with great diligence.

Whether, as the lady had at first persuaded the physicians to believe her ill, they had now in return persuaded her to believe herself so, I will not determine; but she continued a whole month with all the decorations of sickness. During this time she was visited by physicians, attended by nurses, and received constant messages from her acquaintance to inquire after her health.

At length, the decent time for sickness and immoderate grief being expired, the doctors were discharged, and the lady began to see company; being altered only from what she was before, by that color of sadness in which she dressed her person and countenance. . . . [She] conducted herself through the whole season in which grief is to make its appearance on the outside of the body, with the strictest regard to all the rules of custom and decency, suiting the alterations of her countenance to the several alterations of her habit: for as this changed from weeds to black, from black to grey, from grey to white, so did her countenance change from dismal to sorrowful, from sorrowful to sad, and from sad to serious, till the day came in which she was allowed to return to her former serenity.

You will note that in this long passage the satire on doctors is capped by satire on widows, another favorite subject for the satirists time out of mind. I end these illustrations with a passage in mockery of lawyers, who, like the doctors, are perennial subjects for satire.

Mr Dowling was indeed very greatly affected with this relation; for he had not divested himself of humanity by being an attorney. Indeed, nothing is more unjust than to carry our prejudices against a profession into private life, and to borrow our idea of a man from our opinion of his calling. Habit, it is true, lessens the horror of those actions which the profession makes necessary, and consequently habitual; but in all other instances, nature works in men of all professions alike; nay, perhaps, even more strongly with those who give her, as it were, a holiday, when they are following their ordinary business. . . . An attorney may feel all the miseries and distresses of his fellow creatures, provided he happens not to be concerned against them.

In this passage Fielding pretends to be defending the lawyers against their traducers; he used the same tactics, you will remember, in satirizing the doctors when he gave it as his opinion that these gentry quite possibly cured more people than they killed. This device is one that satirists have always used to great effect.

Such examples as those that I have read to you might be added to almost indefinitely. There is hardly an aspect of eighteenth century English life which Fielding does not touch upon. His masterpiece, *Tom Jones*, may be called, in his own terms, a treatise on human nature. He studies that noblest and basest of animals, man, as he appears in eighteenth-century England. In this long history of eighteen books, he explores every avenue and lays open to our gaze the life of the period in all its manifestations. And he is not merely a reporter of what he sees; he is a commentator as well. He satirizes what he does not like, and praises what he does like. More than that, he is a reformer; he attacks with vigor and fervor the many abuses of the time. And yet, somehow or other he manages to escape the deadly seriousness, the repulsive fanaticism of the reforming type of mind. Like Chaucer, he is amused rather than indignant at most of what he satirizes. His satire is tolerant, not savage. Even those characters, like Blifil, for whom he feels contempt, are let off with little or no punishment. Enough that their evil schemes have been thwarted. His hero is generous and forgiving to a fault, and here he reflects his creator, Henry Fielding, or at any rate his creator's ideal.

The attitude toward morality which dominates this work, and all the works of Fielding, is essentially that of the enlightened man. The sins of the flesh, such as sexual overindulgence and drunkenness, are taken lightly; it is the sins of the spirit which receive condemnation: Blifil, the villain of the piece, is a man of the greatest respectability and outward piety. It is interesting to note that Fielding leaves him as he found him; he has no change of heart, does not turn over a new leaf at the end—on the contrary, we find him turning methodist, not for his soul's welfare but because thereby he hopes to marry a rich widow of the methodist persuasion. Here is exemplified the technique of the novel, not of the romance.

Fielding wrote other novels, though *Tom Jones* is his masterpiece. Another ambitious work of his is *Amelia*. In the dedications he describes thus his reason for writing it:

The following book is sincerely designed to promote the cause of virtue, and to expose some of the most glaring evils, as well public as private, which at present infest the country.

The tone of the reformer here is manifest, and *Amelia* in fact outdoes *Tom Jones* in this department. But Fielding's hatred of wrongdoing and wickedness comes out most strongly in *Jonathan*

Wild, the Great, a novel little read nowadays but astonishingly recent in its point of view. The hero is a criminal, who comes to a criminal's proper end, viz., death by hanging. Fielding explains as follows why he calls such a character great:

We must endeavor to remove some errors of opinion which mankind have, by the disingenuity of writers, contracted: for these, from their fear of contradicting the obsolete and absurd doctrines of a set of simple fellows, called, in derision, sages or philosophers, have endeavored, as much as possible, to confound the ideas of greatness and goodness; whereas no two things can possibly be more distinct from each other: for Greatness consists in bringing all manner of mischief on mankind, and Goodness in removing it from them. It seems therefore very unlikely that the same person should possess them both; and yet nothing is more usual with writers, who find many instances of greatness in their favorite hero, than to make him a compliment of goodness into the bargain; and this, without considering that by such means they destroy the great perfection called uniformity of character. In the histories of Alexander and Caesar, we are frequently, and indeed impertinently, reminded of their benevolence and generosity, of their clemency and kindness. When the former had with fire and sword overrun a vast empire, had destroyed the lives of an immense number of innocent wretches, had scattered ruin and desolation like a whirlwind, we are told, as an example of his clemency, that he did not cut the throat of an old woman, and ravish her daughters, but was content with only undoing them. And when the mighty Caesar, with wonderful greatness of mind, had destroyed the liberties of his country, and with all the means of fraud and force had placed himself at the head of his equals, had corrupted and enslaved the greatest people whom the sun ever saw, we are reminded, as an evidence of his generosity, of his largesses to his followers and tools, by whose means he had accomplished his purpose, and by whose assistance he was to establish it.

Now, who doth not see that such sneaking qualities as these are rather to be bewailed as imperfections than admired as ornaments in these great men; rather obscuring their glory, and holding them back in their race to greatness, indeed unworthy the end for which they seem to have come into the world, viz., of perpetrating vast and mighty mischief.

We hope our reader will have reason justly to acquit us of any such confounding ideas in the following pages: in which, as we are to record the actions of a great man, so we have nowhere mentioned any spark of goodness, which had discovered itself either faintly in him, or more glaringly in any other person, but as a meanness and imperfection, disqualifying them for undertakings which lead to honor and esteem among men.

As our hero had as little as perhaps is to be found of that meanness, indeed only enough to make him partaker of the imperfection of humanity, instead of the perfection of Diabolism, we have ventured to call him *The Great*; nor do we doubt but our reader, when he hath perused this story, will concur with us in allowing him that title.

Here Fielding reveals himself as a thoroughgoing pacifist, and as a bitter satirist indeed. One is reminded of Swift, but Fielding's later works (for *Jonathan Wild* was written earlier in his career) show that he grew more mellow, more tolerant of mankind, with the years. And with this glimpse of another, more serious-minded Fielding I will close this review of one of our very greatest novelists.